Translated Texts for Historians

This series is designed to meet the needs of students of ancient and medieval history and others who wish to broaden their study by reading source material, but whose knowledge of Latin or Greek is not sufficient to allow them to do so in the original languages. Many important Late Imperial and Dark Age texts are currently unavailable in translation and it is hoped that TTH will help to fill this gap and to complement the secondary literature in English which already exists. The series relates principally to the period 300-800 AD and includes Late Imperial, Greek, Byzantine and Syriac texts as well as source books illustrating a particular period or theme. Each volume is a self-contained scholarly translation with an introductory essay on the text and its author and notes on the text indicating major problems of interpretation, including textual difficulties.

Editorial Committee

Sebastian Brock, Oriental Institute, University of Oxford
Averil Cameron, Keble College, Oxford
Henry Chadwick, Oxford
John Davies, University of Liverpool
Carlotta Dionisotti, King's College London
Peter Heather, University College London
Robert Markus, University of Nottingham
John Matthews, Queen's College, Oxford
Raymond Van Dam, University of Michigan
Michael Whitby, University of Warwick
Ian Wood, University of Leeds

General Editors

Gillian Clark, University of Liverpool
Mary Whitby, Royal Holloway, London

Front cover: Representation of the Ezra portrait

A full list of published titles in the Translated Texts for Historians series is printed at the end of this book.

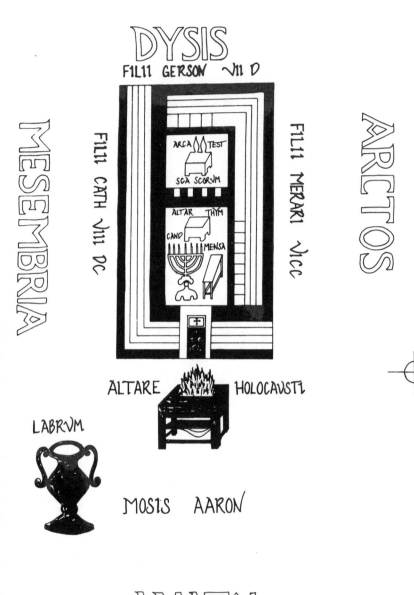

DYSIS

FILII GERSON ꝟ11 D

MESEMBRIA

FILII CATH ꝟ11 DC

ARCA TEST

SCA SCORꝟM

ALTAR THYM

CAND MENSA

FILII MERARI ꝟ1cc

ARCTOS

ALTARE HOLOCAVSTI

LABRꝟM

MOSIS AARON

ANATOL

drawn by Gail Heather

NOTE TO FRONTISPIECE

Codex Amiatinus, fol. IIr-IIIr. Wearmouth-Jarrow, late seventh century. Plan of the tabernacle of Moses, perhaps based on a diagram in the sixth-century Codex Grandior of Cassiodorus. A doorway (INTROITUS) on the east leads into an outer chamber which contains a seven-branched lampstand (CAND), the table (MENSA) of showbread and the altar of incense (ALTAR THYM). Inside the holy of holies (SCA SCORUM) stands the ark of the covenant (ARCA TEST) surmounted by two winged cherubim. In front of the tabernacle stand a bronze laver (LABRUM) in which the priests wash themselves and the altar of burnt offerings (ALTARE HOLOCAUSTI), below which are inscribed the names of Moses and Aaron. The four cardinal directions are given in Greek words (ARCTOS = North), the initial letters of which spell ADAM. On three sides of the tabernacle are written the names of the sons of Levi (Gershon, Kohath and Merari) with the enumeration of their clans as in num. 3. Not pictured here is an outer colonnade surrounded by the names and numbers of the twelve tribes of Israel.

Translated Texts for Historians
Volume 21

Bede: On the Temple

Translated with notes by SEÁN CONNOLLY
with an introduction by JENNIFER O'REILLY

Liverpool
University
Press

First published 1995 by
LIVERPOOL UNIVERSITY PRESS
Senate House
Abercromby Square
Liverpool
L69 3BX

British Library Cataloguing-in-Publication Data
A British Library CIP Record is available
ISBN 0-85323-049-8

Printed in the European Union by
Page Bros, Norwich, England

To Cláirín

The truly capable woman – who can find her?
She is far beyond the price of pearls...
Give her a share in what her hands have worked for,
And let her works tell her praises at the city gates.
Proverbs 31:10–31

CONTENTS

Acknowledgements ix

Abbreviations xi

Translator's Preface xiii

Introduction xvii

Prologue 1

On the Temple

    Book 1 5

    Book 2 65

Select Bibliography 118

Index of Biblical Quotations and Allusions 130

Index of Patristic and Classical Sources 141

ACKNOWLEDGEMENTS

I acknowledge my indebtedness to all those who have helped me make this translation of *De templo* available in print. First among these are Prof Éamonn Ó Carragáin, Head of the Department of English, and Dr Jennifer O'Reilly, Head of Medieval History, in whose departments at University College, Cork it has been my pleasant duty to teach, and who encouraged me to submit the work for publication in the first place. Dr O'Reilly, at very short notice and despite heavy demands on her time, generously agreed to write the Introduction and so share with us the insights gained through years of reflection and lecturing on the works of Bede.

I should also like to thank Sr Benedicta Ward of the Department of Theology at Oxford, whose work on St Bede is acknowledged as one of the best comprehensive treatments of his writings, for so kindly reading the first draft of this version and recommending it to Liverpool University Press for publication. On some points of translation I am indebted to Dom David Hurst, O.S.B. who edited the Latin text on which the version is based, and to my former colleague and Head of Classics at the Oratory School, Woodcote, Oxford, Mr Tom McIntyre, M.A., a fellow-Celt whose knowledge of Latin and feel for its genius few can equal. I also owe much to Mr Diarmuid Scully, M.A., currently doing his doctoral research on Bede in our Department of Medieval History, at whose request I originally taught the course on Bede, and who has made many invaluable suggestions.

In producing camera-ready copy of the manuscript for the press I have used the computer typesetting program TEX, and in this regard it will be difficult if not impossible to repay the debt I owe to my UCC colleagues, Peter Flynn of the Computer Centre and Prof Niall Ó Murchú of the Department of Physics, who selflessly shared with me their considerable expertise in the use of this complex program, to say nothing of their precious time.

More personally I must thank my wife Cláirín without whose support, encouragement and constructive criticism, not to mention the countless hours of eye-strain entailed in proof-reading, it would have been immeasurably harder to bring this work to completion.

Seán Connolly
Palaeography, Greek and Medieval Latin
Department of English
University College Cork, Ireland.
24th July, 1995

ABBREVIATIONS

ACW   *Ancient Christian Writers*
ANF   *Anti-Nicene Fathers*
CCSL *Corpus Christianorum, Series Latina*
CSEL *Corpus Scriptorum Ecclesiasticorum Latinorum*
FOTC *Fathers of the Church*
GCS   *Die Griechischen Christlichen Schriftsteller*
LCL   *Loeb Classical Library*
MGH   *Monumenta Germaniae Historica*
NPNF *Nicene and Post-Nicene Fathers*
OCD   *The Oxford Classical Dictionary*
PL   *Patrologia Latina*
SC   *Sources Chrétiennes*

TRANSLATOR'S PREFACE

The translation of *De templo* offered in the following pages came about as a result of a Latin course on Bede given to our graduate students in Medieval History. In view of the ever diminishing number of students with even the rudiments let alone a good command of Latin, I have designedly opted for a rendering that adheres to the original as closely as the genius of English will allow. In consequence the reader may feel that the pull of the original has at times distorted the English wording, but here I can cite eminent precedents, notably the RSV, where the idiom of the original Hebrew or Greek is at times distinctly evident in the English. Bede's architectonic sentence structure, a feature of his style and a reflex of the density of his thought, has occasionally resulted in rather lengthy sentences in the English, and may require closer concentration on the reader's part, if not perhaps even a second reading. Here and there it has been necessary for clarity to repeat a noun or pronoun, verb or adverb which the Latin requires only once in a long sentence or succession of clauses. Otherwise I have made few concessions to the reader. While endeavouring to offer a version that was accurate and idiomatic, rather than a readable but reductive paraphrase, I have favoured fidelity over elegance for two reasons: first with a view to allowing the reader with little or no Latin to taste something of the flavour of Bede's language and appreciate his mindset; secondly with a thought for the serious student of medieval history whose Latin is either rusty or sketchy or otherwise inadequate, but who would still like to be able to compare the translation with the original and see at least how the English version was arrived at. I also had in mind those who, like myself, have to teach such students how to read a Latin text of this complexity and have a very limited amount of time in which to do so. Anyway readers must not forget that even for those competent enough in Latin to read the original text with relative ease, Bede's involved periodic sentences still have to be wrestled with, sometimes long and hard, before yielding up their meaning. Surely English readers cannot reasonably complain if no less is demanded of them than Bede's Latin demanded of readers of his own time.

Putting English on the architectural terminology relating to the Temple and its precincts posed difficulties of its own. The textual uncertainties reflected in divergent readings in the Hebrew Massoretic text and the Septuagint Greek of 3 Kings are evidence that even the Hebrew and Greek editors or translators of the texts as they have come down to us encountered somewhat similar problems. Writing, as they did, long after the event, they inevitably reworked the text, and their depiction Solomon's Temple was understandably coloured by the much modified post-exilic Temple familiar to them. The problem is compounded by the fact that in Ch. 17 of our text Bede is drawing upon Cassiodorus who in turn is drawing upon Josephus. Now, we know that Cassiodorus organized a Latin translation of *Jewish Antiquities* which Bede must have known and be quoting here in his description of the Temple. But Josephus probably based his account of the Temple courts on what he knew of the much later Temple of Herod. All of this the reader must bear in mind.

The word *porticus* used in the Vulgate and equally by Bede is a particular case in point. It is a multi-purpose rendering of several words differing more or less in meaning. The commonest of these is αἰλάμ (*ailám*), the Septuagint Graecization of Hebrew אֵילָם (*'ūlām*), usually rendered 'vestibule'. Others are Greek πυλών (*pulōn*), 'gateway', 'gatehouse', προθύρον (*prothúron*), 'space before the door', 'front door', 'porch', and στοά (*stoá*), (the word used by Josephus and rendered *porticus* by Bede) 'roofed colonnade, cloister, portico' etc. Dom David Hurst, editor of the Latin text of *De templo*, on which this translation is based, very kindly agreed to look at this chapter of my translation where, as elsewhere, I had originally rendered *porticus* as 'portico'. In a private communication he remarked that this "use of 'portico' might be misleading. Here in the United States, 'portico' or 'porch' is used to describe a veranda, whereas abroad it denotes a covering of the main door of a large house." Yet, while, of course, I deeply appreciate his kindness in vetting my translation and suggesting improvements, there are two observations which, with great respect, I feel I must make: (a) I have seen *porticus* or its Hebrew or Greek counterparts in the context of 3 Kings 6 rendered 'portico' and even 'porch' in quite recent publications by several biblical commentators, mainly North Americans; and (b) not only in the most modern English dictionaries of British provenance but even in Webster's Dictionary (New York, 1988) the word 'portico' is defined 'as a colonnade or covered passage-way in classical architecture.' (See the footnote on the Loeb translator's rendering of the Greek *stoá(s)* at Ch. 17.1). Nevertheless I have taken Dom Hurst's point and, in deference to what he assures me is current North American usage, have in some instances used the translation 'colonnade', notably in Chapter 17.2. But it did not seem necessary or advisable to adopt this rendering uniformly throughout the work. And the same applies to the rendering of several other expressions in *De templo*. As the panel members of the body of 54 that produced the 'Authorized Version' or King James Bible of 1611 stated in their Preface:

> 'An other thing we thinke good to admonish thee of (gentle Reader) that wee haue not tyed our selues to an vniformitie of phrasing, or to an identitie of words, as some peraduenture would wish that we had done, because they obserue, that some learned men some where, haue beene as exact as they could that way... That we should expresse the same notion in the same particular word; as for example, if we translate the Hebrew or Greeke word once by *Purpose*, neuer to call it *intent*; if one where *Iourneying*, neuer *Traveiling*, if one where *Thinke*, never *Suppose*; if one where *Paine*, neuer *Ache*; if one where *Ioy*, neuer *Gladnesse*, etc. Thus to minse the matter, wee thought to sauour more of curiositie then wisedome, and that rather it would breed scorne in the Atheist, then bring profite to the godly Reader. For is the kingdome of God become words or syllables? why should wee be in bondage to them if we may be free, vse one precisely when wee may vse another no lesse fit, as commodiously?'

Not that I am suggesting any comparison between the present modest undertaking and that of the authors of the King James Bible; but I am fully in accord with their principle and in the light of such a precedent one feels no apology is needed for adopting it. In the last analysis the context and one's own judgement must be one's guide. Readers will have to decide for themselves in the light of the original Latin, Greek or Hebrew and their own regional English usage.

The following editorial features of this translation should be noted:

1) Scripture texts are identified according to the abbreviation system of the *Jerusalem Bible*, with two exceptions: to avoid confusion the Vulgate nomenclature used in *De templo* is consistently followed here, i.e. the titles 3 and 4 Kings (3 and 4 K) are used instead of 1 and 2 Kings, and Paralipomenon (Paralip) instead of Chronicles. For quotations from the Psalms the Vulgate enumeration is followed. The translations of the scripture texts are based on the

Vulgate but the wording is adapted to that of Bede who occasionally follows a version other than the Vulgate.

2) To make it easier to check the English against the original, the page numbers of Hurst's critical edition of the Latin, *CCSL* vol. 119A, are given in the margins.

3) Cross-references, *supra* and *infra* within the work are indicated in the footnotes by means of a double asterisk.

4) Bede's chapter headings, (*Capitula*), have been inserted into the appropriate places in the text. This seemed preferable to page after page of unrelieved text as in the Latin edition. Moreover, the chapters have been broken up into sections for ease of reference, the sections, in all but one or two cases, corresponding to the paragraphs of the Latin.

Readers of the original Latin will be aware that, although the work is divided into two books, the chapters are numbered as if it formed a single book. This arrangement, which was Bede's own, I have retained to preserve uniformity and facilitate reference to the original; which explains why the first chapter of Book 2 is not Chapter 1 but Chapter 17. Twice the text of the Latin traverses the chapter break, viz. at 13/14 and 24/25. To ensure a smoother transition in each instance I have transferred the link phrase from the end of the preceding chapter to the beginning of the next.

INTRODUCTION

The theme of the Tabernacle and Temple recurs throughout Bede's exegetical writings and provides the main subject for three homilies and three of his biblical commentaries, *De tabernaculo* (c.721–25), *In Esram et Neemiam* (c.725–31) and *De templo* (c.729–31)[1]. At first sight this interest in defunct Jewish buildings and their associated cultic ritual and priesthood may seem antiquarian and strangely at variance with the vital contemporary concerns of the *Ecclesiastical History of the English People* (731), with which his reputation is identified for most modern readers. During the past twenty years or so, however, scholars have shown that Bede inherited rhetorical traditions from Late Roman Christian historiography and that his historical writings share some of the preoccupations and even the techniques of his Old Testament commentaries[2]. Henry Mary-Harting has argued that the description of the universal Church in *De templo* and the account of the building of the Church among the *gens Anglorum* in *Historia Ecclesiastica* (*HE*) in particular 'form a kind of diptych'.[3]

In the autobiographical note appended to the *HE*, Bede (673–735) testifies that throughout his monastic life, which was spent in the joint foundation of Wearmouth-Jarrow in Northumbria, he had applied himself to the study of the scriptures. Partly for the benefit of his monastic brethren, he made 'brief extracts from the works of the venerable Fathers on the holy Scriptures' and added notes of his own 'to clarify their sense and interpretation'. This modest disclaimer may give a misleading impression of his biblical commentaries, especially his later work. Bede was immensely well read in patristic exegesis in which the theme of the Tabernacle and Temple frequently occurs but *De templo* is very far from being a mere pastiche. Not only has its modern editor identified few direct patristic quotations in the text but in the Latin tradition it appears to be the first sustained allegorical

---

[1] See Bibliography for details of editions and translations of primary texts cited. *Homiliae* 2.1, 2.24, 2.25; Holder 1989, 1994.

[2] Ray 1976, 1982, 1985; Kendall 1979; Davidse 1982; Thacker 1983; McClure 1983.

[3] Mayr-Harting 1976, 13.

commentary on the description of Solomon's Temple in 3 K 5:1–
7:51, just as Bede's earlier commentaries on the description of the
Tabernacle in Ex 24:12–30 and on the account of the Second Temple
in Ezra and Nehemiah also fill gaps in the patristic legacy. As will be
seen, the theme of the Temple was peculiarly suited to Bede's well-
known objective of supplying teaching materials for the purposes of
monastic formation and the education of spiritual teachers who had
a crucial role in his vision of the regeneration and inner conversion
of contemporary society. The inspiration of Gregory the Great is
evident but both the form in which *De Templo* is cast and Bede's
handling of individual features reveal a work of originality and insight,
marking the culmination of a lifetime's thought and writing on the
subject: the closest parallels to *De Templo* occur in three of Bede's
own Gospel homilies.

The key to understanding the significance of the Temple image for
Bede and his monastic contemporaries lies in the huge importance
of the image in Scripture itself where its Christian interpretation is
already well established. An indication of the major links in the
chain of biblical texts concerning the Temple (which are all in some
way used or assumed in *De templo*) may therefore give some idea
of the scale and complexity of the materials at Bede's disposal and
of the allusive subtlety with which he used Scripture to comment on
Scripture in the light of his patristic reading.

THE TABERNACLE AND TEMPLE IN SCRIPTURE

1. The Old Covenant House of God

The Book of Exodus describes the pivotal event in Jewish history,
namely the deliverance of God's chosen people from slavery in Egypt
and his covenant with them. It recounts their crossing of the Red Sea
and forty-year exile in the wilderness before their final homecoming
to the Promised Land. In the New Testament these events were read
as having an underlying and continuing significance for Christians
who perceived in the literal text divinely ordained prefigurings of
their own deliverance from sin through baptism, and of their journey
through this earthly life to the heavenly Promised Land and the new
Jerusalem (1 Co 10:1–4, 11).

The Exodus story was recalled and appropriated in the early liturgy
for the Easter vigil and baptism of catechumens so that the new

chosen people, gentile as well as Jewish converts to the Church, became the spiritual inheritors of the covenant made between God and his people in the desert and of the divine promise that they would become 'a kingdom of priests and a holy nation' (Ex 19:6; 1 P 2:90–10). That deliverance and covenant had been graphically epitomised in the Tabernacle which God had instructed Moses to build, a tent-like structure in which the sacred shrine of the Ark of the Covenant could be housed during the long sojourn in the desert. Two golden cherubim were placed over the Ark in the innermost Holy of Holies and God promised, 'I will speak to you over the propitiatory and from the midst of the two cherubims' (Ex 25:22).

When the Jews became a settled people in the Promised Land, the Ark was transferred to the Holy of Holies in the Temple which David's son Solomon had been divinely inspired to build in Jerusalem (3 K 8:1–20). Both the Tabernacle and its successor the Temple were seen as the house of God, the place of God's presence with his people. As well as the detailed accounts of the Tabernacle in Ex 25–30, 35–40 and of the Temple in 3 K 5–8, the image of God's dwelling-place recurs right through the Old Testament in supplementary descriptions of the two successive buildings and their cults, in many allusions in the psalms and the prophets and in historical accounts of the fortunes of the Israelites typified in foreign desecrations and subsequent re-building of the Temple. The image carries the whole history of God's relationship with his people.

In a homily Bede chronicles this process from the construction of Solomon's Temple to its destruction by the Babylonians four hundred and thirty years later; from the return of the chosen people after their seventy-year exile, and the rebuilding of the Second Temple in forty-six years under Zerubbabel and Joshua, to its profanation with idolatrous images by Antiochus the Greek three hundred and fifty-six years later and its subsequent purification and re-dedication under Judas Maccabeus. Bede's summary ends with a quotation from St Paul: ' "All these things were done as an example for us" (1 Co 10:11) and were written down for us, and so we must scrutinise them carefully for their spiritual meaning'[4]. Paul's text, originally applied to the account of the Exodus, encapsulates an entire methodology of interpretation and was frequently cited in exegesis and applied to the whole of the Old Testament. It is quoted at the opening of *De*

---

[4] Homily 2.24, Martin and Hurst 1991, 248–49.

tabernaculo to explain why Bede's exposition extends to all the circumstantial details of time, place, objects, deeds and words contained in the description of the Tabernacle in Exodus. Similarly, immediately after the introduction to *De Templo*, Bede explains he will be discussing all the details of the Temple's construction contained in the biblical account of Solomon's Temple 'for these matters too are pregnant with scriptural mysteries according to the testimony of the Apostle: "All these things happened to them (in the Old Testament) by way of example, and they were recorded in writing to be a lesson for us" '.

2. The New Covenant and the Heavenly Sanctuary

While the magnificent Temple of Solomon in Jerusalem, filled with the glory of the Lord, is a powerful image of Isaiah's experience of the presence of God (Is 6:1–6), the prophet was also aware that the Creator of heaven and earth could not be circumscribed (Is 66:1, cf. Ps 10:5) and his words were taken up in the New Testament to show that God who made the world 'dwells not in temples made with (human) hands' (Ac 4:8–9; 17:24; Jn 4:21–24). The Epistle to the Hebrews gives an extended exegesis on the replacement of the entire Old Covenant by the New which greatly influenced patristic expositions of the Tabernacle and Temple. The 'former Tabernacle' (including, by extension, the Temple) is revealed to have been but an earthly shadow or copy of the heavenly reality shown to Moses (Heb 8:5,9; 10:1), its priesthood and blood sacrifices now superseded by Christ's priestly offering of himself which has enabled him to pass through the veil of the Holy of Holies, not into the inner sanctuary reserved for the High Priest in the earthly Tabernacle, but into the *heavenly* sanctuary 'not made with hands' which is the abode of God (Heb 9:11–12, 24).

A roll-call of honour reviews Old Testament history and heroes, including Abraham and other faithful patriarchs from even before the Mosaic Law, who desired not simply a homeland but a city 'whose builder and maker is God' (Heb 11:10); these are the spiritual ancestors of all Christians (cf. Ga 3:5–29). As in the prophetic visions of the Temple in Isaiah, Ezekiel, the psalms and the Apocalypse, the image of the heavenly sanctuary here broadens and merges with that of the walled citadel of the heavenly Jerusalem to which all the faithful will eventually be drawn (Heb 12:22). For the faithful there can be no lasting earthly tabernacle or city: 'We seek one ⟨yet⟩ to come' (Heb 13:14); when 'the earthly house of this habitation be dissolved, we have a building of God, a house not made with hands, eternal in the heavens' (2 Co 5:1). The text forms part of the closing image in *De templo*.

The idea that the Church has already, since the Incarnation and Passion of Christ, spiritually replaced the Tabernacle and Temple on earth but is itself incomplete, awaiting its future fulfilment in heaven whose eternal joys can only be glimpsed and desired by the faithful still on earth is a fundamental assumption underlying Bede's *De templo*. This does not mean that the Jewish Temple is to be reviled; rather it is to be revered because, like the Tabernacle, it had been divinely ordained in its day as a shadow or prefiguring of the divine temple 'not made with hands' and therefore a proper spiritual interpretation of its features still has much to teach the present Church. As well as looking back at the material structure of a building in the past, Christian exegetes also looked at scriptural accounts of the heavenly sanctuary yet to be revealed. Discussion of the heavenly Jerusalem was shaped by knowledge of the earthly sanctuaries which were held to prefigure it. The heavenly Jerusalem is thus built foursquare, recalling the Holy of Holies in the Temple of Solomon (Rv 21:6; 3 K 6:20); it has twelve gates inscribed with the names of the twelve tribes of Israel, recalling the encampment of the twelve tribes around the Tabernacle in the desert (Rv 21:13; Nb 2:3–31; Ezk 48:30–35). The theophany of the Ark of the Covenant in the heavenly sanctuary and the vision of the glory of God filling the heavenly Temple of the new creation (Rv 11:19; 15:5,8) evokes the scenes of God taking possession of his Tabernacle in the desert (Ex 40:34–35) and of his Temple in Jerusalem (3 K 8:10–11; Is 6:4). All three sanctuaries — the Mosaic Tabernacle, Solomon's Temple and the heavenly Jerusalem — signify God's presence with his people. Clearly there is no suggestion in the New Testament of a particular church building as the replacement of the Temple: how, then, was God's presence among his new chosen people expressed?

3. The Temple of Christ's Body

In John's gospel Jesus is challenged by the Jews to give some sign of the divine authority by which he had presumed to cleanse the Temple in Jerusalem of its traders and money-lenders. He replied: 'Destroy this temple and in three days I will raise it up'. They understood him literally, but, explains the evangelist, 'he spoke of the temple of his body' (Jn 2:13–18). In Mark's account of Christ's trial his Jewish priestly accusers say, 'We heard him say, I will destroy this temple made with hands and within three days I will build another not made with hands' (Mk 14:58; cf. Mt 26:61; 27:40). The new Temple, the place of the divine presence, is here presented as the incarnate body of Christ.

4.　The Living Temple of the Church

The Old Testament Tabernacle and Temple were seen, therefore, in the New Testament itself as prefiguring both the eternal heavenly sanctuary, the destined homeland of the faithful into which Christ passed after his atoning sacrifice, *and* his incarnate body in which that propitiation had been made. The allegorical interpretation of the Temple was further enriched, however, by New Testament texts visualising the Church on earth in terms of architectural images which merged with the Pauline metaphor of the Church as the body of Christ, its various members having different spiritual gifts and functions as the limbs of the body variously serve its head. Two texts are of particular importance here. Ep 2:19–22 describes the formation of the new people of God, gentiles as well as Jews, as an organic building which is still growing, 'built upon the foundation of the apostles and prophets, Jesus Christ himself being the chief corner-stone, in whom all the building is framed together, grows up into an holy temple to the Lord... in whom you also are built together into an habitation of God in the Spirit.'

The second text, 1 P 2:4–10, describes all the members of the Church as inheriting God's promises made to their spiritual ancestors in the desert before the construction of the Tabernacle: 'You are a chosen people, a royal priesthood, a holy nation' (cf. Ex 19:6). It is therefore the community of the faithful, not a material church building, which forms the new household of God; its members are exhorted to be 'as living stones built up, a spiritual house, a holy priesthood, to offer up spiritual sacrifices to God by Jesus Christ'.

Individual scriptural images offer the possibility of extending the building metaphor still further. Both Ep 2:20 and, more fully, 1 P 2:4–8 incorporate the Old Testament image of 'the stone which the builders rejected', destined to become the cornerstone of the build-

ing (Ps 117:22) and the precious stone laid in the foundation of Zion
(Is 28:16), explicitly identified with Christ in the synoptic gospels
and Acts. The new 'holy temple to the Lord' built of living stones
upon the apostles and prophets also has Christ as its one foundation (1 Co 3:11).

This spiritual building can be viewed from various perspectives. It
is the continuing community of all the faithful on earth, awaiting its
completion in the heavenly sanctuary of which it is but a reflection.
But individual Christians can also be seen as building up the Church
from the foundation which has been divinely laid (1 Co 3:10). Each
Christian is exhorted not only to become a living stone or a pillar
in the new temple (Ga 2:9; Rv 3:12) but at baptism to become that
temple and remain worthy of being so: 'Know you not that you are
the temple of God and that the Spirit of God dwells in you?' (1 Co
3:16; 2 Co 6:16). The faithful thus strive to become like Christ whose
body, filled with the Holy Spirit, forms the new temple of the divine
presence with his chosen people on earth.

It will by now be evident that the great chain of scriptural texts
using the architectural metaphor to describe the incorporation of the
faithful into Christ reveals insights into the multiple meanings of the
term 'the body of Christ' – incarnate, sacramental, ecclesial, mystical.
Though already, through baptism, forming part of the body of Christ,
the community of the Church on earth longs to be fully joined with
Christ and united with all the faithful who have gone before.

THE TEMPLE THEME IN PATRISTIC EXEGESIS

The interpretation of the Temple as a figure of the incarnate body
of Christ, the community of the Church on earth, the individual soul
and the heavenly sanctuary or city of the New Jerusalem was therefore not the invention of patristic or medieval exegesis but is already
contained within the New Testament. The Fathers were important,
however, in demonstrating the simultaneity of these modes of interpretation, and in popularising exegetical chains of texts featuring
elements of the image. A few examples must suffice to illustrate
something of the range of other scriptural texts to which the Temple exegesis was applied, with a variety of rhetorical approaches and
differences of theological emphasis.

The interpretative method of **Origen** (185–254/5) was of fundamental importance to the history of the allegorical interpretation of

Scripture. In the first of his sixteen surviving Homilies on the Book
of Leviticus, translated by Rufinus, he argued that, just as the human
flesh of the Word of God veiled his divinity from most eyes, so the
underlying spiritual meaning of the Word of God as expressed in
the Old Testament is veiled by the literal letter of the Law and the
prophets. It follows that the literal text is inspired and important:
Moses really was shown 'heavenly things' but the Tabernacle and later
the Temple and its cult were merely copies of that reality, 'a shadow
of things to come', (citing 1 Co 10:1–4; Col 2:17; Heb 10:1).[5] The
regulations governing the ritual purification, ordination, vestments,
sacrifices and altar vessels of the Old Covenant priesthood described
in the book of Leviticus therefore have a continuing importance for
the Christian because they represent divine precepts to be understood
spiritually, although no longer practised literally. Scripture is used to
explain Scripture; the Epistle to the Hebrews transformed Origen's
reading of Leviticus and the associated Old Testament accounts of
the Tabernacle and Temple. Particularly influential was the exposition of the 'twofold sanctuaries' in both buildings: the outer one,
visible and open to the Aaronic priesthood, represents the present
Church on earth which is open not only to the ordained but to all
the elect through baptism, while the inner sanctuary, invisible and
entered only by the Jewish High Priest, is a figure of heaven itself.[6]
The distinction is a major element in Bede's *De templo*.

   Ambrose (c.339–97) was important in mediating this Alexandrian
allegorical interpretation of Scripture to the Latin West. He applied
the scriptural texts of the architectural metaphor to the interpretation of the opening chapters of Luke's gospel, which itself uses the
image of the Temple in Jerusalem as a means of showing how the
Old Covenant priesthood and sacrifices were superseded by Christ.
In the third book of his commentary Ambrose links several key texts
concerning the Temple. Christ is 'the priest who is to come...who
would not offer sacrifice for us in a temple made with human hands
(Heb 9:11, 24; Acts 17:24) but he would offer propitiation for our
sins in the temple of his body' (Jn 2:19–22). He very briefly describes the Temple built by Solomon as the type of the church built
by God and describes its origin and nature, its growth and vocation through the New Testament metaphor of the spiritual building

---

[5] *Homilies on Leviticus*, Barkley 1990, 29, 141–2, 205.
[6] Barkley 1990, 195–6.

formed of living stones (1 P 2:5), built upon the foundation of the apostles and prophets, with Christ as its cornerstone 'in whom all the building framed together grows into a temple' (Eph 2:20–21). Ambrose applies this exegetical chain, however, not to an exposition of the Old Testament Temple building but to his discussion of the genealogy of Christ in Lk 3:23–38 which immediately follows the account of Christ's baptism[7]. Bede's commentary on Luke's gospel was influenced by Ambrose's so it may seem surprising that he did not incorporate book three of Ambrose's work in his own discussion of the Lucan genealogy. However, it may well have been an important source of inspiration, particularly its treatment of the faithful who lived before the Incarnation, which is a favourite theme with Bede and is fully integrated into the architectural metaphor of Solomon's Temple in *De templo*. Ambrose shows that the royal and priestly human lineage taken on by Christ at his Incarnation is also that of his Church. Christ's Old Testament ancestors are therefore the spiritual ancestors of all those, whether Jew or gentile, who in baptism share in Christ's anointing as prophet, priest and king and who 'in time past were not a people but are now the people of God' (1 P 2:9–10, citing Ho 1:10). The pastoral theology of baptism is fundamental to an understanding of *De templo* where it signifies not only initial conversion into the unity of faith and membership of the household of God but is an image of the process of continuing inner conversion which characterises the Christian life and the monastic vocation in particular.

The Temple metaphor permeates the work of **Augustine** (354–430), not only in his commentaries on texts such as Jn 2:19–21 which were links in the exegetical chain, but in his influential commentaries on the psalms which in a monastic society were intimately known through the daily divine office. Ps 86:1–2, for example, ('The foundations thereof are in the holy mountains: The Lord loves the gates of Sion above all the tabernacles of Jacob'), prompts a dazzling rhetorical display.[8] Augustine deploys the usual texts, such as Ep 2:19–22, 1 P 2:5–9, 1 Co 3:11, to reveal the psalm's spiritual allusion to the present Church, the heavenly Jerusalem and Christ himself and its direct relevance to his readers and listeners: 'These words apply to us'. Augustine then stands the figure on its head to show its incon-

---

[7] *Expositio evangelii secundum Lucam*, Book 3. O'Reilly 1994, 355–69, 383–88.

[8] *Enarrationes in psalmos*, 1198–1203; Ladner 1983, 180–81.

sistencies and even absurdities: how can the prophets and apostles be the foundations of this spiritual building if its one foundation is Christ? How can Christ possibly be described as a door, such as is made by a carpenter? This introduces the key exegetical concept that divinity is present in all places and the likeness of all things can simultaneously be applied to it, but in reality it is none of these things. Having justified the use and the necessity of paradox and of the mixed metaphor in attempting to give some glimpse of an ultimately unknowable mystery, he shows how the spiritual building of the Church is that part of the body of Christ still in pilgrimage on earth, Christ having 'gone ahead'. The theme, central to Bede's world view, underlies *The City of God*.

Commenting on the idea that Old Testament references to Jerusalem as the city of God seem to be fulfilled when Solomon builds the Temple, but are also a symbol of Jerusalem in heaven, Augustine notes: 'Now, this class of prophecy in which there is a compounding and commingling, as it were, of both references, is of the greatest importance in the ancient canonical books which contain historical narratives and it still exercises the wits of those who examine sacred Scripture'.[9] The divine promise made to king David about the building of the future Temple, literally fulfilled by Solomon, also refers to 'the one that was to come, who would build God a house not of wood and stone, but of human beings...you are that temple' (cf. 1 Co 3:17). This is very much Bede's approach in *De templo*.

The influence of **Gregory the Great** (c.540–604) on Bede's exegesis and his vision of the Church and its reform is well known.[10]. Arthur Holder has noted some points of comparison between Gregory's homilies on Ezekiel 40 and Bede's *De tabernaculo* and *De templo* and the general influence on Bede of Gregory's practical spiritual application of the scriptural text, particularly regarding pastors and teachers.[11] In a homily on Lk 19:41–47, Gregory noted how Christ's prophecy of the destruction of Jerusalem and his cleansing of the Temple showed that 'the downfall of the people arose principally from the sins of the priests'.[12] Bede shared Gregory's view

---

[9] *De civitate Dei*, 17.3 (Bettenson 1972, 714, cf 734–35, 768). Temple theme also in Bk 17.20; 18.45; 18.48; 21.26.
[10] Thacker 1983; 1992, 152–59; McClure 1985, 17
[11] *Homiliae in Ezechielem* Bk 2; Holder 1989 244; McClure 1983, 81, n 27.
[12] *Homiliae in euangelia*, 39; Hurst 1990, 358.

and incorporated the passage into his own commentary on Luke. In Ezekiel, Gregory found the prophetic figure of a priest aware of the responsibilities and contemporary shortcomings of the pastor. In the context of the Israelites' exile from Jerusalem, Ezekiel's vision is not simply of rebuilding the physically desecrated Temple in Jerusalem abandoned by God, but of reconstituting his people through thoroughgoing religious reform so that God could dwell with them again. The image of Ezekiel's visionary Temple, partly based on the description of Solomon's Temple in the books of Kings and Chronicles, is called into imaginative being through the incantatory measurement of its features reiterated in the Apocalyptic vision of the new Jerusalem (Ez 40–42; Rv 21:15–17). Gregory's and Bede's use of the common exegetical tool of numerology in discerning the concealed meanings of architectural features is particularly appropriate in their exposition of the Temple whose dimensions have such an important role in both its historical description and visionary evocations in scripture.

In his preface Gregory notes that Ezekiel's vision of the Temple is veiled in clouds of obscurity. His ten homilies, which are confined to Ez 40 alone, are extremely diffuse and only partly concerned with the interpretation of the Temple's architecture but contain a number of features which were to be assimilated by Bede in *De templo*. Several parts and dimensions of the Temple, for example, are interpreted as denoting the triad of faith, hope and charity and the numerology of the decalogue is used to expound the perfection of combining the active and contemplative life, the love of God and one's neighbour.

Gregory interprets Ezekiel's reconstituted Temple and city of Jerusalem as both the heavenly Jerusalem and the Church 'which labours on earth before it will reign in heaven'. He cites the usual New Testament texts to reveal this as a spiritual building made of living stones laid on the foundation of Christ (1 P 2:5; 1 Co 3:9, 11,17). As in *De templo* the faithful are variously described as living stones in the Temple fabric or as being the Temple in which God dwells or as entering the Temple to contemplate their heavenly end. The holy teachers are seen as weighty squared stones supporting others and as builders laying stones in the Temple building. The emphasis is on elucidating the building up of the spiritual life, aspects of which are illustrated from the experience of the early Church in the Acts of the Apostles and the Epistles. Like Bede in *De templo*, Gregory shows that 'He enters the building of the heavenly city who meditates by imitating the ways of the good in the Church' and stresses it is the function of priests to guard the Temple through keeping watch over the faithful, praying, preaching, administering the sacraments and correcting the lives of the worldly. Preachers in particular are the very gateways into the Temple; like Bede, Gregory is emphatic on the importance of their knowing and interpreting Scripture, the standard of measurement for the spiritual life and good works. Like Bede, Gregory distinguishes between models of the spiritual life and those still in thrall to their carnal senses who do not know how to burn with inward love and yearning towards the heavenly. He distinguishes between levels of spiritual perfection and between the compunction of fear and love represented by the Temple's two altars of sacrifice and incense but shows that there is one life of blessedness promised to all the faithful, little and great (Ps 113:13) for 'in my Father's house are many mansions' (Jn 14:2). Both quotations are cited in *De tabernaculo* and resonate through Bede's *De templo*.[13]

BEDE'S OBJECTIVES AND APPROACH

What, then, is distinctive about Bede's handling of a traditional theme? In his early handbook on rhetorical figures, *De schematibus et tropis* (c.700/701), Bede explains that one word or historical event or place in Scripture can at the same time figuratively designate several kinds of understanding. The historical temple built by Solomon, for example, can be seen allegorically as the body of Christ or his Church; tropologically it can refer to the life of the individual soul, the dwelling-place of the Holy Spirit, and anagogically, 'leading us to higher things', it can signify the joys of the heavenly dwelling in the new Jerusalem (120–121). He concludes: 'My discussion of the Church in accordance with the allegorical interpretation has followed the example of that most scholarly commentator, Gregory, who in his *Moralia*, while he did not apply the specific name of allegory to those deeds and words about Christ or the Church, nevertheless interpreted them figuratively'.[14] Gregory taught the literal meaning of the Old Testament text, 'its bearing on the mysteries of Christ and the Church, and the sense in which it applies to each of the faithful'. (*HE* 2.1) Similarly, although Bede does occasionally use a formal fourfold or threefold interpretation of a scriptural passage, in practice he had a

---

[13] Gray 1990, 184, 197; Holder 1994, 22; *De templo*, Prologue; 11.3, 16.2, 18.14, 25.3.

[14] Tannenhaus 1973, 121.

far more flexible approach, particularly in his later work, usually only
distinguishing between the historical meaning of the literal text and
its underlying spiritual significance for the present reader which he
variously termed the allegorical or mystical or figurative sense.[15]

The opening of Book I of *De templo* is a tour de force in which
Bede succinctly demonstrates his command of the temple metaphor's
entire range by citing or alluding to scriptural texts from each level of
its traditional interpretation, though without using rhetorical terms.
The house of God built by Solomon in Jerusalem 'was made as a
figure of the holy universal Church' built by Christ. The obvious
limitations of describing the Church through the static image of a
building are immediately confronted. The architectural metaphor
spans vast time and space and is animated and articulated through
attributing to it the characteristics both of a pilgrim people and the
limbs or members of a body. Thus the Church is still in the process
of being built, part of it is still in exile in this earthly life, part already
'reigns with him in heaven where, when the last judgment is over, it
is to reign completely with him'. It is further shown to be the temple
of Christ's incarnate and risen body (Jn 2:21) and the temple of the
Holy Spirit dwelling in each of the faithful (1 Co 3:16); thus 'it is
quite clear that the material Temple (of Solomon) was a figure of
us all, that is, both of the Lord himself and his members which we
are. But it was a figure of him as the uniquely chosen and precious
cornerstone laid in the foundation (Is 28:16; 1 P 2:5–10) and of us
as the living stones built upon the foundation of the apostles and
prophets (Ep 2:20), that is, on the Lord himself' (cf. 1 Co 3:11). The
figure of Solomon's Temple can therefore apply to Christ in some
respects, in others to all the elect, collectively and individually, both
those on earth and those already in heaven.

In his homily on Jn 2:12–22 and in two homilies for anniversaries
of the dedication of his own monastic church at Jarrow, Bede had
already discussed texts in this exegetical chain and had allegorically
expounded certain physical features of Solomon's Temple.[16] In *De
templo* he proposes a systematic verse-by-verse consideration of Solomon's Temple as it is described in 3 K 5:1–7:51, just as in his earlier
work *De tabernaculo*, he had provided a sustained commentary on
the description of the Mosaic Tabernacle in Ex 24:12–30:21. Another

---

[15] Jones 1969–70, 131–151; Holder 1994, xviii, 25, 104; Ward 1990, 41–87.
[16] *Homiliae* 2.1; 2.24; 2.25.

claim to originality is that Bede established a distinction between Tabernacle and Temple which considerably refined his exegesis of the Temple.[17] Each can show us 'an image of the universal Church which is the one Church of Christ', but whereas the Tabernacle was a temporary portable structure built in the desert 'on the route by which one reaches the promised land', the stone Temple was built in that land of promise, in Jerusalem, so 'the former can be taken to represent the toil and exile of the present Church, the latter the rest and happiness of the future Church' in the heavenly Jerusalem (**1.1,2**).[18]

De templo is without the digressions of Gregory's exegesis on the enigmatic 'profound mysteries' of Ezekiel's vision; instead, it is based on a historical account of an actual building, from which it draws mysteries. The Old Testament passage expounded in *De templo* describes King Solomon building a house for the Lord in fulfilment of his father David's intentions, and God's promise to dwell in the midst of his people Israel if they will keep all his commandments. 3 K 5 describes in detail the provision of the building materials and organisation of the workforce. Ch 6 chronicles the gradual construction of the outer porch, the floors, walls, doors, windows and roof, the building's dimensions and the rich embellishment of all the interior surfaces; it also describes the construction of an inner oracle to house the sacred Ark of the Covenant enshrining the Law and set beneath two golden cherubim. Ch 7 details particular features of the building, notably the two massive pillars set up at its entrance, various Temple furnishings such as the water laver and, finally, the Temple treasure chambers into which, at the completion of the building work, Solomon brings all the precious vessels dedicated by his father. Bede's commentary therefore expounds a description not of the anatomy of a building but of its organic growth through time. The building of Solomon's Temple in seven years and its dedication, presumably in the following year, facilitated its allegorical application not only to the spiritual growth of the individual faithful, but to the whole historical development of the universal Church and its future completion and dedication in the eighth age of the world. It is a remarkably focused, coherent piece of work with persistent themes which further identify it as an original creation within a tradition.

---

[17] cf. *De tabernaculo* 2,1; Holder 1994 xv, xiv, 45; Homily 2.25.

[18] Numbers given in bold refer to the chapter and section divisions of *De templo*.

Some insight into these preoccupations is given in the third prologue. It is addressed to Bede's close friend, Acca, who was abbot
and bishop of Hexham (709–31). He was a very learned theologian
who had built up a large and noble library (*HE* 5.20) and had for
long encouraged Bede in his exegetical writing to help create an ed-
ucated Anglo-Saxon clergy. Several of the earlier commentaries are
dedicated to Acca[19], whom Bede describes as one accustomed in this
transitory life to find consolation in the vision of 'the land of the living' revealed in the study of Scripture and the writings of the Fathers.
Bede sent *De templo* in spiritual friendship to this seasoned monastic
reader, who fulfilled the Gregorian ideal of the teacher and of those
in spiritual authority by combining the active and contemplative life.
Concern for orthodoxy and authorial humility alike prompted Bede
to describe the work as following in the footsteps of the Fathers yet
it is also self-confessedly 'novel', designed to present afresh familiar
truths whose contemplation would then reveal further consolatory
mysteries of Christ, the Church and of the heavenly mansions (Jn
14.2) which are the desire and the destination of the Christian life
and the monastic vocation. Acca is invited to emulate the example
of St John, the author of the Apocalypse, whose intense contemplation of 'the heavenly mansions' of the new Jerusalem enabled him
while still in his literal exile on Patmos and the figurative exile of this
earthly life, to share in the angelic discourse of heaven. Patristic and
early medieval exegesis interpreted the Apocalypse ecclesiologically,
that is, as a commentary on the contemporary Church.[20] Bede in
De templo paradoxically seeks 'the spiritual mansion of God in the
material structure' of Solomon's Temple (**2.1**).

The sublime objective of the work is pursued through the exposition of the scriptural account of Solomon's Temple, its construction,
materials, layout, dimensions, its decoration and liturgical furnishings and vessels. Although the Temple had long since been superseded by the Church and indeed physically destroyed, like the earlier
Tabernacle its original construction had been divinely ordered and
planned. The prologue opens with St Paul: 'Whatever was written
in former days was written for our instruction' (Rom 15:4).[21] Even
circumstantial details are therefore of importance: 'the writing of

---

[19] McClure 1985, 17–20; Ward 1990, 51–73.
[20] Matter 1992, 49.
[21] cf. the opening of *De tabernaculo*.

the Old Testament overflows with such perfection that, if one considers it properly, it contains in itself all the mysteries of the New Testament' (**5.2**). Bede shows respect for the inspired literal text and its historical meaning, trying to resolve any ambiguities or apparent inconsistencies between the descriptions of the Temple in the Book of Kings and in Chronicles and consulting the work of the Jewish scholar Josephus and of Cassiodorus for clarification of particular features of the building (**8.2; 17.1–3**).

In his homily on the cleansing of the Temple in Jerusalem, Bede had already explained that because 'that temple made with hands prefigured our Lord's most sacred body (Jn 2:19–21)... and likewise pointed to his body the Church', he would like to record some details of its construction so that 'this fraternal gathering may recognise how everything that is written about it is applicable to Christ's Church'. Bede's description of the building contains echoes of other scriptural accounts of the Temple. As in *De templo* **8.1**, for example, the door to the spiral stairway on the right side of Solomon's Temple suggests the means of spiritual ascent offered to the faithful by the wound opening Christ's side, the source of the sacraments, an allusion to the water of life which flowed from the right side of the Temple in Ezekiel's vision.[22]

The idea of expounding Solomon's Temple, sketched in the Lenten homily, grows immeasurably in *De templo* in concept and technique. The mental tour of the great building opens vistas on the historical journey of the chosen people journeying to the Promised Land, on the continuing journey of the new people of God towards the heavenly Jerusalem, a journey accomplished by the individual believer at death but continuing for the Church as a whole until the end of time. The work describes how the Church on earth can be built up spiritually to become more like that heavenly dwelling. It ends where it begins with the longing for the heavenly mansions but with the reader's understanding of that image extraordinarily enriched.

Bede does not simply treat the figure of the Temple as a mnemonic framework but exploits the function of its architectural components and the characteristics of its building materials. The initial straightforward exposition of the portico and outer part of the Temple respectively as the faithful of old and the faithful born after the Incarnation, for example, is transformed by the information that access to the in-

---

[22] Homily 2.1; Ezk 47:1; O'Reilly (1992) 173–4.

ner Holy of Holies, representing the joys of the heavenly kingdom, is granted to both groups. The same lesson is then differently taught by exposition of the three materials from which the walls and floors of the building are constructed, 'for in the different materials there is a manifold repetition of the same figures': stone, denoting the ancient people of God and the Law, a timber lining, representing the new chosen people and the Gospel, and finally gold leaf covering all surfaces and symbolising the heavenly reward open to all. The reader is drawn into a deeper understanding that these three categories do not merely refer to three different periods of time. Some people who lived 'before the era of the Gospel led the life of the Gospel', while there are 'a great many at the present time who are content with the precepts of the Law' (i.e. with its literal observance, not its spiritual interpretation); they 'are but at the beginning of spiritual life' (**11.3**).

The historical function of the Temple's structure in delineating areas accessible only to certain categories of people has been quite overturned to reveal spiritual truths about the nature of the universal Church. Similarly the Old Covenant priests who were ritually purified in the bronze water laver and could alone enter the Temple court do not just represent ordained Christian priests or religious but prefigure all those who, through baptism, share in Christ's priesthood (**19.1**); 'After all, it was not only to bishops and priests but to all God's children that the Apostle Peter was speaking when he said, "But you are a chosen people, a royal priesthood"' (**17.4**; 1 P 2:9).

DE TEMPLO AND THE ECCLESIASTICAL HISTORY

There is here no debate over the dating of Easter, the nature of Petrine authority or the rites of baptism and consecration; there is no discussion of synods and councils, the creation of dioceses or the rules of abbatial succession. There is only a brief commendation of the role of kings in increasing and supporting the Church (**2.2**). Bede's vision of the building up of the universal Church in *De templo* is, however, of the greatest interest in casting light on his account of the building of the Church among the *gens Anglorum* in *HE*.[23]

---

[23] Mayr-Harting 1976, 19–22.

1. Evangelization

The same evangelizing imperative underlying the *HE* is described in Bede's exposition of the large bronze water laver which stood in the Temple for ritual purification as prefiguring Christian baptism (**19.1**; 1 Co 10:1–2). It was supported by twelve bronze oxen arranged in groups of three looking outwards to the north, south, east and west (**19.5**). Bede interprets the oxen not only as the twelve apostles but as their successors as well, 'all the ministers of the word' taking belief in the Trinity to the four corners of the world, teaching and baptizing all nations *(omnes gentes)* as directly commanded by Christ (Mt 28:19–20). In a letter of 624 which Bede quotes in *HE* 2.8, Pope Boniface commends Justus, archbishop of Canterbury, for his work among the gentiles, namely the peoples subject to King Eadbald, commenting that the Matthean text 'has been fulfilled in your own ministry, opening the hearts of nations to receive the mystery of the gospel through your preaching'.

In *De templo* the distinction between the apostles Paul and Barnabas who took the Gospel to the gentiles and the apostle James who was ordered to remain in Jerusalem to strengthen the Church already established there is directly applied to the different roles of Augustine, Paulinus and the rest of the mission to the Anglo-Saxons and to Pope Gregory who had to remain in Rome (**20.7**). Gregory is acclaimed as combining both roles, however, in the laudatory biography in *HE* 2.1, which describes both the continuing need for Gregory's pastoral work in Rome, 'long converted to the true faith', and his active role in sending and supporting the English mission so that he may properly be called 'our apostle' who 'made our nation, till then enslaved to idols, into a Church of Christ'.

Part of Bede's distinction between the Tabernacle and the Temple is that the Jews alone built the Tabernacle in the desert but Solomon was assisted in constructing the Temple by the gentile workforce sent by Hiram king of Tyre (**2.3**). Though both structures are 'an image of the universal Church', in *De templo* the Tabernacle is particularly associated with 'the ancient people of God' and the Temple with the Church assembled from the gentiles as well as the Jews. In the *H.E.* the process by which the *gens Anglorum* were initially brought to the faith and then drawn ever more fully into the universal Church is presented as a continuation of the conversion of the gentiles recorded in the Acts of the Apostles in response to Christ's command to teach all nations.[24] If the Anglo-Saxons are the gentiles, the question may reasonably be asked: who in this context are the Jews? The native British Christians whose 'unspeakable crimes' and refusal to share their faith with the pagan invaders Bede so deplores, are presented by the latter-day Old Testament prophet Gildas, whom Bede cites, as a people who have broken the covenant. God therefore appointed 'much worthier heralds of the truth' to bring the Anglo-Saxon people, whom he foreknew, to the faith (*HE* 1.22; Rom 11:2). The following chapter immediately introduces the Gregorian mission, and Augustine and his monastic community settled at Canterbury are specifically described as imitating 'the way of life of the apostles and of the primitive church' (*HE* 1.26).

But Bede shows that this apostolic way of life was also adopted by the Irish monks engaged in converting and ministering to the Anglo-Saxons and, indeed, by some of their Anglo-Saxon disciples, as is made clear in the memorable pen-portraits of Aidan, Colman and the community at Lindisfarne, and of Chad. Similarly in *De templo* Bede notes that the skilled stonemasons of Solomon and Hiram are equally engaged in building the Temple at Jerusalem, both successfully hewing large dependable foursquare living stones which can be laid on the foundation of the apostles and prophets (Ep 2:20) and of Christ himself (1 Co 3:11): Bede directly relates this to the building up of the early Church by both Jewish and gentile Christian evangelists as recorded in the Acts of the Apostles. However, he notes that Hiram's woodcutters were at first supervised by Solomon's workmen: they needed instructions, not on how to fell trees, but on how long to cut the planks required in building the Temple! In the same way, Bede argues, 'the first teachers from among the gentiles needed the apostles themselves who had received training... lest, were they to begin to teach without masters, they might turn out to be teachers of error'.

2. The Easter Controversy

The theme of the building of the universal Church in *De templo* is informed by Bede's reading of the building of Solomon's Temple in the light of the early history of the Church as recorded in Acts. The historical narrative in Acts provided him with exemplifications of the

---

[24] Ray 1982 19–20; Olsen 1982.

heavenly qualities described in the Epistles and needed in the construction of the present Church. He was probably engaged in revising his early commentary on Acts (with careful attention to its literal text and problems of composition) at the same time that he was working on *De templo* and the *HE*. Reading Bede's account of the building of the Church among the *gens Anglorum* in the light of *De templo* casts into relief certain underlying themes in the *HE* which have sometimes been obscured by attempts to reduce the evangelization process to a contest between Roman and Irish (or Columban) missionaries and to regard Bede's treatment of the Easter controversy as curiously inflated or triumphalist.

The British Christians do not represent the Jews of the Old Covenant depicted in *De templo*. Rather, they are faithless Jews, meaning the obdurate and spiritually blind: 'no healing or benefit was obtained from their ministry'. Augustine heals the blind and shares the faith (*HE* 2.2). The Gregorian missionaries and those, regardless of racial origin, who are in harmony with them, are the spiritual descendants of those faithful Jews, the apostles, who recognised in Christ the fulfilment of inspired Old Testament prophecy.

Columba's monastic descendants are also consistently honoured in the *HE* for their belief, their apostolic way of life and for sharing the faith. Bede explicitly clears them of the false charge of being Quartodecimans, that is, of celebrating Easter on the same day that unconverted Jews celebrate the Passover (*HE* 3.4,17). However, in his account of the famous meeting at Whitby in 664, Bede shows the Columban monks were charged with obduracy in still preferring their own local customs in the dating of Easter rather than the 'truth' as now manifested in decrees of the apostolic see, in the practice of the universal Church and 'confirmed by the holy Scriptures' (*HE* 3.25). Bede describes the eventual conversion of the last of the Columban monks on Iona in 716 as the climax of his story. They are converted by one who had been divinely diverted from the apostolic task of preaching the gospel to nations who had not yet heard it and were still practising heathen rites (*HE* 5.9,22). Bede does not, of course, mean the Ionan monks needed converting from pagan idolatry, but he is describing a further process, a deeper level of conversion of those already far advanced in the spiritual life who had long ago overcome the earthbound fleshly desires which St Paul describes as 'the service of idols' (Col 3:5). The text is quoted in *De templo*'s account of the veil of the Temple at the entrance to the Holy of Holies which signifies entry into the heavenly city, the same veil of the Temple which was rent at the Crucifixion to show that 'the figures of the Law thereupon came to an end and the truth of the Gospel and the heavenly mysteries and the very entrance to heaven were no longer a matter of prophecy or figurative meaning' (16.2–3). The Ionan monks, at the very entrance to the Holy of Holies, are converted from a lingering spiritual idolatry of their own customs. They are converted 'from the deep-rooted tradition of their ancestors to whom the apostle's words apply: "They had a zeal of God but not according to knowledge"'; Bede is here quoting, for the second time, St Paul's comment on Jews who do not submit to God's justice through Christ but seek to establish their own (Rm 10:2–3; *HE* 5.22; 3.3).

At Whitby Wilfrid explains that the early apostles had been unable to bring to a sudden end the entire observance of the Mosaic law, including the custom of circumcision, among their Jewish converts in the way they had been able to insist that gentile converts abandon the worship of idols (Acts 15:1–6). Although Wilfrid does not specifically mention the Council of Jerusalem's agreement to abandon this custom which was threatening the universal mission of the Church, there is the clear implication that 'in these days when the light of the gospel is spreading throughout the world', persistence in this Judaising custom would be a form of idolatry. As with early diversity of practice in the calculation of Easter, that which had once been accepted was now 'not even lawful' (*HE* 3.25).

The Columban monks' recalcitrance at Whitby could not, in this view, be accommodated as a harmless expression of the Gregorian ideal of diversity in unity but is designated a sin because it violated unity. Every instance of Bede's careful preparation of the Easter controversy theme in *HE* is accompanied by reference to the ideal of Church unity. Notwithstanding their manifold virtues, in their persistent spiritual blindness over this matter the Columbans might be compared with the British Christians who had refused to respond to Augustine's exhortation that Christ 'makes men to be of one mind in his Father's house' (*HE* 2.2). The true diversity in unity runs throughout *De templo*'s repeated insistence on the fellowship of all the faithful in the one house of God in which it imitates heaven: 'In my Father's house are many mansions' (11.3, 16.2, 18.14, 25.3). The Columbans, like the British, were in effect refusing to break bread in the same house of God with other Christians at Easter, thereby violating the Church's incorporation into the one body of

Christ (1 Co 10:16–17).

Significantly it is Egbert, an Anglo-Saxon whose religious formation is Irish, who becomes God's agent in finally convincing the Ionan
community of its error concerning Easter and it is Cuthbert, another
Anglo-Saxon conforming to post-Whitby teaching about Easter dating but formed in the Irish monastic tradition, who is presented as
Bede's culminating example of pastoral monastic bishops; Cuthbert's
form of monastic life at Lindisfarne is traced back both to the time of
Aidan and to the practice of Augustine in Kent on the directions of
Pope Gregory 'our apostle' whose instructions, quoted again by Bede
at this point, cite the practice of the early Church (*HE* 1.27; 4.27).

The 'Jewish' and 'gentile', Mediterranean and barbarian spiritual
and cultural traditions are inextricably entwined in the conversion
and building up of the Church among the *gens Anglorum*. In *De
templo* Bede repeatedly uses the theme of the Jews and gentiles
as the archetypal New Testament image of reconciliation and of all
peoples and estates being drawn into the Church. In describing the
laver in the Temple court which is an image of baptism, Bede shows
that 'it is here that the circumcised and the uncircumcised are made
one in the Lord through faith, hope and love' (**19.8**; Col 3:11). The
living stones of the Temple are cemented together 'for in Christ Jesus
there is no circumcision nor lack of it', only 'the faith which works
through love' (**11.2**; Ga 5:6). The evenness of the floor in Solomon's
Temple denotes that 'though there are Jews and gentiles, barbarians
and Scythians, freeborn and slaves, high-born and low-born, they all
boast of being brothers in Christ and of having the same Father in
heaven' (**14.3**; Col 3:11). The decorative chains woven together and
linking the tops of the columns in the Temple show that all believers,
'quite removed from each other though they may be in space, time,
rank, status, sex and age, are nevertheless linked together by one and
the same faith and love' (**18.9**).

The new people of God in the *HE* are not the Anglo-Saxon race
but all members of the universal Church of which the Anglo-Saxons
form but a tiny part at the ends of the earth. But the Church that is
established among them in a manner recalling many features of the
early Church of the apostles discussed in *De templo*, is also presented
as a microcosm of that universal Church and itself undertakes the
apostolic task of the evangelization of other Germanic gentiles (*HE*
5.9–11). The ancient chosen people of God mystically prefigured the
universal Church but the Old Testament's historical account of their

society and kingship seemed to the Anglo-Saxons to bear many points of comparison with their own. Like the Jews, the Anglo-Saxons' sense of their own identity grew with their knowledge and service of God. It is in this sense that Bede presents them as a chosen people of God, but an inclusive one.

Their royal protectors hold sway over the speakers of four languages: British, Pictish, Irish and English (HE 3.6); in the opening chapter of the whole work Bede notes that in addition Latin is now in use among them all 'through the study of the scriptures'. He finds a parallel to the five languages in the fact that 'the divine (Mosaic) law is written in five books, all devoted to seeking out and setting forth one and the same kind of wisdom, namely the knowledge of sublime truth and of true sublimity'. *De templo* reveals this to be an important image for Bede of the unity and harmony of the Church itself which casts further light on his arrangement of the history of the new people of God in five books, like the account of the chosen people in the Pentateuch. Constantly in the architectural features and dimensions of the Temple, in its liturgical furnishings such as the two cherubim and the altar of sacrifice, Bede discerns some allusion to the concord of the Old and New Testaments and particularly to the five books of the Mosaic law whose divine precepts are summarised in the gospels as love of God and one's neighbour (**13.2**). Everything Moses said 'bore testimony to the sayings of the four Evangelists so that, as a result of the harmony of both, our common faith and love of Christ might strengthen the hearts of all' (**20.8; cf.18.8; 22.3**).

The theme of harmony and unity is concealed beneath every surface in Solomon's Temple: doorways, pillars, units of measurement ingeniously render up their inner meaning as figures of the joining together of Jews and gentiles, the Old and New Testaments, the apostles and prophets which in turn prefigure not only particular groups of people in the present Church but, more profoundly, point to spiritual qualities necessary in the building up of the universal Church: 'Variously and in many ways the self-same mysteries of our salvation are prefigured' (**20**). The reader gradually becomes aware that these are not isolated features but part of a vast coherent plan in the design of God's providence.

3. Pillars of the Church

The walls of the Temple 'are all the peoples of the holy Church laid

upon the foundation of Christ'; the Church it prefigures is still being
built, new precious stones are being added but they represent not
only the inclusion of people from every nation and background but
the variety of spiritual gifts which make up the body of Christ (**8.6**; 1
Co 12:8–10; Ga 5:22). The only hierarchy is in the practice of charity
and the progress of the spiritual life which is marked out by faith and
good works, love of God and one's neighbour and the longing for
the heavenly life. The real division is between 'the carnal', who are
'beginners in the way of righteousness' and still have to wrestle with
base cravings of the flesh and 'the perfect' who as well as the faith,
hope, charity and good works required of all, 'also, like the apostles,
labour in preaching the word, distribute all their goods to the poor,
give themselves to vigils, fasting, hymns, spiritual canticles as well as
to sacred reading ...' (**17.7**). By their teaching and ministry of the
sacraments they open the doors of the Temple to the carnal. They
already imitate the life of angels on earth and constantly contemplate
the heavenly sanctuary. These are the successors of the apostles and
prophets who evangelize at various levels, by exhortation and stern
reproof, and especially by their example and by their knowledge of
Scripture 'without which we can have neither hope of heaven nor
love of neighbour on earth', neither can the teachers' manner of life
nor their word be sound (**20.5**).

Alan Thacker has drawn attention to the crucial role of the teacher
and of the monastic pastorate in Bede's Gregorian vision of reform
in Church and society 'which is a key to the understanding of all
Bede's later works', and has studied Bede's prose *Life of Cuthbert*
as an exemplification of the type.[25] Bede's treatment of Aidan also
offers an extremely interesting example of the translation from pre-
cept to practise and of the expression of common preoccupations in
the different literary modes of the *De templo* and the *HE*. Aidan is
first and foremost in the gallery of good examples in the *HE* who
wonderfully embody the various virtues of the elect found in every
feature of the building fabric of the Temple in *De Templo* making it
most like the heavenly sanctuary.

Yet the portrait of Aidan illustrates the tension which Glenn Olsen
identified between Bede's view of the primitive apostolic Church as a
golden age in which he believed the monastic life to have been formed
and which he consciously recalled in his description of the more

---

[25] Thacker (1983).

recent golden age of seventh-century pastors and monastic bishops, and his historical understanding of the growth and maturation of the Church, partly evidenced in its periodic eradication of Judaising tendencies[26].

In his letter to Egbert bishop of York (734) Bede adopts the exhortatory and denunciatory tone of an Old Testament prophet to give a dire warning that contemporary developments in episcopal and monastic life threaten the spiritual well-being of the Church.[27] Already in De Templo this tone had briefly broken through in his condemnation of 'the sluggishness of our time when some want to have the appearance and name of being teachers, priests and pillars of the house of God though they have absolutely none of the firm faith needed to despise worldly ostentation and make invisible goods their ambition' (**18.16**). In contrast, he who observes and teaches everything which the Lord commanded the apostles, without adding or omitting anything, 'such a one is indeed a pillar in God's house which is the Church and a bulwark of truth such as the apostle Paul admonished Timothy to be (**18.7**; 1 Tm 3:15). In the HE 3.5 Aidan's pastorate is offered 'in great contrast to our modern slothfulness'. His role as a pillar of the Church is perhaps figured in HE 3.17 in the story of the miraculous survival through successive fires of a church buttress which Aidan had leaned against as he died; eventually the buttress was set up not as a physical support to the rebuilt structure, but as a memorial inside the church where it effected miraculous cures.

Bede's criticism of Aidan's monastic successors at Whitby in 664, only thirteen years after Aidan's death, and his stricture in De templo that anyone who 'despises the apostolic decrees or proposes something novel on his own whim' is not a fit pillar for the temple of God (**18.7**), at first sight may seem to question Aidan's credentials as a pillar of the Church. But De templo is here condemning those motivated by laziness or arrogance. Immediately after the story of the church buttress which was Aidan's memorial, Bede, while censuring Aidan's rustic ignorance regarding the Easter dating, entirely exoner-

---

[26] Olsen 1982, 525–26

[27] Gildas had used the scriptural architectural metaphor, quoting the whole of 1 Co 3:11–16, in denouncing the priests of his day who had violated the temple of God through neglect of their pastoral charge: Winterbottom 1978, 73, 78; cf. Gregory, *Regulae pastoralis liber* 2.7, Davis 1950, 71.

ates him from any suspicion of slothfulness, heresy or obduracy and
stresses that 'in his celebration of Easter he reverenced and preached
no other doctrine than we do'. He emphasises Aidan's diligence in
the study of Scripture which informed his teaching and example: 'He
made it his business to omit none of the commands of the evangelists,
the apostles and prophets, but he set himself to carry them out in his
deeds'. In his chapter on Whitby Bede shows that, far from threatening church unity, Aidan had been deservedly loved and respected
by all, including those who had other views on the dating of Easter,
such as bishops Honorius of Kent and Felix of the East Angles. He
had diligently laboured to practise the works of faith, piety and love,
'which is the mark of the saints'. By implication he is to be included
among those holy forefathers of Colman's community whom Wilfrid
said would have followed the proper dating if anyone had instructed
them 'as they are known to have followed all the laws of God as soon
as they learned them' (*HE* 3.25).

The Pauline image of the apostles and their followers as pillars of
the Church (Gal 2:9) is very fully developed by Bede in *De templo*. It
also appears in Gregory's homilies on Ezekiel's vision of the Temple.
What has not been noticed is that Gregory's exposition has a sub-
stantial commentary on the Judaising crisis in the apostolic Church.
In Gal 2:9 James, Cephas and John are described as pillars; unlike
some commentators, Gregory insists that Cephas here refers to Peter, who is described by that form of his name in the previous two
verses, where the missions of Peter and Paul to the Jews and the gentiles respectively are designated the gospels of the circumcision and
of the uncircumcision. Gregory actually quotes Paul's condemnation
of Peter for continuing to preach the circumcision of converts: 'I
withstood him to his face because he was to be blamed... And to his
dissimulation the rest of the Jews consented' (Gal 2:11,13). Gregory
upholds Paul's action and describes Peter's subsequent acknowledge-
ment (in 2 P 3:15–16 after he had read Paul's epistle!) that Paul had
been right. The spiritual lesson Gregory derives from this episode
is that Peter was the friend of truth even when he was blameworthy,
that he yielded 'to his lesser brother for harmony and thereby became
a follower of his inferior so that he even excelled in this, in that he
who was the first in the leadership of the apostles was also the first in
humility': Peter refrained from reminding Paul that he had received
the keys of the kingdom. For Gregory this is not incompatible with
his earlier acclamation of Peter as the first of the apostles and 'a great

pillar in the true Tabernacle'[28].

Nothing of this background to the Council of Jerusalem appears in Wilfrid's reference to the Judaising issue in his speech at Whitby where Petrine authority is strongly argued as the safeguard of Church unity. Peter is shown to have been right about Easter (or at least from the time of his arrival in Rome). Bede's exegesis, however, shows he was aware that the Council of Jerusalem had other spiritual lessons to teach. Ironically, these lessons are in the *HE* taught by Aidan and the Columban community on Lindisfarne whose apostolic life is eulogized in the chapter immediatley following the debate at Whitby.

Roger Ray has argued that although 'the synod of Whitby was to Bede what the Council of Jerusalem was to Luke: the point at which a new Church went on record for catholic faith', Bede made sophisticated use of the rhetorical arts of *inventio* in adapting this material for his purposes[29]. His exegesis on the New Testament material suggests other considerations were also involved. At a meeting of apostolic missionaries in Jerusalem it was decided that gentile converts, saved by faith and the grace of Christ, no longer needed to submit to the requirements of the Jewish Law concerning circumcision and dietary observances; they were however, to distance themselves from pagan practices and at least 'refrain from the pollutions of idols and from fornication and from things strangled and from blood' (Acts 15:20). In his commentary on Acts, Bede scarcely mentions the accounts in Galatians ch 2 and 5 which show there was considerable dissension between the apostles over this question and he completely omits any mention that Paul had roundly denounced the Judaising stand of Peter himself and had said of those continuing to practice circumcision: 'You are made void of Christ you who are justified in the law; you are fallen from grace' (Gal 5:4). Instead, Bede stresses the agreement reached by the apostles at Jerusalem in moving to the next stage in the Church's growth: because of the diversity of those early times, 'the sacramental signs could be diverse, though nevertheless reverting most harmoniously to the unity of the same faith'[30]. He also explains the modest minimum standard required of gentile converts was a concession 'in view of their rudimentary faith and the long-standing custom of the gentile world'. Gradually, as they continued

---

[28] Homily 6, Gray 1990, 221–22

[29] Ray 1986, 80.

[30] L.T. Martin 1989, 130.

to gather to read the law and the prophets (for Bede says he is aware the primitive Church still practised Jewish customs including Jewish readings in their sabbath celebrations), the converts would receive the principles of life, meaning a more rigorous understanding and practice of the Christian faith. Little by little, they will receive 'the rules requiring the keeping of mutual love', a process repeatedly described in *De templo* as a movement from the literal precepts of the Law to an understanding of its spiritual interpretation (**11.3**).

In *De templo* Bede's reflections on Acts 15 are also pastoral and not concerned with ecclesiastical politics. The Temple's outer court or great hall and portico formed a sacred precinct for the admission of all who had fulfilled 'the basic requirements of ritual purity and observance of the prescriptions of the law' but who were not allowed to enter the main sanctuary reserved for the ritually cleansed Jewish priests (**17.1**). From the literal text and the historical building Bede draws various lessons for the contemporary Church. The outer court offers 'a figure of those of the gentiles who were believers in Syria and Antioch and other provinces and cities on whom the apostles and elders who were in Jerusalem imposed no further burden than that they refrain from that which has been offered to idols and from blood and from things strangled and from fornication' (**17.7**;Acts 15:20). Bede specifically likens this example from the primitive Church to the distinction in the contemporary Church between 'the carnal', possessed of only the most elementary virtues, and the full rigour of the Christian life required of 'the perfect'. The Temple's outer court thus 'suggests figuratively the life and behaviour of the carnal in the holy Church to whom the Apostle says "But I, brethren, could not address you as spiritual people but as people of the flesh, as little ones in Christ, I fed you with milk, not solid food"' (**17.5**; 1 Co 3:1–2). Similarly Pope Gregory had applied the Corinthians text to the apostles who form both the outer and inner gates of Ezekiel's visionary Temple. They give 'the little ones of Christ milk to drink not meat', instructing them in the first entrance into faith and, as they advance inside the Temple, lead them 'through subtler perception to inner truths'[31]. In the *HE* Bede has the apostolic figure of Aidan express St Paul's view at a meeting of the Columban monastic elders on Iona gathered to discuss problems encountered in the evangelisation of the Anglo-Saxons. Aidan observes that,

---

[31] Gray 1990, 246.

because of their ignorance, the pagans should have been 'offered
the milk of simpler teaching, as the apostle recommends, until little
by little, as they grew strong on the food of God's word, they were
capable of receiving more elaborate instruction and of carrying out
the more transcendent commandments of God' (*HE* 3.5). Despite his
own failure, whether through ignorance or custom, to observe Easter
'at the proper time' Aidan is shown to be an exemplary missionary
pastor (*HE* 3.17). When read from the perspective of Bede's exegesis
on Acts 15 and on the Temple's outer court, the account of the
meeting on Iona has clear parallels with the meeting at Jerusalem.
His interpretation of both meetings as points of growth not division
for the Church informs his portrait of Aidan in the *HE* and his
exposition of the pillars in *De templo*.

Bede associates the apostolic pillars of the Church in Gal 2:9 with
the two great bronze pillars erected at the entrance to Solomon's
Temple: 'There are two of them so that they may bring together both
gentiles and circumcised into the Church by preaching'; Peter is not
named but Paul is described as 'a most eminent pillar of the house
of the Lord' (**18.5**). The pillars also denote spiritual teachers, 'strong
in faith and work and elevated to heavenly things by contemplation',
who follow the apostles and the norm of apostolic teaching. Their
dimensions conceal an arcane allusion to the name of Jesus, whom
the saints imitate (**18.4**). Bede had already cited these columns in
his early commentary on the Apocalypse (c.703–09) by way of expounding Rv 3:12, 'He that shall overcome, I will make him a pillar
in the temple of my God'. The saints as Christ-bearing figures are
therefore of importance to the Church on earth and in heaven and
provide a fundamental connection between the two, a basic assumption of hagiography which, interestingly enough, is made particularly
clear in the imagery of Adamnan of Iona's late seventh-century *Life
of Columba*.[32]

The tenth-century Anglo-Saxon Benedictine reformers depicted
saints, including their own monastic leaders, as living stones and pillars of the Church in art and hagiography[33], and the Benedictional
of St Aethelwold, Bishop of Winchester, makes particularly lavish

---

[32] Anderson and Anderson 1991, 15, 107, 225, 227, 229.

[33] Deshman 1986, 273–78. For the use of the architectural metaphor elsewhere in early
insular culture, including the Book of Kells, f 202v, see Farr 1989, 32–191; O'Reilly
1994.

use of the architectural metaphor in its pictorial exegesis. The various heavenly choirs are depicted as human columns, standing on 'living stones' and the opening scene of the Confessors shows the Church supported by St Benedict flanked by Pope Gregory and St Cuthbert. The Benedictine reformers identified themselves with the seventh-century monastic bishops whom Bede descrioes in the *HE* but his extensive exegesis on the Temple theme may also have been an important influence.

LIVING STONES

In an oration on the dedication of the cathedral of Tyre in 317, Eusebius had applied almost the entire catena of scriptural texts on tabernacle, temple and the living stones etc. to the magnificent new church and hailed its patron-bishop as a new Solomon. The topos, if not that particular example, was certainly known to insular writers. 'As Moses built an earthly tabernacle made with hands ... according to the pattern shown by God' so Wilfrid built and gloriously adorned a columned stone church at Ripon whose dedication is compared by his biographer with the dedication of Solomon's Temple.[34] In the *HE* Bede notes the building of stone churches as part of the evangelization of the Anglo-Saxons and probably as one aspect of increasing Roman and Gaulish cultural influences in their further conversion. But, as Arthur Holder noted, for all Bede's interest in the architectural metaphor for describing the Church, he never gives a church building an allegorical interpretation.[35] Again *De templo* and related scriptural exegesis can throw light on Bede's historical work.

The allegorical exposition of the figural ornament in Solomon's Temple led Bede to his often-quoted defence of religious art as providing 'a living writing' for the illiterate (**19.10**). Less quoted is the section which immediately follows where he shows that what the Law forbids is not the making of images but the idolatrous purposes to which impious Jews and pagan gentiles alike may put them (**19.11**). In the Acts of the Apostles the deacon Stephen addresses the Jewish Sanhedrin to answer charges of blasphemy against the Temple and

---

[34] Colgrave 1927, 35, 37; Connolly 1995 for the example of Cogitosus' description of Kildare as fulfilling the prophecy of Isaiah 2:2–3.

[35] Holder 1989, 121–31.

the Law. He argues that the idolatry of their forefathers in worshipping 'the works of their own hands' when they made the bronze calf in the wilderness at the time of Moses is paralleled by their own over-materialistic understanding of the Temple and its cult, and, by implication, their failure, though professional interpreters of the Law, to recognise in Christ the fulfilment of Old Testament prophecy: 'The most High dwells not in houses made by hands, as the prophet says: "Heaven is my throne and earth my footstool. What house will you build me?" says the Lord' (Ac 4:8–9 quoting Is 66:1). Significantly, the same quotation from Isaiah is later cited in St Paul's speech before the assembly of the Areopagus in Athens: 'God who made the world and all things therein, he being Lord of heaven and earth, dwells not in temples made with hands' (Ac 17:24). Before this pagan gentile audience the prophetic warning is directed against idolatrous worship of the man-made. The Creator in whom we live and move and have our being is not 'like unto gold or silver or stone, the graving of art and the device of man' (Ac 17:28–9).

Bede's reflections on these passages, first expressed in his commentary on Acts in 709, underlie his vignette of King Oswy succeeding in converting a fellow-'gentile' where the Roman missionaries had failed. Using reasoned argument 'in friendly and brotherly counsel' like St Paul, not forcing his will on a tributary king, Oswy explains to Sigeberht of the East Saxons that 'objects made by the hands of men could not be gods' and that the Creator of heaven and earth, incomprehensible in his majesty and invisible to human eyes, has his abode 'in heaven, not in base and perishable metal' (*HE* 3.22). The argument had already been rehearsed, directly citing psalms 95.4 and 113, in Pope Boniface's letter to King Edwin which Bede quotes in *HE* 2.10. Throughout the book Bede tackles idolatry at various levels from initial conversion from paganism through further inner conversions from preoccupation with man-made possessions and worldly values. The movement away from attachment to 'carnal desires', which characterise those clustered at the doorway into the Temple, and the drawing closer to the hidden Holy of Holies seeking what 'eye has not seen nor ear heard' is also repeatedly described in *De templo* (cf. **12.4; 18.14**).

In *De templo* Bede extols the spiritual qualities of St Stephen which made him a pre-eminent pillar of the Church. Some twenty years earlier, commenting on Stephen's speech to the Jewish Sanhedrin in Ac 7:44,49 (the companion passage to Paul's speech to the gentiles in Ac

17:24), Bede showed that Stephen was here explaining to the Jews 'that the Lord does not place a high value on dressed stone, but rather desires the splendour of heavenly souls'. He interprets the successor to the Temple, the Christian Church, as a community not a building, and one not confined to this earth. Bede says of Gregory the Great, 'Other popes applied themselves to the task of building churches and adorning them with gold and silver, but he devoted himself entirely to winning souls' (*HE* 2.1). Similarly, Augustine's successor at Canterbury, Archbishop Lawrence, 'strove to build up the foundations of the Church which had been so magnificently laid (cf 1 Co 3:10–11) and to raise it to its destined height; this he did by frequent words of holy exhortation and by continually setting a pattern of good works', including his pastoral care of 'the new Church which had been gathered from among the English' (*HE* 2.4; cf 2.6). The 'living stones of the Church' gathered together in Chad's exemplary monastic community at Lichfield are described as being translated at death 'from their earthly sites to the heavenly building' (*HE* 4.3). In contrast 'the lofty buildings' of Coldingham are reduced to ashes as a direct consequence of the community's failure to abandon worldly occupations and cultivate the desire for heaven (*HE* 4.25, and *De templo* 7.3).

These observations have all the more force coming from one whose whole life had been spent among the monastic buildings of Wearmouth-Jarrow, which must have constituted a wonder of the northern world. In the *HE* and the *Lives of the Abbots* Bede chronicles as acts of religious zeal his founder's labours in securing stonemasons and glaziers from Gaul for the building of St Peter's church at Monkwearmouth, 674, and his repeated trips to Gaul and Italy to secure 'everything necessary for the service of church and altar' — sacred vessels, vestments, reliquaries, books and pictures. There is no sense of profligacy in this seemly honouring of the house of God, but neither does Bede suggest Benedict Biscop was a second Solomon: on his deathbed Benedict avers that he would rather his foundation revert to the wilderness it once was than endanger its monastic life.[36]

In a homily for the anniversary of the dedication of Jarrow, in which so many of the themes in *De templo* are already sketched, Bede urges his monastic community, 'We must not suppose that only the building in which we come together and pray and celebrate the mysteries is the Lord's temple, and that we ourselves are not more

---

[36] Farmer 1965, 196.

fully his temple and are not so named, since the Apostle clearly says, "You are the temple of the living God"... If we are the temple of God, let us take great care and busy ourselves with good deeds so that he may deign... to make his dwelling place here'. Bede gives the brethren a condensed tour of Solomon's Temple in the course of the second dedication homily, 'so that the marvellous workmanship that went into the construction of the Lord's earthly house might delight you and so that these details, spiritually understood, might arouse our minds to more ardent love of the heavenly dwelling place. Therefore, my brothers, let us love whole-heartedly the beauty of the eternal house we have from God in the heaven and let us seek... that we may be worthy to dwell in his house all the days of our life'[37].

Other insular churchmen could justify a different use of the Temple imagery. In invoking the models of Moses' Tabernacle and Solomon's Temple in the account of the foundation of Ripon, Wilfrid's biographer said it was to stir up the faith of the people and to honour Christ. The allocation of lands and consecrated places to the bishop for the service of God as part of the celebrations at the dedication of Ripon strongly recalls the assigning of sanctuary lands to the Temple priesthood and Levites in Ezk 45:1–6. Wilfrid's response to the ruinous state of Paulinus's church at York is that of the prophets Daniel and Jeremiah in denouncing the desecration of the Temple; his rebuilding of the church is presented as a cleansing of the Temple; Wilfrid is another Samuel in whose work the house of God is honoured. The biographer runs out of superlatives in describing Hexham and says that Wilfrid was 'taught by the spirit of God' in its construction; so too was Bezalel, the builder of the Tabernacle, (Ex 35:30–33).[38] Wilfrid's biographer draws attention to the dressed stone, the great height as well as the length of the church at Hexham and to its different levels connected by spiral stairs. These are all general features yet also figure in the description of Solomon's Temple in the Book of Kings. Richard Bailey has suggested that the remarkable crypts at Hexham and Ripon, notwithstanding their rectangular plan, carry an iconographic reminiscence of the church of the Holy Sepulchre in Jerusalem.[39] It may be added that although a Christian counterpart to the Jewish Temple in Jerusalem had not been erected in

---

[37] Homilies 2.24;25, L. Martin and D. Hurst 1991, 242, 267.

[38] Colgrave 1927, 33–37, 45–7.

[39] Bailey 1991, 20–21.

the period of the New Testament, in the changed circumstances of
the Constantinian era the church of the Holy Sepulchre, as pre-
eminently the church of the Resurrection, came to be viewed (and
may originally have been intended) as 'the keystone in founding the
New Jerusalem'.[40] By the sixth century various symbols, relics and
even holy sites once associated with the Temple had migrated to the
Holy Sepulchre complex, and early representations on coins and pil-
grims' souvenirs represent the front elevation of the Temple (or the
Holy of Holies) and the church of the Holy Sepulchre in a similar
schematized manner, despite their very different ground plans.

In his lengthy appreciation of the work of Wilfrid, Bede does not
once refer to Wilfrid's role as a patron of splendid church buildings
(*HE* 5.19). Yet in the following chapter he notes that Wilfrid's long-
time priest Acca, who succeeded him as bishop of Hexham, enriched
the fabric of the church there with all kinds of decoration and works
of art, gathering relics of the apostles and martyrs of Christ, putting
up altars for their veneration and establishing various chapels for this
purpose within the walls of the Church. Furthermore, Acca 'zealously
provided sacred vessels, lamps and many other objects of the same
kind for the adornment of the house of God'. Wilfrid's biographer
had also noted that Acca provided 'splendid ornaments of gold and
silver and precious stones' for the enrichment of Hexham.

Acca was banished from his see in 731; if the prologue to *De templo*
was written then or later it would have had the extra dimension of
offering consolation to one literally in forced exile like St John on
Patmos, but this is hardly its primary purpose[41] nor is it attempting to
convert Acca from an undue regard for church fabric. Acca combined
a proper respect for the beauty of God's house in this transitory world
with an active concern for the education of its pastors and therefore
the spiritual welfare of the people of God, evidenced in his library and
his long-standing involvement with Bede's exegetical work. There is
a clear consistency between Bede's refusal to allegorize man-made
church buildings in the *HE* and his spiritual interpretation in *De
templo* of the Temple building which is described in holy scripture 'for
our instruction' and built according to a divine plan. The churches

---

[40] Kühnel 1986–87,150; Ousterhout 1990, 44–7.

[41] The monastic consolatory tradition used by Bede also appears in the correspon-
dence of Anglo-Saxons in voluntary exile for Christ, who requested copies of Bede's
exegetical works for teaching purposes 'and for our consolation in exile'. Parkes
1982, 15.

built by human hands and the attempts to identify them with the
Temple in Jerusalem are but figures or copies of the true Jerusalem
and can themselves become an earthbound preoccupation or idol.
The true building of the Church, discernible beneath the figure of
the Temple building, is the spiritual growth of the whole diverse
community of the body of Christ and its journey through the exile of
this life to the new Jerusalem.

Bede's view, sustained through exhortation and example in *De
templo* and the *HE*, had been stated by the Fathers, notably in Augustine's comment that the prophecy of Haggai 2:9, 'The glory of this
latter house shall be greater than the former', was not fulfilled in the
restoration of the Temple in Jerusalem built of wood and precious
stones and metals but in this house, the Church 'whose stones are
of more worth because they are living stones'.[42] But the Church
'was symbolized in the restoration of that Temple, because the very
renewing of the Temple symbolizes in a prophetic message the New
Covenant'. The glory of this latter house will be seen to be even
greater, however, when it is dedicated (i.e. completed, at the end of
time), 'for then will come the one who is longed for by all nations',
Christ, the master-builder himself. In 3 K 7:51 the earthly master-
builder, Solomon, finishes building the Temple in Jerusalem ready for
dedication and finally brings into it his father's consecrated vessels of
gold and silver to be stored in various treasuries within the building.
This is interpreted in *De templo* **25.2–3** as prefiguring the time after
the universal judgement when Christ will bring into the joys of his
heavenly kingdom all the elect, the company both of teachers and the
rest of the faithful of diverse spiritual gifts, to be laid up like consecrated vessels in the treasuries of his Father's house. Bede then turns
to Gregory's meditation on Ezekiel's vision of the Temple to explain
the reason why Solomon made one house of the Lord but furnished it
with various treasuries to accommodate the vessels of different kinds
(3 K 7:51): 'there is one house of the Father not made with hands
that will last eternally in heaven (2 Co 5:1), but many mansions in
it (Jn 14:2) to receive all who fear him, and, the Lord blesses those
that love him, both little ones and great' (Ps 113:13).

---

[42] *City of God* 18.48, Bettenson 1972, 830–31.

APPENDIX: THE CODEX AMIATINUS

In the famous Codex Amiatinus produced at Bede's monastery is a diagram which has been variously described as the Tabernacle and the Temple.[43] The huge manuscript, a pandect or single-volume copy of the whole Bible, is the survivor of three such copies made for the joint foundation of Wearmouth-Jarrow under the direction of Ceolfrith, during his abbacy from 688–716, and was the copy which Ceolfrith eventually, in 716, took with him on his final pilgrimage to Rome to present to the pope.[44] The book's format and illustrations have often been seen as modelled on another pandect, the now lost Codex Grandior produced in the monastery of Cassiodorus (d.598) at Vivarium in Italy, which has usually been identified with the pandect 'of the old translation' brought back to Northumbria from Rome in 678, a year or two before Bede's admission to the monastery as a child of seven.[45]

In *De tabernaculo* 2.12 Bede mentions details of the altar of holocausts that he himself had seen depicted in Cassiodorus's book; he notes that the learned Cassiodorus derived his knowledge of this and of the layout of Tabernacle and Temple from teachers among the Jews. In *De templo* Bede describes details of the Temple enclosures in the picture which Cassiodorus had 'put in the pandect, as he himself mentions in his exposition of the psalms' **(17.2)**. In the relevant passage, Cassiodorus refers to Josephus's *Jewish Antiquities* as a source of information on the Temple building. But although Bede is here clearly interested in discovering information about the historical fabric of the Temple[46] it is as a preliminary to the spiritual interpretation of its features and the passage he refers to in Cassiodorus's psalm commentary is on Ps 86, a psalm which had already in Augustine's influential commentary attracted the whole range of scriptural texts interpreting the Tabernacle and Temple as figures of the Church and the heavenly sanctuary.

There has been considerable scholarly debate on the diagram in the Codex Amiatinus. It has, for example, been suggested that there were

---

[43] Florence, *Biblioteca Medicea Laurenziana* MS Amiatinus I; Alexander 1978, cat. 7, pl 23–27; Bruce-Mitford 1967; Webster and Backhouse 1991, cat. 87–88.

[44] *Historia abbatum auctore anonymo* (=*Life of Ceolfrith*) 20.

[45] *Historia abbatum*, 15.

[46] *Expositio psalmorum*, 789–90; Henderson 1980, 5–6.

two separate pictures of the Tabernacle and Temple in Cassiodorus's Codex Grandior and that the diagram in the Codex Amiatinus is a direct copy of one of them, the Tabernacle, strictly as described in Exodus.[47] Others, however, have noticed discrepancies, both between the Codex Amiatinus diagram and the Exodus account of the Tabernacle, and between the diagram and Bede's description of the picture he had seen in Cassiodorus's book.[48] A third approach has been to see the Codex Amiatinus diagram as derived from a single picture in the Codex Grandior which was not a literal depiction of either Old Testament building but was cast in the Jewish and Early Christian tradition of architecturally ambiguous images. In this tradition a representation of the Tabernacle might also allude to the Temple and, in Christian versions, to the sanctuary of the heavenly Jerusalem as well.[49] The issues underlying the debate are complex and only a few observations on the diagram in the Codex Amiatinus may be made here.

Certain liturgical furnishings shown in the diagram were common to Tabernacle and Temple, as Bede makes clear when he refers readers of *De templo* **24.4** to his section on liturgical vessels in the *De tabernaculo*; the two buildings also had a similar division between the sanctuary and inner Holy of Holies. While additional details in the Codex Amiatinus diagram, such as the inscription of the names of Moses and Aaron and the sons of Levi around the sanctuary and of the twelve tribes of Israel encamped around the outer court, suggest it is the Tabernacle in the desert, the positioning of the water laver is that prescribed for the Temple court (**20.15**; 3 K 7:39), not for the Tabernacle. Moreover, Bianca Kühnel has noted that the tiny cross placed over the entrance to the building transforms this sanctuary of the Old Covenant into the eternal temple and city of the New Covenant.[50] The four words written in golden capitals on the four sides of the diagram conceal a further level of allusion. The initial letters of these Greek words for the four cardinal directions - Anatole, Dysis, Arctos and Mesembria - spell out the name of Adam. As

---

[47] Meyvaert 1979, 71–2, n 7; Ferber 1976, 27, 29, 41 also points to other Jewish sources probably underlying Cassiodorus's work.

[48] Corsano 1987 9–11; Holder 1994, 92 n 1.

[49] Kühnel 1986–87, 164–166. For early Christian and insular pictorial exegesis of the Tabernacle-Temple theme see Farr 1989; O'Reilly 1994; Verkerk 1995.

[50] Kühnel 1986–87, 166.

Greek letters they also have a numerical value and add up to forty-six, the number of years it took to rebuild the Temple in Jerusalem, and hence they can allude to the temple of Christ's body (Jn 2:19–21). This numerology, frequently used by Augustine, is used by Bede in his homily on the cleansing of the Temple and in his exposition on the rebuilding of the Temple in the time of Ezra and Nehemiah.[51] The building in the Codex Amiatinus diagram may therefore be read as referring simultaneously to the Tabernacle and Temple of the Old Covenant, which prefigured the Church of the New Covenant, and to the Temple as the body of Christ and the sanctuary of the heavenly Jerusalem.

The diagram does not appear in isolation. The book's well-known frontispiece depicts Ezra, the scribe who had restored and interpreted the Jewish scriptures as an essential foundation to religious reform and the rebuilding of the Temple in Jerusalem after the Babylonian Captivity. He is shown in Jewish priestly dress but in front of a book-cupboard containing all the books of the Bible, both from the Old and New Testaments. The combination of historical detail and visual exegesis continues in the diagram of the Tabernacle and the sanctuary vessels which spans a double opening (originally ff. 4v–5r). This is followed by a series of ingenious diagrams depicting the books of the Pentateuch within the shape of a Cross and the harmony of the three standard classifications of all the books of the Bible in conjunction with the depictions of the Trinity. George Henderson has questioned whether these are either copies of diagrams in the Codex Grandior or directly derived from Cassiodorus's work in his *Institutiones* and has persuasively suggested they could include a considerable element of Northumbrian editing and interpretation.[52]

The whole enterprise of producing the Codex Amiatinus and its two sister pandects, in Roman uncial script and from the best available manuscripts, based not on the Old Latin translation but on 'the Hebrew and Greek originals by the translations of Jerome' (including his third revision of the Psalms, *iuxta hebraicos*), was an astounding feat of scholarship and scribal activity.[53] It may well have been completed before Bede began his biblical commentaries and certainly

---

[51] Berschin 1989, 95–102; for Adam's name as a cosmic tetragrammaton in the Fathers, McNally 1971, 115–16.

[52] Henderson 1993 82–6; Bruce-Mitford 1967, pl 2,7, 9–12, C.

[53] *Life of Ceolfrith*, 37; Ward 1994, 6; Parkes 1982, 3–6.

provides their background. The centrality of a proper understanding of Scripture to the process of building up the Church through further levels of conversion is strongly sketched in the letter explaining the dating of Easter to the Pictish king Nechtan c.710 which rightly forms part of the climax of the *HE*. The rejection of Columban customs by Nechtan and his reformed nation is here presented as the prelude to the final conversion of Iona. Modern commentators have often assumed Bede wrote the letter but he specifically ascribes it to his revered abbot Ceolfrith and it is entirely compatible with the interests already manifested in the Codex Amiatinus. The explanation of the true date of Easter, unlike its implementation, is based not on Petrine authority or Easter tables but on rules divinely laid down in the law of Moses and the Gospel 'which no human authority can alter' (*HE* 5.21). Ceolfrith proceeds to establish at some length the historical meaning of the literal text of Exodus on the Passover of the Old Covenant, then to seek its spiritual significance through reading it in the light of the New Covenant Passover sacrifice, then to show its relevance to the present Church, as did the apostles.

Bede had been formed in a monastic community where the spiritual interpretation of the Old Covenant Law, priesthood and sacrifice, Tabernacle and Temple provided a focal image for understanding the universal Church and the inspired authority of the whole of Scripture. He was to return to the theme time and again, culminating in one of the most important exegetical works of his maturity, the *De templo*.

I wish to thank Alan Thacker for his helpful reading of this introduction.

Jennifer O'Reilly
University College Cork

PROLOGUE

Prol. 1   The vessel of election and teacher of the gentiles exhorts   *[143]*
us to read the word of God, affirming truthfully that *whatever was*
written in former days was written for our instruction so that by steadfast-
ness and the encouragement of the scriptures we might have hope.[12] In
this passage he quite rightly declares that to secure the hope of heavenly goods we must have patience, and contemplate the consolation
of the scriptures; patience, that is, to bear with an attitude of humble
submission the adversities that befall us as punishments imposed by a
just judge and compassionate father whether for the enhancement of
our virtue and increase of merit, should we be punished, even though
upright and innocent, or for the correction of our conduct should we
be enmeshed in vice; on the other hand, we need the consolation of
the scriptures so that by frequent meditation on them we may call to
mind how much dark affliction those eminent Fathers of the Church
and the bright luminaries of the Church have often borne even during this life, how much glory they have enjoyed with their master in
the life to come through the merits of their fidelity and patience, and
how much unfailing praise and fame they have left behind among the
faithful even in this life; as scripture says, *the memory of the righteous*
is a blessing,[13] and again, *Their bodies were buried in peace and their*
name lives to all generations,[14] and the apostle James, *Behold, we call*
those happy who were steadfast. You have heard of the steadfastness of
Job, and you have seen the purpose of the Lord.[15] Now it is not for
nothing that, after mentioning the afflictions of the just, he added:
and you have seen the purpose of the Lord, because even he who lived
his life here below without fault, did not depart from this life without
chastisement, and he who appeared in the world to heal the sick and
raise the dead, chose to return from the world in the weakness of

---

[12] Rm 15:4
[13] Pr 10:7
[14] Sir 44:14
[15] Jm 5:11

1

death to set us an example of patience. Hence after saying, *Our God is a God of salvation,* the psalmist directly added in wonder or rather in astonishment, *and to the Lord belongs escape from death.*[16]

[144]   Prol. 2   Therefore, through patience and the consolation of the scriptures may we also have hope of consoling ourselves after the afflictions of our distress when we too have been patient in tribulation and call to mind the actions of those who have far excelled us in righteousness and merit and borne far greater trials of adversity than we. For they, on account of the righteousness in which they were quite exemplary, often suffered the persecution of the unrighteous, in order that, by their exercise of righteousness, they might receive the crown of invincible patience, and might, moreover, leave behind for all who followed them the glorious footprints of their perseverance to mark their way. We, on the other hand, are more often chastised for our transgressions by the merciful providence of our creator. Let us look into our conscience again with wholesome compunction and earnestly wash away with a bath of tears what in our laxity we have committed by yielding to insidious allurements, and so, corrected and restored to the hope of eternal life with the Lord's assistance, may we merit to attain the fellowship of those who suffered in innocence. For this too we find in the consolation of the scriptures that *he has blessed those who fear the Lord, both little and great,*[17] and declared that there are many mansions in store for us in his Father's house.[18]

Prol. 3   I have no doubt that now, thanks to the consolation they afford, you too, most beloved of bishops, daily gain relief from[19] the present worries of temporal affairs,[20] and are fired with a lofty am-

---

[16] Ps 67:21

[17] Ps 113:21

[18] cf. Jn 14:2. It is worth noting how Bede uses these two texts John 14:2 and Psalm 113:21 as an *inclusio* or catchword with which to articulate the entire text; or to put it in terms of symphonic composition, these texts in juxtaposition form a theme one hears at key points in the opus, viz. here in the Prologue, again at chapter 18.14, a little over half way, and then significantly, in the very last two sentences by way of finale.

[19] The text here has *alleuare,* lit. 'lighten', 'ease', which I have rendered by the phrasal verb 'gain relief from' as being more in accord with English usage while safeguarding the original meaning.

[20] The 'present worries' here alluded to are assumed to refer to 'Acca's trials and

bition to see the good things of the Lord in the land of the living,[21] having risen above the evils of human beings which reign in the land of the dying, inasmuch as ⟨this consolation⟩ is to be found in abundance not only in the pages of God's word but also in the devout expositions which the revered writing of the Fathers has left us. But because what is novel is sometimes more appealing, it seemed good to me to send to your holiness for perusal the little work that I had recently written in the allegorical style on the construction of the temple of God, following in the footsteps of the great treatises. If you read it attentively, then the more you find the mysteries of Christ and the Church contained in its ancient pages and the more liberally you see there the gifts of God bestowed upon us in this present time or promised us in the future, the more tolerable and less worthy of concern will you consider both the favourable and unfavourable vicissitudes of perishable things, after the example of blessed John who, held captive as he was by a wicked emperor within the confines of a tiny island, was immediately introduced by the merciful creator through the Spirit to the contemplation of the unfathomable mysteries of the heavenly mansions; and in the very place where the deluded enemy imagined him to be deprived of the help and companionship of human friends, he was privileged to enjoy the sight and [145] conversation of angelic friends. By these he was taught and the more he learned that the allurements and bitter experiences of the world are to be despised, the more loftily did he contemplate the things

---

persecutions' which are recorded in the *Historia Ecclesiastica* as having arisen at the beginning of Ceolwulf's reign in 729 (cf. D. Whitelock, 1976, p.27). However, this interpretation of the expression 'present troubles' is not the only possible one. 'Present' in Bede is often used in the eschatological rather than the historical sense. Which is particularly true of *De templo*. So the expression 'present troubles' could arguably mean simply the trials of this present life as in *De templo* 1.2; 8.2; or 10. In 8.2 he writes: '. . . after the *present hardships* of the faithful, and after their souls receive their rest in the life to come, the complete happiness of the whole Church will be achieved in the glory of the resurrection.' Again in 10: 'this number (i.e. forty cubits) is often used to signify the *present labour* of the faithful, just as the number fifty stands for the rest and peace to come.' Indeed, of the twenty-seven occurrences of 'present' as an attributive adjective in *De templo,* the sense is eschatological in at least twenty-five, twelve or more of which apply to the Church and the rest to its members. Admittedly the analogy with John's exile on Patmos is striking, but there is nothing in the context to show conclusively that the phrase 'the present worries of temporal affairs' is to be understood as an allusion to the contemporary situation.

[21] cf. Ps 26:13

which, because of their magnitude and eternity, everyone knows are far more worthy of being feared or loved. Farewell my ever most beloved friend and intercede for us.

BOOK ONE

1. THAT THE BUILDING OF THE TABERNACLE AND THE TEMPLE SIGNIFY ONE AND THE SAME CHURCH OF CHRIST

1.1 The house of God which king Solomon built in Jerusalem was   *[147]* made as a figure of the holy universal Church which, from the first of the elect to the last to be born at the end of the world, is daily being built through the grace of the king of peace, namely, its redeemer. It is still partly in a state of pilgrimage from him on earth, and partly, having escaped from the hardships of its sojourn, already reigns with him in heaven, where, when the last judgement is over, it is to reign completely with him. To this house belong the chosen angels, whose likeness is promised us in the life to come on the Lord's word: *Those who are judged worthy of a place in the other world and in the resurrection from the dead do not marry because they can no longer die, for they are on a par with the angels, and being children of the resurrection, they are children of God;*[1] to it belongs the very *mediator between God and men, himself a human being, Christ Jesus,*[2] as he himself attests when he says, *Destroy this temple, and in three days I shall raise it up.*[3] To which the evangelist by way of explanation added: *But he was speaking of the temple of his own body.*[4] Furthermore, the Apostle says of us, *Do you not realize that you are a temple of God with the Spirit of God living in you?*[5] If, therefore, he became the temple of God by assuming human nature and we become the temple of God *through his Spirit dwelling in us,*[6] it is quite clear that the material temple was a figure of us all, that is, both of the Lord himself and his members which we are. But ⟨it was a figure⟩ of him as the uniquely chosen and precious cornerstone laid in the foundation,[7] and of us as the living stones built upon the

---

[1] Lk 20:35–36
[2] 1 Tm 2:5
[3] Jn 2:19
[4] Jn 2:21
[5] 1 Co 3:16
[6] Rm 8:11
[7] cf. Is 28:16

5

foundation of the apostles and prophets, i.e. on the Lord himself.[8] This will be clearer if we consider the actual building of the temple systematically. That is to say, in this way the figure will apply to the Lord himself in some respects, in others to all the elect. In some respects it describes the unclouded happiness of the angels in heaven, in others the invincible patience of mankind on earth, in others the help of the angels bestowed on mankind, and in others again it will show the struggles of mankind rewarded by the angels.

[148] **1.2** The tabernacle once made in the desert by Moses also symbolizes the same spiritual house of the Lord.[9] But that house was built on the route by which one reaches the land of promise, whereas this one was built in the land of promise itself and in the city of Jerusalem; the former so that after being frequently carried from place to place by the ministry of the Levites, it might at length be brought into the land of the promised inheritance; the latter that it might afterwards stand in the fatherland itself and the royal city built on an ever inviolable foundation until it fulfilled the task of the heavenly figures imposed upon it. For these reasons the former can be taken to represent the toil and exile of the present Church, the latter the rest and happiness of the future Church. At all events because the former was made by the children of Israel alone, the latter by proselytes also and by gentiles, the former can be taken chiefly as a symbolic expression for the Fathers of the Old Testament and the ancient people of God, the latter for the Church assembled from the gentiles, although the building of both houses, when it has been discussed in greater detail in the spiritual sense, can be shown in many ways to suggest symbolically both the daily labours of the present Church and the everlasting rewards and joys in the future and the salvation of all nations in Christ.

2. HOW KING HIRAM HELPED SOLOMON IN THE WORK OF THE TEMPLE

2.1 Therefore, as we, with the Lord's help, set about treating of the building of the temple and seeking the spiritual mansion of God in the material structure, it seems opportune to say something first

---

[8] cf. Ep 2:20; 1 P 2:5–6

[9] cf. Ex 25:8–9

about its builders, who they were, and where they were from, and at the same time something about the material itself and what it was made of. For these matters too are pregnant with spiritual mysteries according to the testimony of the Apostle who says, *all these things happened to them by way of example, and they were recorded in writing to be a lesson for us.*[1]

2.2 The history of the Kings[2] tells how Solomon, as he was about to build a house for the Lord, sought help from Hiram king of Tyre who was a long-standing friend of David's and had started off on peaceful terms with Solomon himself too after he had taken over the kingdom, and later proved so willing to help him in all his undertakings that he gave him craftsmen, timber and gold as the project required. In return for this favour Solomon used to give him each year a great many kors of wheat and oil as provisions for his house.[3] Nobody doubts that Solomon, which means 'peacemaker',[4] signifies, both by his very name and the extremely peaceful state of his reign, the one of whom Isaiah said, *his empire shall be multiplied, and there shall be no end of peace.*[5] Hiram, on the other hand, which in Latin means 'living exaltedly', represents figuratively believers from among the gentiles and those who are distinguished both by reason of their life and of their faith.[6] And since Hiram was a king and used his royal power *[149]* to help Solomon in the building of the house of the Lord, there is nothing to prevent him from typifying masters of ⟨worldly⟩ affairs, themselves converted to the faith, by whose help, as is well known, the Church has quite often been assisted and nobly increased, and has been supported by their imperial decrees against heretics and schismatics and pagans.

2.3 The point in Solomon's seeking help from Hiram in the work of the temple was that when the Lord came in the flesh and arranged to build a favourite home for himself, namely, the Church, he chose helpers for the work not from the Jews alone but also from the

---

[1] 1 Co 10:11
[2] cf. 3 K 5:1–12
[3] cf. ibid.
[4] cf. Jer., *Nom. Hebr. CCSL* 72:138, 5
[5] Is 9:7
[6] cf. Jer., *Nom. Hebr. CCSL* 72:107, 25

gentiles. For he picked ministers of the word from both peoples. Hiram sent Solomon cedar and pine-wood hewn in Lebanon to put in the house of the Lord because the converted gentiles sent to the Lord men once famous in the eyes of the world but now cast down and humbled from the mountain of their pride by the axe of the Lord's reproof, to be trained according to the norm of evangelical truth and given their place in the building of the Church, each according to his merits or age. He also sent craftsmen because the gentiles offered to the Lord philosophers converted to true wisdom, people who because of their learning might deservedly be put in charge of people to govern them. Such, for instance, in the time of the apostles was Dionysius the Areopagite, such too was the most gentle and brave martyr Cyprian and countless others. He also sent gold which can be taken in the same sense, namely, that it symbolizes men renowned for wisdom and ability. For all these offerings the gentiles expect the gifts of heavenly grace from the Lord, namely, the wheat of the word of God and the oil of charity and of the unction and enlightenment of the Holy Spirit.

2.4   It is appropriate to the situation of the Church that in requesting help for his holy undertaking Solomon said to Hiram,

⟨5:6⟩ **Give orders, therefore, that your servants cut me down cedar-trees from Lebanon; and let my servants be with your servants.** For the servants of Hiram who cut down cedars from Lebanon for Solomon are the teachers chosen from among the gentiles whose task it is to fell those who enjoy the goods and glory of this world by correcting their pride and arrogance and convert their ambition into obedience to their redeemer. Now with these servants were also the servants of Solomon and together they set about the work referred to because the first teachers from among the gentiles needed the apostles themselves who had received training by being instructed in the word of faith lest, were they to begin to teach without masters, they might turn out to be teachers of error. For the reason why *[150]* Solomon wanted the servants of Hiram to hew timber from Lebanon for him was that they were more experienced than his own servants in felling, but the reason why he also wanted his own servants to be there with them was that they might show the lumbermen what length the planks ought to be. What this symbolizes is plain, namely, that the apostles had a surer knowledge of how to preach to others the word of the Gospel which they were privileged to hear from the Lord, but the gentiles, converted from error and brought into conformity with the truth of the Gospel, had a better knowledge of the actual errors of the gentiles, and the surer their knowledge the more skilfully they learned to counteract and refute them. Paul indeed had a better knowledge of the mystery of the Gospel, which he had learned through revelation, but Dionysius was better able to refute the false teachings of Athens whose syllogisms as well as errors and all of whose arguments he knew since a boy. With this explanation the statement which follows is fully in keeping:

2.5 ⟨5:6⟩ **For you know that there is not a man among my people who has skill to hew wood like the Sidonians.** For when the Lord was bodily present teaching, there was not one among the Jewish people who knew so well how to refute the errors of the gentiles as the actual gentile converts to the faith and those of the gentiles who had become Christians. For the Sidonians and Tyrians are rightly taken as a type of the gentiles because they were gentile peoples.

3. HOW MANY WORKERS SOLOMON HAD IN THE WORK
   OF THE TEMPLE

3.1 How many slaves our Solomon sent for this work is told in the following verse in mystical terms when it says,
⟨5:13–14⟩ **And king Solomon chose workmen out of all Israel, and the levy numbered thirty thousand men. And he sent them to Lebanon, ten thousand every month in relays, so that they would** *[151]* **be two months at home.** The first thing to note here is that it was not for nothing that Solomon chose workmen from all Israel, nor was there any section of the people from which men fit for such a great task were not taken, because, of course, priests nowadays are not to be chosen from the stock of Aaron alone; rather people are to be sought from the whole Church who, whether by example or word, are competent to build the house of the Lord, and wherever they are found they are to be promoted to the office of teachers without any exception of persons. And when such people are ordained to instruct the infidel and those who are to be called into the joint pastorate of the Church, they are sent as energetic and picked men, as it were, to hew in Lebanon the materials for the temple. And indeed the number of thirty thousand which was the tally of the hewers of wood can be aptly applied figuratively to those who are perfect in the faith

of the holy Trinity, because it is most appropriate for teachers. But because the thirty thousand were organized in such a way that ten thousand should set about the holy work every month, we ought to consider further the mystery of the number ten. For ten thousand men of Israel were sent to hew timber for the work of the Lord's house, because whatever teachers and instructors of the ignorant are to be ordained, must themselves in all things observe the ten precepts of the law and show their listeners what must be observed as well as the future rewards in heaven which are customarily represented by the number ten, and they themselves must hope and always show their hearers what must be hoped for. The three months, the term allotted to each of the lumbermen, represent figuratively the perfection of the three evangelical virtues, namely, almsgiving, prayer and fasting. For when the Lord said in the Gospel, *Beware of practising your piety in public to be seen by people*,[1] in the rest of the same sentence he makes no mention of anything else except almsgiving, prayer and fasting, which were not to be performed for human show but solely for the glory of the one who sees inwardly, otherwise they would remain barren of the fruit of eternity.[2] By these words he openly taught that all the fruits of virtues are intimated by these three, as branches issuing from the one root of charity. For almsgiving comprises all that we do out of goodwill for the brethren to put the love of our neighbour into practice; prayer comprises everything that joins us to our creator by interior compunction, and fasting every means we use to keep ourselves from the contagion of vices and from the allurements of the world so that we can always give ourselves with freedom of spirit and chastity of body to the love both of our creator and our neighbour. And these are the three months of the temple workers. For since the month is completed by the total of the days of the lunar cycle, by it (i.e. by the month) is shown the fulness of each spiritual virtue in which the mind of the faithful is solicitously cared for by the Lord by daily illumination as the moon is by the sun. But the one month when they cut timber for the work of the temple stands for almsgiving, i.e. the work of mercy whereby, through teaching and reproving, sacrificing our temporal comforts and giving the example of a good life, we labour for the salvation of the neighbour that by making good progress people may attain

---

[1] Mt 6:1
[2] cf. Mt 6:2–18

the unity of the holy Church. The two other months, during which they were allowed to stay in their homes and have time to attend to their own needs, are prayer and fasting, whereby in addition to those external activities which we engage in for the needs of the brethren, we concern ourselves with our own salvation, by turning our mind inward towards the Lord.

3.2 And since only those who humbly submit themselves to divine grace attend perfectly to their own or their brethren's salvation, there *[152]* rightly follows the verse:

⟨5:14⟩ **And Adoniram was over this levy.** For whom does Adoniram (which in Latin means 'my lord is lofty'), whom does he more aptly suggest than the one whom by his name he imitates, namely, the Lord our saviour?[3] And Adoniram is put in charge of the temple workers in order that by his arrangement it may be duly determined which months they each go out to work and also which months they return to look after their own home; this happens when our Lord and saviour forms the minds of his holy preachers more intimately by his light to discern when the work of building the Church should be undertaken by preaching or performing other services of piety, and when one ought to return again to the examination of one's own conscience as if to inspect his house, and by prayer and fasting render it fit for the inspector and visitor from above.

3.3 ⟨5:15–16⟩ **And Solomon had seventy thousand to carry burdens, and eighty thousand to hew stones on the mountain; besides, the overseers (three thousand in number) who supervised each operation, and three hundred who were in charge of the people and of those who did the work.** He calls the stonemasons *latomi*. These stonemasons, who also figuratively represent the woodcutters, are the holy preachers who train the minds of the ignorant by the work of the word of God and strive to change them from the baseness and deformity in which they were born, and when they have been duly instructed, endeavour to render them fit to join the body of the faithful, i.e. for the building of the house of God. The fact that the wood and stones were both cut on the mountain, and that, after being cut and dressed, both materials were transferred to the mountain of the house of the Lord, obviously means that all of us human beings were

---

[3] cf. Jer., *Nom. Hebr. CCSL* 72:109, 21

born on the mountain of pride because we take our carnal origin
from the first human being's prevarication which pride was the cause
of; but those of us *preordained to life*[4] by God's grace, who were hewn
by being catechized and by receiving the mysteries of the faith, were
transferred from the mountain of pride to the mountain of the house
of the Lord,[5] and, rescued from the power of darkness,[6] we reached
the citadel of virtues, which is in the unity of the holy Church. But it
is to be noted that the same workers were distributed in such a way
that some cut stones on the mountain, others carried burdens. For
the gifts of the Spirit are different and some have greater constancy
in speaking and refuting the arrogant, others are gentler for the task
of encouraging the timid and lifting up the weak, some are endowed   *[153]*
with the gift of both virtues and are fitted for the work of the house
of the Lord. Such did the Apostle wish those to become to whom he
spoke the words: *Admonish the disorderly, encourage the faint-hearted,
support the weak, be patient towards all.*[7]

3.4   Now the overseers who were in charge of each operation are
the writers of sacred scripture by whose teaching authority we are
instructed in all things as to how best to teach the ignorant and correct the contemptuous, to bear each other's burdens so that we may
fulfil the law of Christ.[8] But the more each one labours in giving his
neighbours support in their needs or in correcting their mistakes, the
more surely may he expect in the life to come the rewards whether
of peace of soul after death or of blessed immortality of body. Consequently, the aforesaid overseers are rightly recorded as numbering
seventy thousand and eighty thousand: seventy thousand because of
the sabbath rest of souls[9] for the seventh day is consecrated to the

---

[4] Ac 13:48
[5] cf. Is 2:2
[6] cf. Col 1:13
[7] 1 Th 5:14
[8] cf. Ga 6:2,5
[9] cf. Heb 4:9 *infra* 8.2 ** The expression "sabbath rest of souls", which also occurs
     below at 8.2, renders the word which appears in the Latin in the form *sabbatissi-
     mum,* (*sabbatissimo* 8.2). The spelling, which at first sight suggests a superlative form,
     is disconcerting until one realises that it is a misspelling of the form *sabbatismum.*
     Whether the misspelling goes back to Bede himself or is the error of a later scribe is
     difficult to say. The *apparatus criticus* of the *Corpus Christianorum* edition on which
     the present translation is based, gives no variants at either point in the text. So

sabbath, i.e. rest, eighty thousand because of the hope of resurrection which on the eighth day, i.e. after the sabbath, has already taken place, in the Lord, and, it is hoped, will take place in us also on the eighth day and in the eighth age to come. The overseers, on the other hand, were three thousand three hundred, doubtless because of faith in the holy Trinity which the holy scriptures proclaim to us. But the fact that in the Book of Paralipomenon the number three thousand is written instead of three thousand three hundred, has to do with the very same perfection of people of sublime virtue.[10] For because the Lord completed the adornment of the world in the number six,[11] the perfect works of good people are rightly wont to be symbolized by the same number[12] and because holy scripture teaches that we must have the works of piety as well as true faith, the overseers of the temple works are rightly said to be three thousand and six hundred. Nor should we pass over the fact that these seventy and eighty thousand hod-carriers and stonemasons with their overseers were not from Israel but from among the proselytes, i.e. strangers who sojourned among them. For it is written in the Book of Paralipomenon: *And Solomon took a census of all the proselytes resident in the land of Israel, on the model of the census which David his father had taken; and it was found that they numbered a hundred and fifty-three thousand six hundred. And he put seventy thousand of them carrying burdens on their shoulders,* and so forth.[13] 'Proselytes' is the Greek name for those who were of other nationalities by birth but accepted

---

the reader can only assume that the codices collated are at one on the spelling as received in our text and that this is how the word appears in the archetype. The term is found in Hebrews 4:9 in the nominative singular, *sabbatismus,* a transliteration of the Greek *sabbatismos* and is a *hapax legomenon,* i.e. it occurs nowhere else in the Greek Bible. The RSV translates it 'sabbath rest'. Properly speaking it means not just 'rest' but 'the observance or enjoyment of rest'. It is a cessation from work in imitation of the creator. Judging from the context of Hebrews 4, the implication is that it is the reward of good works, a well-earned rest from one's labours well done, and a sharing in the beatific vision, an idea which recurs like a refrain in *De templo.* One is reminded of Revelation 14.13: *'Blessed are the dead who die in the Lord henceforth.' 'Blessed indeed,' says the Spirit, 'that they may rest from their labours, for their deeds follow them!'* Leonard, (1952), 936a.

[10] cf. 2 Paralip 2:2,18
[11] cf. Gn 1:31; 2:1 *infra* 6.1 **
[12] cf. Greg., *Hom. in Ezech. PL* 76:952D; 992A
[13] 2 Paralip 2:17–18

circumcision and converted to the faith and fellowship of the people of God.

3.5 The workmen of the house of the Lord were drawn from among the sons of Israel, the proselytes and the gentiles; i.e. from the sons of Israel came the thirty thousand who were sent to fell the cedars of Lebanon; from among the proselytes came the stonemasons of whom we have just spoken; from among the gentiles came Hiram himself and his slaves who together with Solomon's slaves cut the timber. Therefore, every kind of person by whom the Church was to be built had already gone before in the building of the temple. For the Jews and proselytes and gentiles converted to the truth of the Gospel build one and the same Church of Christ whether by upright living or by teaching as well.

4. WHAT KIND OF STONE THE TEMPLE WAS MADE OF

4.1 ⟨5:17⟩ **And the king commanded that they bring great costly stones for the foundation of the temple and square them.** The foundation of the temple is to be understood mystically as none other than that which the Apostle points out when he says, *For there is no other foundation anyone can lay than the one which has been laid, namely, Jesus Christ.*[1] Consequently, he can rightly be called the foundation of the house of the Lord, because, as Peter says, *There is no other name under heaven given to men by which we must be saved.*[2] Into this foundation great and costly stones are carried when men eminent in deeds and sanctity adhere by their habitual sanctity of spirit to their creator, so that the more firmly they place their hope in him, the greater is their capacity to direct the life of others, which is to act as a broad foundation supporting a massive building. Therefore, the stones which were laid as the foundation of the temple to bear the whole structure, are properly speaking the prophets and apostles who either visibly or invisibly received the word and mysteries of truth from the very wisdom of God. Hence of us too, who, in our modest way, strive to imitate the life or teaching of these men, the Apostle says we are supported *on the foundation of the apostles and prophets.*[3]

---

[1] 1 Co 3:11
[2] Ac 4:12
[3] Ep 2:20

But even in general all the perfect who have learnt to adhere faithfully to the Lord himself and bear with fortitude the needs of their brethren which are laid upon them, these too can be symbolized by these great and precious stones. And they are fittingly ordered first to be squared and so placed in the foundation. For whatever is squared is accustomed to fit no matter which way it is turned.[4] To this figure are likened the hearts of the elect which have learnt to stand firm in the faith so that no adverse occurrence, not even death itself, can make them deviate from their way of uprightness. Such for instance are the teachers whom the Church has received in great numbers not only from Judaea but also from the gentiles. Hence concerning such great and precious stones is fittingly added:

4.2 ⟨5:18⟩ **And the masons of Solomon and the masons of Hiram hewed them.** For precious stones are hewn when, as a result of the *[155]* instruction and zeal of the saints who have gone before them, each of the elect gets rid of whatever is harmful or vain in himself, and in the sight of his creator exemplifies only the norm of righteousness implanted in him as the stable form of a square. However, it was not only Solomon's masons but also those of Hiram that hewed the stones because there were teachers of the holy Church from both groups. In fact there were some from both groups so eminent that they were rightly teachers even of the eminent teachers and, as it were, by squaring them, prepared them to erect the building of the house of the Lord. For not only Jeremiah and Isaiah and the other prophets of the circumcision but also blessed Job with his sons who were of the gentiles, afforded teachers of the succeeding age the greatest example of lifestyle or patience, and the greatest proclamations of salutary teaching so that they gave up vain words, acts and thoughts and were deemed worthy and competent to bear the responsibility of the holy Church.

4.3 ⟨5:18⟩ **Furthermore the men of Biblos prepared wood and stones to build the house.** Biblos is a city in Phoenicia which Ezekiel mentions saying, *Your skilled men, Tyre, were your pilots. The elders of Biblos and its skilled men,*[5] for which ⟨city⟩ in Hebrew is written Go-

---

[4] cf. Greg., *Hom. in Ezech. PL* 76:1044C

[5] Ezk 27:8–9

Gobel or Gebal which means 'defining' or 'limiting'.[6] This word is very appropriate to those who prepare people's hearts for the spiritual edifice which is built of the virtues of the soul. For they are only equal to the task of teaching their hearers faith and the works of righteousness when they themselves have first been instructed by the Sacred Page and thoroughly learnt from a clear definition of the truth what belief one must hold, and on what path of virtue one must walk. For he who does not know what is definitely catholic faith is wasting his time assuming the office of teacher, and those who try to teach others the norm which they themselves have not learned, do not build a sanctuary for the Lord but ruin for themselves.

4.4   In building the house of the Lord, first of all the wood and stones must be hewn from the mountain because those whom we seek to train in the true faith we must first teach to renounce the devil and escape, by being reborn, from the fate of the first transgression in which they were born. Then we have to look for large, precious stones and lay them in the foundation of the temple, so that after they have renounced their former way of life, we may remember in all things to watch over their life and conduct, and set before our hearers for imitation those whom we know to cling in a special way by *[156]*   the virtue of humility to the Lord, people whom we see persevering unflinchingly with invincible constancy of spirit like squared stones, in a certain sense, and whom by their merit and repute we have found to be large and precious stones. But after the foundation which is made up of stones of such quality and size, the house must be built with wood and stones very carefully dressed and laid in the proper arrangement, ⟨wood and stones⟩ which had once been removed from their original position or roots, because, after the first rudiments of the faith and after the foundations of humility have been laid in us after the example of men of high virtue, there remains to continue upwards the wall of good works, superimposing on each other, as it were, courses of stones by the life we lead and by advancing from virtue to virtue.[7]   Or at all events the large precious square stones are, as I said above, the first masters of the churches who heard the word of salvation from the Lord himself. The courses of stones or timber laid upon them were the priests and teachers who followed,

---

[6]   cf. Jer., *Nom. Hebr. CCSL* 72:119, 20; *Sit. PL* 23:884B

[7]   cf. Ps 83:8

each in his own time, and by whose preaching and ministry the fabric of the Church grows or by whose virtues it is shaped.

4.5 What colour the stones were with which the temple was made is openly stated in the Book of Paralipomenon when David said to Solomon on showing him the materials of the temple which he had procured, *I have prepared all manner of precious stones and marble of Paros in great abundance.*[8] White marble is called Parian marble because it was produced on the island of that name. Hence the poet writes of it:

> *(past the) Isle of Olives, and then past snow-white Paros and the Cyclades sprinkled about the sea we sped o'er the waters tossed by many a wind.*[9]

4.6 The reason why Paros is called 'snowy' is that it produces a brilliant white variety of marble. That the temple was made of this stone, Josephus hints when he says, *Therefore, he built the temple of white stone up as far as the room; it was a hundred and twenty cubits high.*[10] Nor is the meaning of the mystery obscure. For it is obvious to everyone that the white marble of which the house of the Lord was built denotes the pure manner of acting of the elect as well as their conscience purified of all blemish of corruption, such as that wise architect wanted those stones to be which he laid upon the foundation of Christ, precious stones adorned with gold and silver. *Dearly beloved,* he said, *let us cleanse ourselves of every defilement of flesh and spirit, achieving our sanctification in the fear of God.*[11] *[157]*

5. WHEN AND WHERE THE TEMPLE WAS BUILT

5.1 ⟨6:1⟩ **Therefore, it came to pass in the four hundred and eightieth year after the children of Israel came out of the land of Egypt, in the fourth year of Solomon's reign over Israel, in the month of Zio, which is the second month, he began to build a house to the Lord.** Where it says, *in the fourth year in the month of Zio, which is*

---

[8] 1 Paralip 29:2
[9] Virg. *Aen.*, 3:126–127
[10] Josephus *Ant.*, 8.3.2
[11] 2 Co 7:1

the second month of the reign of Solomon over Israel, the intended order is, in the fourth year of the reign of Solomon in the month of Zio, i.e. the second month. He calls the second month May, for April in which the Pasch, the principal feast among the Hebrews, is held, was the first month of the year.[1] From this it is quite clear that later when the Pasch was over he began to build a house for the Lord, and after they had been consecrated by the mystical solemnity, the people set their hands to the mystical task. A commemoration is made of the exodus from Egypt when work began on the building of the tabernacle so that the reader may be made aware what a period of time had passed between the building of both houses, and also learn the spiritual mystery attaching to this period of time. For four times a hundred and twenty make four hundred and eighty; now four is very appropriate to evangelical perfection on account of the actual number of the evangelists; a hundred and twenty is appropriate to the teaching of the law on account of the same number of years of the legislator.[2] It was also in this number of men that the primitive Church received the grace of the Holy Spirit,[3] clearly showing that those who use the law legitimately, i.e. those who recognize and embrace the grace of Christ in it are deservedly filled with the grace of his Spirit so that they may become more ardent in his love.

5.2 Now we have said that the Synagogue could be denoted by the tabernacle which Moses and the children of Israel built in the desert, but the Church of the gentiles by the temple which Solomon and the children of Israel erected with the help of the proselytes and gentiles. The worship and religion of the tabernacle lasted four hundred and eighty years and then work began on the building of the temple because the writing of the Old Testament overflows with such perfection that, if one understands it properly, it contains in itself all the mysteries of the New Testament. Besides, a great many of the patriarchs of the Old Testament attained such a peak of perfection by the way they lived that they are not in any way to be considered inferior to the apostles or apostolic men. The tabernacle remained among the people of God for four hundred and eighty years, until the construction of the temple, i.e. for a hundred and twenty years

---

[1] cf. Ex 12:2
[2] cf. Dt 34:7
[3] cf. Ac 1:15

[158]   multiplied by four, because from the time the Law was given until
the Lord's incarnation and the time of the revelation of grace there
was no lack of people who were grounded in the Law and observed
evangelical perfection in all things in outlook and action; and there
was no lack of scripture to intimate by its prophetic words the grace
of the New Testament in the Old. But the fact that it was in the fourth
year of Solomon's reign that work began on the house of the Lord
can be applied mystically to the fact that after the completion of the
dispensation of the Lord's incarnation which was treated in the four
books of the Gospel, the construction of the holy Church began when
the Holy Spirit was sent from heaven. And the fact that it was begun
in the second month can be applied to the election of the gentiles
that undertook the creator's building in the second place after Israel.
Hence also the second month was granted for celebrating the Pasch
to those who, because they were unclean in soul or lived at a distance,
were unable to attend the Pasch in the first month.[4] This obviously
refers to us who, because we are unclean on account of the death of
our soul and still live far from the people of God, cannot hold the
first Pasch which was celebrated with the flesh and blood of a lamb.
But we celebrate today the second Pasch which is enacted with the
body and blood of our redeemer by whom we were sought and have
been cleansed.

5.3   Where the temple was built is shown rather clearly in the Book
of Paralipomenon where it is written: *And Solomon began to build
the house of the Lord in Jerusalem, on Mount Moriah, where David his
father had had a vision at the place which David had prepared on the
threshing-floor of Ornan the Jebusite.*[5] The reason why the house of
the Lord is built in the vision of peace is that the Church which is
spread throughout the world consists in one and the same faith and
fellowship of universal truth. For God is not in division of minds;
rather *his place is in peace and his dwelling in Sion.*[6] It is built on the
mountain, that is to say, on the Lord the saviour himself of whom
Isaiah says, *And in the last days the mountain of the house of the Lord
shall be set up on the top of the mountains,*[7] and he says of himself

---

[4] cf. Nb 9:10–11
[5] 2 Paralip 3:1
[6] Ps 75:3
[7] Is 2:2

in the Gospel, *a city set on a hill cannot be hidden.*[8] For he himself
is the mountain of mountains that rose indeed from the earth as a
result of his taking flesh but transcends the power and holiness of all
the earth-born by the peak of its singular dignity. That is to say, on
this mountain the city or house of the Lord has been built because
unless it fixes its root in him, our hope and faith are nothing. He is
rightly called Mount Moriah, that is, the mountain of vision, because
he deigns to watch over and help his elect whom he preserves for the
eternal vision of his glory as they toil in this passing life. For he is   *[159]*
the place in which Abraham offered his son Isaac to the Lord and
merited by the devotion of his obedience to be seen by him; which
is also how it received its name.[9] Finally where the Lord says, *Take
your only begotten son Isaac and go into the land of vision and offer
him as a holocaust,*[10] for 'the land of vision' he has in the Hebrew
'the land of Moriah'. And because the immolation of Isaac is a type
of the Lord's passion it is right that the temple should be built on
the site of the same sacrifice because it is by the faith and mysteries
of the Lord's passion that the Church is dedicated and grows into a
temple which is holy in the Lord.

5.4   About this mountain are aptly added ⟨the words⟩: *which was
shown to David his father,* for to David and the other prophets was
shown the Lord who was to come in the flesh and who through the
mysteries of his own very incarnation would cleanse from her sins the
Church which was called from the gentiles, and consecrate her as a
house faithful and dear to himself. And the phrase *in the place which
David had prepared* is fittingly added. For David had prepared by
singing psalms, and the other prophets too by prophesying prepared
for the Lord who was indeed the true Solomon, a place in which he
might build a house, because they taught the hearts of their hearers
by true faith, earnestly urging them to receive with faith and devotion
the Son of God who was coming in the flesh. Indeed that is why the
Lord said to his disciples concerning the peoples prepared to believe
in him, *Lift up your eyes and see the fields because they are white for
the harvest. He who reaps receives wages, and gathers fruit for eternal*

---

[8] Mt 5:14
[9] cf. Gn 22:14
[10] Gn 22:2

life, so that sower and reaper may rejoice together,[11] in other words, as
if he were speaking about the building of the temple: lift up your
eyes and see the place because it is already prepared for building the
house of the Lord, and he who builds by teaching receives a reward
and gathers precious stones for eternal life, so that both the one who
prepares the site for the building and the one who builds it rejoice
together, i.e. the prophet who foretells the one who is to come, and
the apostle who proclaims the coming Lord, share in him together
the one reward.

5.5   It is appropriate that this place should be on the threshing-floor
of Ornan the Jebusite because the Church is customarily designated
by the word threshing-floor as John says of the Lord: *His winnowing
fork is in his hand, and he will clear his threshing-floor.*[12]   Ornan
whose name means 'enlightened' and who was a Jebusite by origin,
signifies the gentiles by his origin,[13] and by his name he indicates
these same ⟨gentiles⟩ who were to be enlightened by the Lord and
transformed into children of the Church to whom the Apostle rightly
says, *once you were darkness, but now you are light in the Lord.*[14]
Jebus is the same city as Jerusalem.[15] Now Jebus means 'trampled   *[160]*
upon' but Jerusalem 'the vision of peace'.[16] As long as the gentile
Ornan reigned there it was called Jebus; but when David bought a
place of holocaust there,[17] when Solomon built a temple to the Lord
there, it was no longer called Jebus but Jerusalem, because, that is,
as long as the gentiles continued in ignorance of divine worship they
were trampled upon and made a mockery of by the unclean spirits,
following mute idols according as they were led to do;[18] but when
they called to mind the grace of their creator they immediately found
in themselves both the place and the name of peace, as the Lord
says of them, *Blessed are the peacemakers for they shall be called the*

---

[11] Jn 4:35–36
[12] Mt 3:12
[13] cf. Jer., *Nom. Hebr.* CCSL 72:83,29
[14] Ep 5:8
[15] cf. Jer., *Sit.* PL 23:904C
[16] cf. Jer., *Nom. Hebr.* CCSL 72:67,13; 121,9–10
[17] cf. 1 Paralip 21:25–26
[18] cf. 1 Co 12:2

children of God.[19] Therefore, while Ornan still held sway in this city it was called Jebus, but when he sold the site of his threshing-floor together with his oxen and threshing-sledges to king David, it took the name Jerusalem because the gentiles who still persisted in their obstinacy were trampled upon as worthless and contemptible by the wicked spirits; but when they learned to sell all they had and offer it to the true king they could no longer be trampled upon by the demons and vices, but were given a greater share of inner peace which they possessed with their creator.

6. WHAT ITS DIMENSIONS WERE

6.1 ⟨6:2⟩ **And the house which king Solomon built to the Lord was sixty cubits long, twenty cubits wide, and thirty cubits high.**[1] The length of the house stands for the long endurance of the holy Church, whereby in the exile of this sojourn of endurance she bears with all adversities until she reaches her country which she looks forward to.[2] The breadth suggests the charity whereby she is happy to open wide the bosom of her soul and for God's sake to show her love not only to her friends in God but also to her enemies until the time comes when either they are converted to her peace or else are completely dead and she rejoices with her friends alone in God.[3] The height denotes the hope of a future reward in view of which she gladly despises all things here below whether attractive or trying, until, having risen above both, she merits *to see the good things of the Lord in the land of the living.*[4] Hence the length of the house is fittingly expressed by the figure of sixty cubits. For the number six whereby the world was made,[5] conventionally denotes the perfection of good works.[6] And it is necessary that we should endure the trials of our sojourn with forbearance so that we may deservedly be able to enter the promised land of good works when it appears. The breadth is determined by the number twenty because of the twofold dimension of the same

---

[19] Mt 5:9

[1] *infra* 22.3 **

[2] cf. Greg., *Hom. in Ezech. PL* 76:957C; 963A–B

[3] *infra* 9.3 **

[4] Ps 26:13

[5] cf. Gn 1:31

[6] *supra* 3.4 **

charity wherewith we love both God and neighbour;[7] the height is
determined by the number thirty because of belief in the holy Trinity
[161]   which is one God in the vision of whom all our hopes and desires
have their fulfilment. So six has to do with the perfection of the
work, two with the love of God and neighbour, and three with the
hope of the vision of God. Each number is rightly multiplied by ten
because it is only through faith and the observance of the decalogue
of the law that our patience gets salutary exercise or our charity burns
profitably or our hope is rapt aloft to yearn for the things of eternity.
Here it must be noted that the thirty cubits of height did not reach
as far as the roof of the temple but as far as the lower supper-room.
For in the Book of Paralipomenon it is clearly written that *the height
was a hundred and twenty cubits.*[8] It will be more appropriate to treat
of the mysteries of this matter in what follows, where the course of
the reading takes us as far as the middle and third supper-room.[9]

**6.2 ⟨6:3⟩ The portico in front of the nave of the house was twenty
cubits long, equal to the width of the house, and ten cubits deep in
front of the house.** The same is not written about this in the Book
of Paralipomenon: *The portico in front of the nave of the house was
twenty cubits long.*[10] It is obvious, therefore, that this portico was
built on the east side of the temple. For the temple faced eastwards
just as the tabernacle did, and had the vestibule door on the east
opposite the temple door according to what Josephus the Jewish
historian quite explicitly tells us, so that the equinoctial sunrise could
shed its rays directly on the ark of the covenant through the three
doors, namely, that of the portico, the temple and the oracle.[11] But
because the temple designates the holy Church, what could be more
aptly typified by the portico which was in front of the temple and used
to be the first to receive the light of the sun than that part of it which
preceded the times of the Lord's incarnation?[12] And in it are the
patriarchs and prophets who were the first to welcome the sun rising
on this world and bore witness by their lives and preaching, their

---

[7] *infra* 9.3 **
[8] 2 Paralip 3:4
[9] *infra* 8.2 **
[10] 2 Paralip 3:4
[11] cf. Josephus *Ant.* 8.3.2
[12] *infra* 11.3 **

birth and even their death, to the Lord who was born in the flesh. The reason why the door of the temple is the Lord is that *no one comes to the Father except through* him,[13] and as he says elsewhere, *I am the door; whoever enters through me will be saved.*[14] The door of the portico is prophetic speech which led as if by a straight path those going in at the door of the temple by the grace of the Lord the saviour whereby he proclaimed that he was to redeem the world. The whole structure of the portico, therefore, signifies the faithful of that time, but the door in the portico stands for the teachers who shone the light of life for the others and held the door open for them to enter into the presence of the Lord. And rightly was there *[162]* one door because of the harmony of faith and love of the truth in all the saints. That is to say, this portico was twenty cubits long to correspond with the breadth of the temple, because, of course, the just of ancient times awaited with much patience and forbearance the time when the Lord would appear in the flesh and bring to the world the new grace of the Gospel though they themselves did not receive the promises but beheld and greeted them from a distance. By their length they equalled the breadth of the temple because through the forbearance of their devoted spirit they longed for the coming of the expansion of the Church in *the love of God in Christ Jesus Our Lord*[15] for, although still separated in time from the mysteries of the Lord's incarnation, nevertheless by their faith and preaching they were very near. In the forefront of this most sacred portico were the blessed martyr, Abel, and Seth and Enos and the other just men of the world's beginning. On the other hand, in its inner sanctum and, as it were, near the mystical wall of the temple were placed the parents of the blessed forerunner of the Lord, Simeon and Anna and the others who, though they were privileged to see his birth, nevertheless were unable to get to hear his teaching and partake in his mysteries. And this portico was fittingly ten cubits wide because fine people such as these, even though they had not yet received the words or mysteries of the Gospel which were handed down by the Lord, nevertheless observed the precepts of the decalogue which they received with the perfect love of a heart which was open to the Lord.

---

[13] Jn 14:6
[14] Jn 10:9
[15] Rm 8:39

7. ITS WINDOWS AND STRUCTURES ALL THE WAY ROUND

7.1 ⟨6:4⟩ **And he made for the temple slanting windows.** The windows of the temple are the holy teachers and all the spiritual people in the Church to whom when in divine ecstasy it is granted more specially than to the others to see the hidden mysteries of heaven. And when they reveal publicly to the faithful what they have seen in private, they fill all the inner recesses of the temple as windows do with the sunlight they let in. Hence these windows are appropriately said to have been slanting, i.e. wider on the inside, because, of course, whoever receives a ray of heavenly contemplation even for a moment must expand the bosom of his heart more fully by mortification and prepare it by resourceful asceticism to strive for greater things.

7.2 ⟨6:5–6⟩ **He also built floors upon the wall of the temple all the way round and on the walls of the house running right round the temple and the inner sanctuary; and he made side chambers all the way round. The top floor was five cubits broad, the middle one six cubits broad, and the third seven cubits broad.**[1] In the Gospel where the Lord is tempted by the devil these floors are called the pinnacles of the temple.[2] But we also read that the apostle James, the brother of the Lord, was lifted to the pinnacle of the temple from which to address the people.[3] Whether it was the practice of teachers *[163]* to deliver their address to the people standing around below them while they sat on these floors is something we find nowhere in the scriptures. So what the mystery obviously means is that these three floors denote the corresponding number of levels of the faithful, namely, married people, those who practise continence, and virgins, levels distinguished according to the loftiness of their profession but all of them belonging to the house of the Lord and intently clinging to him by reason of their fellowship in the same faith and truth.

7.3 There it is beautifully put that the top storey was five cubits broad, the middle one six and the third seven. The reason why the top storey was narrower than the rest, the middle one wider than

---

[1] *infra* 8.4 **

[2] cf. Mt 4:5

[3] cf. Rufinus, *Hist. Eccl.* 2, 23 *GCS* 9:169,17–21

the top but made narrower than the bottom one was that the higher profession of virtue ought to follow a higher way of life. For those who have renounced the bond of marriage and consecrated their virginity to the Lord ought to give evidence of behaviour consonant with virginity, abstain from useless talk, anger, quarrelling, detraction, immodest dress, carousing, drinking, strife and jealousy, and earnestly give themselves instead to holy vigils, prayer, divine readings and psalms, to doctrine and almsgiving and the other fruits of the Spirit[4] so that those who by profession follow the state of the life to come in which *they will neither marry nor be given in marriage but be as the angels in heaven*[5] may strive to imitate the state of that life so far as is possible for mortals in the present life. But the bottom storey was of greater width because married people are not told, *Go, sell what you possess and give it to the poor,*[6] but, *If you would enter life, keep the commandments: you shall not kill, you shall not commit adultery, you shall not steal, you shall not bear false witness,*[7] and so forth. Those who practise continence occupy a place midway between these, as far below virgins as they are higher than married people, whose most glorious portion built the original church in Jerusalem, as Luke puts it when he writes that *the multitude of the believers had but one heart and one soul,*[8] and so forth, and the fact that the majority of them had renounced the embrace of their wives is attested by the story of St Stephen where he calls the women who professed the same religion not their spouses but their widows.[9]

7.4 Each floor, however, had sides all round it, i.e. little breastworks, in case anyone standing or sitting on these floors should fall on to the lower ones, which, as we read, happened to king Ahaziah in Samaria.[10] These sides not inappropriately denote the safeguards of God's daily protection of us of which the psalmist says, *The angel of the Lord shall encamp around those who fear him, and shall deliver*

[164]

---

[4] cf. Ga 5:20–22; Rm 1:28–32

[5] Mt 22:30

[6] Mt 19:21

[7] Mt 19:17–18

[8] Ac 4:32

[9] cf. Ac 6:1

[10] cf. 4 K 1:2

them.[11] Ahaziah king of Samaria who had separated himself from the house of David did indeed go up to the upper-room, but he fell through the railings because, although heretics or schismatics seem to scale some peak of good work, nevertheless, because they lack the structure of the Church's unity, the protecting side-walls are, as it were, gaping wide open and weak, and consequently, they ⟨the heretics and schismatics⟩ are continually falling back into the depths of their vices until, deprived of God's help, they perish through their arrogance and obstinacy.

7.5 The technique used to attach the aforesaid floors to the temple walls is made clear in the text which follows:

⟨6:6⟩ **He put beams in the house all the way round on the outside, that they might not be fastened in the walls of the temple.** Therefore, the the beams which reinforced and adorned the house inside were of such a length that their ends were jutting out seven cubits in the bottom level, six in the middle one and five in the top one, and in these ends the floors were set, not in such a way that they were inserted into the temple walls but laid on beams which were beside the walls and protruded from the walls. Who then except preachers are typified by the beams of the house which supported the floors? And while occupying a lofty and privileged place in the Church of God, they enable all the weaker and frail ones by their sermons to rise above the cravings of the basest and raise them to long and hope for heavenly things and also help them by their intercession to persevere in what they have undertaken.

7.6 On the other hand, we read in the Book of Paralipomenon that the beams of the temple like the rest of its interior were adorned with gold.[12] There is no doubt that this was done in such a way that those portions of the beams which were inside the temple were covered with gold leaf, but that those which showed outside were not gilded in order to show the actual graining and beauty of the cedarwood while supporting the floors which were laid on them. Therefore, the portion of the beams which protruded outside denotes the life of the saints which could become known to us on earth; the gilded portion which gleamed inside the temple represents figuratively that

---

[11] Ps 33:8
[12] cf. 2 Paralip 3:7

brightness whereby they rejoice in their heavenly country in the sight
of their creator. This golden brightness of the beams was visible
only to those who had entered the temple, because only those who
have merited to enter the kingdom of heaven know how great is the
abundance of the sweetness of God which he has laid up for those
who fear him and has perfected for those who hope in him.[13] And yet
when through contemplating the life, sufferings and teaching of the
saints, or reading of them in books, we are moved by their example,
we are lifted from the earth, as it were, by the outwardly visible ends
of the beams because, although we are as yet unable to see clearly   *[165]*
the inner glory of the saints, nevertheless from what we have been
able to see from the outside we faithfully adhere to the members
of the Church who are in heaven above. We can also apply this to
the saints who are still in this life. The purity of their love which
makes them shine in the recesses of the heart before the Lord we
cannot penetrate; nevertheless we find help for our salvation from
those things which are externally visible whether in word or action or
suffering.

**7.7 ⟨6:7⟩ And when the house was being built it was with stones
hewn and dressed, so that neither hammer nor axe nor any tool of
iron was heard in the house while it was being built.** This properly
pertains to the part of the Church which after the toils and struggles
of this life has merited admittance to eternal rewards. There, indeed,
only the perfect and spotless and those purified from every stain of
iniquity enter. For nothing defiled shall enter that city, nor anyone
who practises abomination or falsehood, as John has written in the
Apocalypse.[14] No hammer, axe or any iron implement is heard
because here below we are hammered by adversities and trained by
the teaching of truth so that there we may be ranged in appropriate
places according to our deserts and so that when our purification is
over we may be filled with the one Spirit and bathed in the glue of
love to bind us to each other. Moreover, although scripture speaks
of *Noah, a man perfect in his generations*[15] and says, *Blessed are the
undefiled in the way,*[16] and other things of the kind, no one can

---

[13] cf. Ps. 30:20
[14] cf. Rv 21:27
[15] Gn 6:9
[16] Ps 118:1

live truly perfect and without stain as long as he is on the road of this life. *There is not a righteous man on earth who does good and never sins.*[17] Nevertheless, in a certain earthly manner of speaking, those are called perfect and undefiled who are truly perfected at the time when they are freed from the bonds of the body and reach the immortal beauty of the Lord's house and ascend to the place of the tabernacle of his glory.

8. OF THE STAIRS AND THE MAKING OF THE MIDDLE AND THIRD TABERNACLE

8.1 ⟨6:8⟩ **The door to the middle section was on the right of the house, and by the winding stairs they went up to the middle storey, and from the middle to the third.** Some misinterpret this and think the door of the temple was facing south, forgetting that if scripture had meant this it would not have said, *The door to the middle section was on the right of the house,* but rather would have said simply, 'And the house had its door facing south.' As it is, it means something quite different. For it calls the right-hand side of the house the south side of the temple, in the east side of which a door had been made in the very corner near the ground, and those who entered it *[166]* went straight up a flight of steps to the upper floors with a stairway along by the very inside of the wall until ⟨following this route⟩ they reached the middle storey and from the middle storey to the third. Nor, although the scripture does not say so, is it to be doubted that those who thus went up had windows on the south at very frequent intervals by whose light they could make their way through all the floors safely and without danger of stumbling. This place, of course, properly refers to the Lord's body which he received from the virgin. For *the door to the middle section was on the right of the house* because when the Lord died on the cross *one of the soldiers opened his side with a spear.*[1] And aptly ⟨does it say⟩ on the right hand of the house because the holy Church believes his right side was opened by the soldier. Here too the evangelist used the appropriate word when instead of saying he struck or wounded his side, said *opened*, that is to say, as it were, the door of the middle side through which a path to heavenly things might be thrown open to us. Finally he added the

---

[17] Qo 7:21

[1] Jn 19:34

following: *and forthwith there flowed out blood and water,* i.e. water
with which we are washed in baptism, and blood with which we are
consecrated in the holy chalice. For it is through this door that we
have a stairway to the middle storey and from the middle storey to the
third, because it is through faith and the mysteries of our redeemer
that we ascend from the present life of the Church to the repose of
our souls after death and then, come judgement day, from the repose
of our souls to the immortality of our bodies too, we shall penetrate,
as it were, to the third storey by a more lofty progress, and from this
point on we shall live for ever in the great happiness of both, namely,
of body and of soul. This journey, of course, was made invisibly so
that only those who entered here knew it, although they used to see
the actual door while they were on the outside, that is to say, because
the actions of the faithful in this world and the celebrations of the
mysteries can be seen even by the wicked, but the mysteries of the
faith and the grace of love in the inmost heart no one knows but
the one who, under the Lord's guidance, mounts by way of these to
heavenly things. For *he who says he knows God and does not keep his
commandments is a liar.*[2]

8.2 It is to be noted, of course, that the thirty cubits of height spoken of above[3] reached to the middle storey; from there up to the
third storey another thirty cubits were added until the portico which
was around the temple on the south and north and east reached the
roof as we learn from Josephus's account;[4] from there to the top
of the temple roof was another sixty cubits, and so the total height
of the house according to the Book of Paralipomenon amounted to
a hundred and twenty cubits.[5] Also the portico which was in front

[167] of the temple to the east, according to the account of the aforesaid
volume was the same number of cubits in height. That is, the porticoes around the temple of which we have just spoken, this book
calls treasuries and inner chambers. David, it says, *gave his son Solomon a plan of the portico, and of the temple, and of the treasuries,
and of the upper room, and of the inner chambers, and of the room for*

---

[2] 1 Jn 2:4
[3] *supra* 6.1 **
[4] Josephus *Ant.* 8.3.2
[5] cf. 2 Paralip 3:4

the mercy seat;[6] here too he refers to the outer houses which were outside the courtyard of the priests surrounding the temple, when he adds, *As also of all the courts which he had in mind, and of the surrounding chambers for the treasuries of the house of the Lord, and for the treasuries for dedicated objects.* The fact that the entire height of the temple was a hundred and twenty cubits refers to the same mystery as when the primitive Church in Jerusalem after the passion and resurrection and ascension of the Lord into heaven received the grace of the Holy Spirit in the same number of men.[7] For fifteen, which is the sum of seven and eight, is sometimes taken to signify the life which is now lived in the sabbath rest of the souls of the faithful[8] but will be brought to perfection at the end of the world by the resurrection of their immortal bodies. Now this fifteen arranged in a triangle, i.e. numbered with all its parts, makes a hundred and twenty.[9] Hence by the number one hundred and twenty the great happiness of the elect in the life to come is aptly represented, and by it the third storey of the Lord's house is aptly completed because after the present hardships of the faithful, and after their souls receive their rest in the life to come, the complete happiness of the whole Church will be achieved in the glory of the resurrection. To this mystery likewise refers, as we have said, the fact that the Lord on rising from the dead and ascending into heaven sent to this number of men in tongues of fire, the Holy Spirit, who enabled them, though

---

[6] 1 Paralip 28:11–12

[7] cf. Ac 1:15; *supra* 6.1 **

[8] cf. Heb 4:9; *supra* 3.4 **

[9] 8.2: At first sight it is difficult to make much sense, mathematically or otherwise, of the statement: 'fifteen arranged in a triangle, i.e. numbered with all its parts, makes a hundred and twenty.' The mathematics of it are that the sum of the integers $1+2+3+\ldots 15$ is 120. The Greeks, as we know from Plutarch, 2.1003f, cf. Nicomachus, *Arithmetica Introductio,* 2.8, spoke of ἀριθμοί τρίγωνοι (*arithmoi trigonoi*) 'triangular numbers', i.e. numbers whose units can be arranged in a triangle. So Bede's 'fifteen arranged in a triangle, i.e. numbered with all its parts' can be represented graphically as follows:

differing from each other on account of the diversity of their languages, suddenly to speak in his praise in a common tongue by giving
them a knowledge of all languages.[10] For the Church too in its own
turn rising from the dead and ascending to heaven in incorruptible
flesh will be fully and perfectly enlightened by the gift of the Holy
Spirit when, according to the promise of the Apostle, *God* will be *all
in all.*[11] Then there will be complete unity of languages universally
for the preaching of the wonderful works of God because all join
with one mind and voice in praising the glory of the divine majesty
which they see before them.

8.3 ⟨6:9⟩ **So he built the house and finished it. And he covered the
house with ceilings of cedar.** Ceilings are boardwork constructed and
adorned with great beauty and fixed to the beams on the lower side,
and because the house of the Lord had been built three times the
double height, naturally it had three ceilings. What is more fitting
for us to believe than that these ceilings signify all the just people of
most exalted virtue in the holy Church? And their work and teaching
is held up as an example to all as being much loftier than any other
and by their intercessions and exhortations they keep the spirits of
the weak from failing in temptation. These ceilings are indeed rightly
described as being of cedarwood. For cedar is by nature a completely
incorruptible tree, of pleasant fragrance and luxuriant appearance
and when it is set on fire it drives away and destroys serpents by
its dazzling brightness.[12] These things are an apt figure of all the
perfect whose patience is indomitable, whose outstanding reputation
for virtue is far more pleasing to the good than that of anyone else,
whose powers of refuting and proving wrong those who resist the
truth are utterly unshakable, and who, both in this life and the life to
come, shine with a resplendence that outshines the rest of the saints.

8.4 ⟨6:10⟩ **And he built a structure over all the house five cubits in
height.** This means the breastworks which were constructed on top
of the roof of the house all round in case anyone who came up to the
upper parts of the building should suddenly fall to the bottom. And
in every house which anyone built, Moses ordered this to be done,

[168]

---

[10] cf. Ac 2:3–4; *supra* 6.1 **

[11] 1 Co 15:28

[12] cf. Isid., *Etymol.* 17.7.33; *infra* 11.1 **; 17.8 **

saying, *When you build a new house, you shall make a parapet for your roof all the way round lest blood be shed in your house and you be to blame should any one slip and fall down headlong.*[13] Now these structures or breastworks are called sides above,[14] where, after the words, *And upon the wall of the temple he built structures all round, running round the walls of the house, both the temple and the oracle,*[15] the following is immediately added: *and he made side chambers all round.* These side chambers, of course, we have understood as denoting the divine protection which helps us not to give up while still struggling in this world and daily striving after higher things according to our capacity. We ought to understand this passage also in the same sense, but with this distinction that in this life, whether amid the frequent temptations of our implacable enemy or the obstacles of our frailty, we are often, indeed constantly, protected by heavenly compassion, but in the life which, as we have stated above, the top of the roof of the temple suggests, we are protected by so great a grace of God who is with us, that we neither want nor are able to sin, nor are we affected by fear of either death or pain or the adversary who tempts us. The Lord himself speaks of the helps he gives us in the present life, as if they were the sides of the structures, when he says of his people, *They will call upon me and I shall hear them, I am with them*

[169] *in their tribulation and I shall rescue them and glorify them.*[16] Of his grace to come whereby that heavenly city is illumined, the prophet says to the same city, *Praise the Lord, Jerusalem*[17] and so forth as far as *peace in your borders.* Now this structure on the roof of the house of the Lord is rightly said to be five cubits high because, of course, the presence of God's glory in that homeland ⟨of ours⟩ fills us in such a way that nothing else is sweet to our sight, our hearing, our sense of smell or taste or touch[18] except to love the Lord our God with our whole heart, our whole soul, our whole mind, and also to love our neighbour as ourselves.[19]

---

[13] Dt 22:8
[14] *supra* 7.2 **
[15] 3 K 6:5
[16] Ps 90:15
[17] Ps 147:12–14
[18] *infra* 15 **
[19] cf. Mk 12:30–31

8.5 ⟨6:10⟩ **And he covered the house with planks of cedarwood.** Here the very top of the roof of the house is meant, i.e. the structure which was laid on top of the beams. The temple did not have a ridge on top any more than the tabernacle did, but was flat, as was the prevailing fashion with all who built houses in Palestine and Egypt. Now this is the very structure with which the house is covered and which denotes the ceilings, i.e. all the people who are most eminent in the glory of the resurrection and who reach the very pinnacle of virtue by their exceptional sanctity, concerning one of whom it is said: *Among those born of women there has not arisen a greater than John the Baptist.*[20] And if you want to know whose greatness I compare him to, listen to what the angel said to his father: *And he shall go before the Lord in the spirit and power of Elijah.*[21]

8.6 ⟨6:15⟩ **And he lined the walls of the house on the inside with boards of cedar; from the floor of the house to the top of the walls and to the rafters of the ceilings he covered it with boards.** On the inside, indeed, the house was lined with cedar, for on the outside, the actual stone it was built of glinted with as much brilliance as if it had been covered with glowing white marble. Taken in the mystical sense, however, the temple walls are the nations of believers of whom the holy universal Church consists and whose widespread distribution throughout the whole world is denoted by the width of the walls, whereas the height denotes the hope and whole upward thrust of the Church towards heavenly things, or at any rate the height of the wall which consists of courses of stones laid one on top of the other denotes the state of the present Church where the elect are all built upon the foundation of Christ and follow each other in succession through the course of the ages and, by supporting each other, fulfil the law of Christ,[22] which is charity.

8.7 For when those who are now being instructed by the masters who precede them, themselves in turn instruct others as courses laid upon each other, thanks to the unshaken firmness of the living stones in the house of God, they are supported by others in such a way that they themselves too are equal to the task of supporting others right

---

[20] Mt 11:11

[21] Lk 1:17

[22] cf. Ga 6:2

down to the last righteous ones to be born at the end of the world.
These, as it were, placed on the very summit of God's house are
[170]   taught and supported by others but they themselves do not have any
⟨others⟩ to teach or any ⟨others⟩ whose frailty they ⟨must⟩ bear with.
That is to say, these walls are lined on the inside with planks of cedar
when the hearts of the faithful overflow with the love of virtue. For
just as the nature of cedar typifies perfect people, as we have said
above, so also there is good reason to say that in the relevant context
it denotes the loftiness of the virtues whereby the same perfection
is reached. Now everything from the floor of the house to the top
of the walls and even to the ceilings is covered with wood when the
elect, from the first rudiments of the faith to the perfection of good
behaviour and even to their entrance into their heavenly homeland,
do not cease in their efforts to perform good works, when from the
first righteous persons to the last at the end of the world, all strive
after virtue and by their merits can justly claim, *We are the aroma of
Christ to God in every place.*[23]

9. HOW THE WALLS WERE COVERED WITH CEDAR AND THE FLOOR WITH FIR

9.1   ⟨6:15⟩ **And he covered the floor with planks of fir.** How this was
done he explains more fully in the Book of Paralipomenon where it
is written: *He also paved the floor of the temple with most precious
marble.*[1]   From this it is clear that he certainly did not lay on the
ground the fir planks with which he covered the floor, but that he
first covered the floor with marble and then laid the planks on top
of that and on these two layers he superimposed a coating of gold
as we read in what follows.[2]   Now just as the height of the wall as
it rises aloft and reaches the ceiling, signifies the progress in virtue
whereby the elect reach the heavenly kingdom, or, at the very least,
the actual choirs of the elect which succeed each other in the course
of the different ages, so the evenness of the floor may with good reason be said to demonstrate their harmonious humility while they are
still in this temporal life and live sociably with each other according

---

[23]   2 Co 2:15

[1]   2 Paralip 3:6

[2]   cf. 3 K 6:22

to the dictates of charity.[3] In other words, this floor was paved with most precious marble of great beauty and this marble was later covered with fir planks because, of course, the life of the righteous must first be fortified in the heart in advance by the firmness of faith and then adorned in action by the wide range of spiritual virtues. Otherwise what good would the beauty of the most precious marble be when covered from view by planks of wood, unless it tacitly signified something mystical, and taught that the abundance of good works had to be grounded on the strength of unblemished faith? But on account of its height and lasting strength the fir tree is a quite appropriate analogy of the mind of the elect which spurns every lowest craving and is ever intent upon the contemplation of heavenly things and moreover, especially excels in the virtue of patience. On the other hand, the gold leaf with which the marble and the fir planks are overlaid is the expansiveness of charity[4] *of pure heart and good conscience and faith not feigned.*[5] Just as gold is more precious than other metals so this is more outstanding than the other virtues and shines forth with a light all its own in the temple of God. Hence the Apostle, enumerating the great many rewards of virtue to be stored up for the humble of heart, the adornments of the floor, so to speak, puts it well when he says, *Put on then, as God's chosen ones, holy and beloved, compassion, kindness, lowliness, meekness, and patience, forbearing one another and, if one has a complaint against another, forgiving each other; as Christ has forgiven you, so you also must forgive*[6] ⟨and⟩, like a veil of gold to be added from above, he immediately added: *and above all these put on love, which binds everything together in perfect harmony.*

[171]

9.2 ⟨6:16⟩ And he built up twenty cubits with boards of cedar at the rear of the temple, from the floor to the top, and made the inner house of the oracle the Holy of Holies. He calls the east side of the temple the rear; for the temple had its entrance on the east and its inner house, i.e. the Holy of Holies, on the west. The fact that he says that the board partitions which separated the inner house

---

[3] *infra* 9.3 **; 14.3 **

[4] *infra* 9.3 **

[5] 1 Tm 1:5

[6] Col 3:12–14

from the outer one were erected from the floor to the top,[7] does not mean they were built to the ceiling which was at a height of thirty cubits from the floor, as has already been said above,[8] but only up to a height of twenty cubits, as one can clearly read in what follows.[9] But the portion above these partitions up as far as the ceiling was left open and empty to a height of ten cubits and a length of twenty cubits across the width of the house, and, of course, through this aperture the smoke of the burnt offerings from the altar of sacrifice used to ascend and penetrate all the way in to cover the ark of the Lord. This division of the Lord's house is a clear figure of a mystery[10] and, thanks to the explanation of the Apostle, is clearer than daylight because the first house into which *the priests* continually *go performing their ritual duties*[11] is the present Church where intent upon works of piety we daily offer sacrifices of praise to the Lord, but the inner house which was built at the rear of the temple[12] is the promised life in heaven which indeed precedes this life of our exile which is celebrated there in the presence of the supreme king as a perpetual solemnity of the blessed, both angels and humankind. Hence it is with reference to it that the servant is quite deservedly told, *Enter into the joy of your Lord,*[13] but it is later in time because it is after the labours of this world that we succeed in entering it.

9.3 Now the board partitions which separate each house from the other are actually the gates of heaven which we daily long to have opened to us and which, in so far as the Lord grants us, we are ever knocking upon with pious importunity until they are opened to let us enter where, even though not yet allowed to enter before the dissolution of our bodies, we nevertheless have open to us the door of divine compassion through which we send ahead of us the incense of our alms, fasting and other works of piety. This is why the cedarwood wall of the inner house had an aperture at the top all the way across whereby the smoke of the burnt offerings might go in because the

[172]

---

[7] *infra* 12.2 **

[8] *supra* 6.1 **; 8.2 **

[9] cf. 3 K 6:20

[10] *infra* 10 **

[11] Heb 9:1–9

[12] *infra* 12.1 **

[13] Mt 25:21

eyes of the Lord are on the watch over his house night and day[14] and his ears listening intently to the prayers of his servants[15] and this ⟨is so⟩ through the whole extent of the Church which is spread over the world. For the altar of incense[16] which indeed stood in the outer compartment but near the doorway, was a type of the inner compartment of the perfectly righteous who though still detained in the world, are nevertheless lifted up to heavenly things by their every desire and who, as it were, with burnt incense send forth smoke which ascends into the Holy of Holies, because being on fire with celestial love they knock upon the ears of their creator with the continual sound of their prayers, and the smoke of their burnt offerings finds the door at the top wide open, because the purer each of them is on earth and the closer they live, so to speak, to their heavenly homeland, the more quickly they receive everything they ask from the Lord. Fittingly then was the inner house made twenty cubits long on account of the mystery of which we have spoken above,[17] the mystery of twofold love which in this interim life enlightens the minds of the majority of the elect but which in that homeland, when the works of other virtues come to an end, alone reigns forever.

10. OF THE EXACT DIMENSIONS OF THE TEMPLE ITSELF AND THE ORACLE

10 ⟨6:17⟩ **And the temple itself before the doors of the oracle was forty cubits long.** We have said that the temple itself before the doors of the oracle was a type of the present Church.[1] Hence it was rightly forty cubits long for this number is often used to signify the present labour of the faithful, just as the number fifty stands for the rest and peace to come. For the number ten contains the precepts, the observance of which leads to life. Likewise the number ten signifies that very eternal life which we desire and for which we live. But the world in which we strive to attain that life is a square. Hence too the psalmist, foreseeing the Church which was to be assembled from the nations said, *He has gathered them out of the countries from the*

---

[14] cf. 3 K 8:29–30
[15] cf. Ps. 129:2
[16] *infra* 12.3,5 **
[17] *supra* 6.1 **; 9.1 **
[1] *supra* 9.2 **

rising and from the setting of the sun, from the north and from the sea.[2]
Now ten multiplied by four makes forty. Hence the people liberated
from Egypt as a figure of the present Church were subjected to many
[173] hardships for forty years in the desert,[3] but at the same time were
also regaled with heavenly bread,[4] and in this way finally reached
the land promised them of old. They were subjected to trials for
forty years in order to draw attention to the hardships with which the
Church contends throughout the whole world in observing the law
of God; they were fed on manna from heaven for those forty years
to demonstrate that the very sufferings which the Church endures in
the hope of the heavenly denarius, i.e. of eternal happiness, are to be
alleviated when those *who* now *hunger and thirst for righteousness will
have their fill*[5] and as the same Church sings to its redeemer, *But as
for me, I will appear before your sight in righteousness; I shall be satisfied
when your glory shall appear.*[6] In the same way then the people of God
is both subjected to adversities and regaled with manna to confirm
the saying of the Apostle: *Rejoicing in hope, patient in tribulation.*[7]
In this figure too Our Lord fasted forty days before his bodily death[8]
and feasted forty more with his disciples after his bodily resurrection
*appearing to them by many proofs and speaking of the kingdom of God,
and eating together with them.*[9] For by fasting he showed in himself
our toil, but by eating and drinking with his disciples he showed his
consolation in our midst. While he was fasting he was crying out,
as it were, *Take heed lest perhaps your hearts be weighed down with
dissipation and drunkenness and the cares of this life,*[10] whereas while
he was eating and drinking he was crying out, as it were, *Behold I am
with you all days even to the consummation of the world;*[11] and: *But
I will see you again, and your heart shall rejoice, and your joy no one
shall take from you.*[12] For as soon as we set our feet upon the way of

---

[2] Ps 106:2–3
[3] cf. Dt 2:7
[4] cf. Ex 16:35
[5] Mt 5:6
[6] Ps 16:15
[7] Rm 12:12
[8] cf. Mt 4:2
[9] Ac 1:3–4
[10] Lk 21:34
[11] Mt 28:20
[12] Jn 16:22

the Lord we both fast from the vanity of the present world and are cheered with the promise of the world to come, not setting our heart on the ⟨life⟩ here below but feeding our heart ⟨on the life⟩ up there.

11. HOW THE WHOLE BUILDING WAS COVERED WITH CEDAR AND GOLD

11.1 ⟨6:18⟩ And the whole house was covered inside with cedar, having its turnings and joints skilfully wrought and carvings in relief. We have said of cedarwood that it betokened the unsurpassable beauty of the virtues.[1] Now the entire house is covered inside with this wood when the hearts of the righteous begin to shine with nothing but the love of good works and the house has its turnings made of cedar boards and its joints skilfully wrought when these elect are joined to each other by the most beautiful bond of charity so that, though the multitude of the faithful is innumerable, they can nevertheless, with good reason, be said to have one heart and one soul on account of the community of the faith and love they share.[2] For the turnings which were attached to the joints of the planks in order that they might all make one partition, are the very services of charity by which the holy brotherhood is bound together and formed into one house of Christ all over the world. Moreover, this house has carvings standing in relief when, far from covering and hiding their works of virtue, the saints, by a clear outward expression, show forth to all, as an example for living, what they themselves are like and what they do, as did the apostle Paul who not only by preaching Christ to the gentiles and by personally suffering for Christ showed how outstanding he was, but also in his letters addressed to the churches declared how many perils he underwent for Christ, and by what great revelations he was raised aloft in a blessed glorification.[3] And when he said to his listeners without any hesitation, *Be imitators of me just as I am of Christ,*[4] what did he show them but the carvings standing in relief in the house of the Lord, which by the exceptional eminence of his virtue showed itself to be within the power of all to imitate?

[174]

---

[1] *supra* 8.3 **
[2] cf. Ac 4:32
[3] cf. 2 Co 11:26ff.
[4] 1 Co 11:1

11.2 ⟨6:18⟩ **All was lined with boards of cedar, and no stone at all could be seen in the wall.** Both the stones of the wall or of the floor and the boards and the gold all denote the life of the saints in the Church, but with this distinction, of course, that when they are compared, the living stones are the saints cemented to each other by the strength of their faith in one and the same rule ⟨of faith⟩; the planks of cedar or fir are the saints joined to each other in one and the same faith by reason of the compass of their various virtues according to the gifts of the Holy Spirit; the sheets of gold leaf are the saints who have a love that surpasses knowledge[5] and rejoice together in its most delightful splendour. These three things the blessed Apostle comprised in one sentence saying, *For in Christ Jesus neither circumcision nor the lack of it is of any use but the faith which works through love.*[6] For the stone was a figure of unconquered faith, the cedar a figure of fragrant action, the gold a figure of all-transcending love, and the stone wall is covered with cedar planks when the profession of faith is adorned with good works, lest without works it be judged useless or dead.[7] But because the law was written in stone[8] whereas the teaching of the Gospel was confirmed by the wood of the Lord's passion, so too the people were circumcised by a flintstone in the foreskin[9] whereas we are consecrated by the sign of the cross on the forehead. The stone walls of the temple or the floor paved with most precious marble can quite appropriately be taken as a type of those who lived faithfully and perfectly in the law, whereas the planks of cedar or fir can signify the righteous of the New Testament who in their desire to go after the Lord deny themselves and take up their cross daily and follow him.[10] And since the common glory of a heavenly reward awaits the righteous of both *[175]* eras, a third kind of material, that of gold leaf, is added to the stones and precious wood.

11.3 Nor should there seem to be any conflict between this and

---

[5] cf. Ep 3:19
[6] Ga 5:6
[7] cf. Jm 2:17,20
[8] cf. Ex 31:18
[9] cf. Jos 5:2-3
[10] cf. Mt 16:24

what we said above[11] to the effect that the portico which was in front
of the temple was a figure of the faithful of old, whereas the temple
is a figure of those who came into the world after the time of the
Lord's incarnation, and moreover, that the inner house prefigured the
joys of the heavenly kingdom which are granted to both groups of the
righteous; but let us now say that the stone walls stand for the ancient
people of God whereas the cedar planks stand for the new (people of
God) and the gold leaf denotes the rewards of both in heaven, since
these temple walls, both in the portico and in the temple itself and in
the Holy of Holies equally were made up of stones and timber and
gold. For in the different materials there is a manifold repetition of
the same figures. But it must also be said that both in the (era of the)
law and before the written law there were a great many who zealously
served the Lord by not killing or fornicating or stealing or bearing
false witness, by honouring their father and mother and loving their
neighbour as themselves.[12] These belong to the stone walls of the
portico. There were others who with greater perfection gave up the
affairs of the world and took up their cross and followed the Lord,
who, as the Apostle writes, *suffered mockery and scourging and even
chains and imprisonment. They were stoned, they were sawn in two, they
were killed with the sword; they went about in skins of sheep and goats,
destitute, afflicted, ill-treated; people of whom the world was unworthy.*[13]
These who before the clear era of the Gospel led the life of the
Gospel, what are they but the cedar boardwork shining in the portico
before the entrance to the temple? The same kingdom of heaven
receives both of these (groups of people) alike, albeit in separate
dwellings, just as the portico of the temple was covered inside with
gold after the stone and cedarwood. There are a great many at
the present time who, content with (observing) the precepts of the
law which we have mentioned above, believe that it will be enough
for them merely if they merit entrance into life; there are others
who, striving for perfection, sell all they have and follow the Lord,[14]
mindful of his promise whereby he foretold that in the resurrection
not only life but special honour would be given: *Truly I say to you, in
the new world, when the Son of man shall sit upon his glorious throne,*

---

[11] *supra* 6.2 **
[12] cf. Mt 19:18–19
[13] Heb 11:36–38
[14] cf. Mt 19:21

you who have followed me will also sit upon twelve thrones, judging the twelve tribes of Israel.[15] The latter belong figuratively to the temple wall made of white stone, the former to the cedarwood boardwork,   *[176]* and both expect from the Lord the rewards of eternal light, the gold leaf, as it were, with which ⟨the walls⟩ are adorned. There are in the recesses of the temple precious stones, planks of aromatic wood, both of them covered with gold because both those who have walked without blemish in the law of the Lord[16] and those who have fully received the grace of the Gospel equally enjoy eternal life.

12. HOW THE ALTAR OF THE ORACLE WAS OF CEDAR AND GOLD

12.1 ⟨6:19⟩ **And he made the oracle in the middle of the house in its innermost part to set the ark of the Lord's covenant there.** The exposition of this has been anticipated[1] to the effect, namely, that the secret inner house of our heavenly homeland designated the ark of the covenant, the Lord our saviour in whom alone we have a covenant of peace with the Father, ⟨our saviour⟩ who ascending into heaven after his resurrection placed at the right hand of his Father the flesh which he had taken from the virgin.

12.2 ⟨6:20⟩ **Now the oracle was twenty cubits long, twenty cubits wide and twenty cubits high. And the altar also he covered with cedar.** What he says about twenty cubits in height signifies the cedarwood which separated the oracle, i.e. the Holy of Holies, from the outer building, as we have said above.[2] Therefore, the oracle where the ark was kept measured twenty cubits in length, breadth and height, i.e. it was square, because in the heavenly fatherland where the eyes of the saints see Christ the king in his glory,[3] the grace of divine and fraternal love alone shines over all. This is added also in the following words when it is said: *And he covered and overlaid it with most pure gold,* which is to state clearly that the grace of charity filled the walls of the heavenly city.

---

[15] Mt 19:28
[16] cf. Ps 118:1
[1] *supra* 9.2 **
[2] *supra* 9.2 **
[3] cf. Is 33:17

12.3   And the altar he also covered with cedar. He means the altar of incense which was in front of the oracle,[4] about which a little further down are added the words: *Also the whole altar which belonged to the oracle he covered with gold.*[5] From this we are given to understand that the same altar was indeed made of stone and overlaid with cedar and then covered with gold. It signifies typically the life of the perfectly righteous who are, as it were, placed near the oracle and giving up the basest pleasures concentrate all their attention merely on entering the kingdom of heaven. Hence quite appropriately it was not the flesh of victims that was burned on this altar but only incense, because such people no longer need to sacrifice in themselves carnal sins or seductive thoughts but only offer up the fragrance of spiritual prayers and heavenly desires through the fire of eternal love in the sight of their creator. Now what the stone, cedar and gold represent in this kind of altar can be easily understood from what has been said above.

[177]   **12.4   ⟨6:21⟩ And the house in front of the oracle he overlaid with most pure gold, and fastened the plates on with nails of gold.** We have said that the house in front of the oracle contained a type of the present Church where we are so on fire with the love of our redeemer that we are not yet able to see him face to face. Hence this house is aptly covered with the purest gold indeed but separated from the oracle by the interposition of a dividing wall. For it is called an oracle when God or an angel addresses human beings to reveal their respective secrets. Hence the oracle was aptly built in a hidden place, i.e. in the inner house, because in the heavenly homeland the sight and the utterance of angels and the very presence of God will be revealed to us according to what he who is Truth itself promises to those who love him when he says, *And he who loves me will be loved by my Father, and I will love him and manifest myself to him;*[6] and again: *The hour is coming when I shall no longer speak to you in figures but tell you plainly of the Father.*[7] The reason why the house in front of the oracle was covered with gold was that all the righteous who are perfect in this life where they cannot hear of the Father plainly, i.e.

---

[4]   *supra* 9.3 **; *infra* 12.5 **
[5]   3 K 6:22
[6]   Jn 14:21
[7]   Jn 16:25

cannot see him plainly, enhance the faith and work of righteousness with divine love through which they may earn the perfect vision and full knowledge of God. The gold leaf with which the house was covered are the manifold works of piety which pure love exhibits in the service either of its creator or of a brother's need. The gold nails with which the gold leaf was attached are the very precepts of charity or promises of eternal glory through which by the gift of the grace of Christ we are kept constant in the exercise and pursuit of virtue in case we should fail. Hence of these nails it is well written in the Book of Paralipomenon: *He also made nails of gold, so that the weight of every nail was fifty shekels.*[8] The number fifty in the scriptures is usually a figure of the remission of sins and the grace of the Holy Spirit and eternal rest since the fiftieth Psalm is a psalm of repentance and pardon; the fiftieth year is the year of jubilee and on the fiftieth day after Easter the Holy Spirit came and consecrated the primitive Church. And each of the nails with which the gold leaf was affixed to the walls of the house of the Lord weighed fifty shekels, no doubt because the heavenly words by which we advance in the love of good works and are saved, promise us the pardon of our sins by the grace of the Holy Spirit, and eternal rest in the world to come. And these indeed are nails of love. But there are other nails ⟨nails⟩ of fear, by

[178]   which, as beginners and not having yet attained perfection, each of us mortifies the enticements of the vices and carnal inclinations; ⟨these nails are⟩ the words of truth by whose instruction we are taught to crucify our flesh with its vices and passions,[9] nails which the prophet desired to have when he said, *Pierce my flesh with your fear as with nails, for I am afraid of your judgements;*[10] and again as he attains greater perfection he says of the nails of love, *But it is good for me to adhere to my God.*[11]

12.5   ⟨6:22⟩ And there was nothing in the temple that was not covered with gold; the whole of the altar of the oracle he also covered with gold. The altar has been spoken of above.[12] But these matters are more fully explained in the Book of Paralipomenon where the

---

[8] 2 Paralip 3:9
[9] cf. Ga 5:24
[10] Ps 118:120
[11] Ps 72:28
[12] *supra* 9.3 **; 12.3 **

portico which was in front of the temple is said to have been gilded on the inside and the rooms too are said to have been covered over.[13] Here the figure of a mystery is in evidence because the whole Church both in this world and the next abounds in the gift of charity more than in the other virtues pleasing to God, and this virtue by itself, inasmuch as it is particularly outstanding, seems to obscure the rest. For the portico in front of the temple was gilded because the Fathers of the Old Testament pleased God by their charity; the temple was gilded because the very same *charity is poured forth in our hearts by the Holy Spirit who is given to us;*[14] the inner house was gilded because in our heavenly homeland charity alone reigns, but there ⟨it does so⟩ the more truly and surely in that God himself who is charity is seen in person;[15] there ⟨it does so⟩ the more certainly in that the very *mediator of God and men*[16] who alone is privy to the secrets of the Father, like the ark of the covenant is contemplated perpetually. And the fact that the rooms too were covered over is to be taken in the same sense. For as the inner house of the Holy of Holies, where the ark was, signifies the eternal life of the saints in the sight of their creator and redeemer according to the saying of the psalmist, *You shall hide them in the covert of your countenance from the disturbance of men,*[17] so the upper rooms denote that this life is above, i.e. in heaven, and not in this world, as the Apostle says, *Seek the things that are above, where Christ is sitting at the right hand of God. Mind the things that are above, not the things that are upon the earth.*[18]

13. THE MAKING OF THE CHERUBIM

13.1 ⟨6:23⟩ And in the oracle he made two cherubim[1] of olive-

---

[13] cf. 2 Paralip 3:4,9

[14] Rm 5:5

[15] cf. 1 Jn 4:16

[16] 1 Tm 2:5

[17] Ps 30:21

[18] Col 3:1–2

[1] 'The cherubim were winged animals with human heads, like the winged sphinxes of Syro-Phoenician iconography. Their name, however, $K^erûb$, comes from the Akkadian, in which the word *karibu* or *kuribu* means a genie who was the adviser to the great gods and an advocate for the throne of Yahweh, just as in 2 S 22:11=Ps 18:11, they served as his steeds, and according to the visions of Ezk 1 and 10, drew his chariot.' de Vaux (1973), 319

wood, ten cubits high.[2] 'Cherubim', as the prophet Ezekiel explicitly declares, is a title of dignity, and in the singular number the form cherub is used, but cherubim in the plural.[3] Hence the figures of the cherubim which were made in the oracle can be appropriately taken to mean the angelic retinues that always wait upon their creator in

[179] heaven. And they are properly said to have been made of olive-wood because, of course, angelic virtues are anointed with the grace of the Holy Spirit lest they should ever grow arid in the love of God. For they are those fellow-companions of ours of whom the prophet speaks in his praise of Christ: *God your God has anointed you with the oil of gladness above your fellows.*[4] In figurative terms it was quite right that those whom their creator later filled with the light of heavenly wisdom, were made of olive-wood. That is why he wanted them called cherub which means in Latin 'a great store of knowledge'. And they are ten cubits high because they enjoy the denarius of eternal life having preserved ever untarnished in themselves the image of their creator by the sanctity and uprightness and truth which they received in the first creation. For a denarius is worth ten obols and customarily bore the name and likeness of the king. Consequently, it also makes a very fitting metaphor for the kingdom of heaven where, on the one hand, the holy angels ever remain in their creator's likeness according to which they were made, and on the other hand, the human elect receive his image which they had lost by sinning.[5] For *we know,* he says, *that when he appears we shall be like him* ⟨and⟩ *see him as he is.*[6]

13.2 ⟨6:24⟩ **One wing of the cherub was five cubits, and the other wing of the cherub was five cubits, that is, in all ten cubits, from the tip of one wing to the tip of the other.** Wings when used as a figure of holy men signify their virtues whereby they delight in always flying to heavenly things and passing their lives in preoccupation with these things. But when wings are used to signify angels, what do they more aptly demonstrate than the grace of perpetual and unfailing happiness of those who persevere continually in heavenly things in the service of their creator? Or at all events because they

---

[2] *infra* 16.8 **
[3] cf. Bede, *De tab.* 1, 513ff; cf. Ezk 10:5–8
[4] Ps 44:8
[5] cf. Jer., *Nom. Hebr. CCSL* 72:63,11; 103,7
[6] 1 Jn 3:2

are endowed with the lightness of spiritual nature so that they can get to wherever they want, as it were, by flying, they are here both figuratively represented with wings and actually shown with wings. Now it has been well said, *one wing of the cherub was five cubits and the other wing of the cherub five cubits,* since the angelic powers keep with untiring devotion the law of God which is written in five books, that is, by loving the Lord their God with all their strength and by loving their neighbours as themselves.[7] *For love is the fulfilling of the law.*[8] Now 'their neighbours' includes both the angelic spirits themselves reciprocally and elect human beings who are equally their fellow-citizens. So the reason each wing is said to be of the same dimensions is that with the same devotion as they love each other in God they also long for our company as we ascend to them, and so ten wings together take up ten cubits when, in a twofold demonstration of love, the angels rejoice in the presence of their maker. *[180]*

13.3 ⟨6:25⟩ **The second cherub also measured ten cubits. The measurement and the shape was the same in both cherubim.** Two cherubim were made in order to signify a sharing in the same love of which we speak, because love cannot exist between fewer than two. Moreover, the reason why the saviour took care to send the disciples in twos[9] to preach was that he might tacitly teach that those who were to preach the word of faith must before all works possess the virtue of love. And the two cherubim were of the same dimensions and shape because there is no difference of will or thought in the heavenly homeland where all are illumined by one and the same vision and glory of God there present.

13.4 ⟨6:27⟩ **And he set the cherubim in the middle of the inner temple, and the cherubim stretched forth their wings. And the wing of the one touched one wall, and the wing of the other cherub touched the other wall, and the other wings in the middle of the temple touched one another.** From what has been said already it is clear why the cherubim, whose abode is always in heaven, were placed in the middle of the interior of the temple. The cherubim, moreover, stretch out their wings as if to fly because angelic spirits always have

---

[7] cf. Lk 10:27

[8] Rm 13:10

[9] cf. Lk 10:1; Bede *in Luc.* 3, 1897–1905; Greg., *Hom. in Eu. PL* 76, 1139A

their mind in readiness to comply with the divine will. But the fact that one cherub's wing was touching one wall and the second cherub's wing the other wall has to do with that ministry of love which the angels perform for us. The fact that the other wings in the middle of the temple touched each other expresses that grace of love with which they embrace each other.

13.5 The text which follows,

⟨6:28⟩ **And he overlaid the cherubim with gold,** is apposite because their creator both elevated their nature with immortal glory and filled their minds with the true light of love and humility. True, it should be noted that Moses, while making the tabernacle, also made two golden cherubim which he placed on the mercy seat which was above the ark,[10] but Solomon added two more much bigger ones to place in the temple so that he might put the ark under their wings in the middle with the mercy seat and the first cherubim, and so it happened that whereas there were two cherubim in the tabernacle, in the temple there were four. However, they both had the same significance but the work was repeated and made more majestic by Solomon also in order that it might be shown in figure that when the Church had multiplied after the Lord's incarnation, the sublimity of the citizens *[181]* of heaven was to be made more widely known to the gentiles, and these ⟨heavenly citizens⟩ extol their creator so highly for the gift of their own blessedness bestowed on them, that they also rejoice with us over our rescue and reception into the same beatitude. For they stretch their wings towards each other over the ark[11] when they refer to the praise of their Lord and saviour every good thing they have received. They stretch the ⟨two⟩ other wings to the walls of the oracle when they are glad to see holy people also with them, and touch, as it were, with the tips of their wings those who, to their delight, have been sharers and imitators of their purity in this life. But equally they touch the two walls with their wings because they consider the faithful of both peoples, i.e. the Jews and the gentiles, to be possessors with them of the heavenly court; not because in that homeland there is distinction of place between each of the two peoples but because the celebration of their inner happiness is enhanced by the fellowship of fraternal union. Why the cherubim stretch their wings to each of

---

10 cf. Ex 25:18-20; 37:7-9

11 *Libri Carolini* I.20 *MGH, Legum S. 3, Concilia 2, Suppl.* ed. Bastgen, 46–48

the two walls of the oracle is that, while rejoicing in their heavenly homeland, they spur on the upright among both peoples to the praise of the creator by the vision of their own glory also. And not only do they rejoice at the happiness of those righteous people whom they inwardly regard as being with themselves the heavenly hosts, but they also show unremitting concern for us who are still on the outside crying from the depths to the Lord.[12]

13.6 Hence in the Book of Paralipomenon it is aptly written of these cherubim: *And they stood upright on their feet, and their faces were turned towards the house outside.*[13] The cherubim, indeed, stood upright on their feet because the angels never strayed from the way of truth in which they were once created. They have their faces turned towards the outer house because they desire us to attain to fellowship with them after we have been rescued from the hardships of this sojourn. The reason why they stand upright on their feet like this and stretch out their wings to the gold-covered oracle walls in such a way that they have their faces turned towards the outer house is that this is how the angels forever preserve their innocence; and they rejoice so much together over the happiness of the holy souls in heaven that they never cease giving assistance to those chosen ones also whom they see still in exile on earth until they bring them too to their heavenly homeland. For *they are all ministering spirits, sent to serve for the sake of those who are to receive the inheritance of salvation?*[14]

13.7 The two cherubim can also stand for the two testaments. These cherubim, no doubt, were made in the oracle because in the design of God's providence, which is, of course, inaccessible and incomprehensible to us, it was arranged before the world began, when and *[182]* how and by what authors sacred scripture was to be written. They were made of olive-wood because the divine books were composed by men *of mercy, whose godly deeds have not failed,*[15] men who were enlightened by the unction of the Holy Spirit. They were made of olive-wood because they afford us the light of knowledge with the

---

[12] cf. Ps 129:1

[13] 2 Paralip 3:13

[14] Heb 1:14

[15] Sir 44:10

help of the flame of God's love which is poured forth in our hearts by the Holy Spirit.[16] They are ten cubits high because by the observance of the decalogue of the Law they preach that God is to be served since they show that those who serve God faithfully are to be rewarded with the denarius of an everlasting kingdom. They have twin sets of wings because they proclaim that the testaments have always, both in adversity and in prosperity, pursued heavenly things with tireless resolve and attained to them, because they point out to their listeners that they must do exactly the same. Five cubits is the length of one cherub's wing and five the length of the other's since in all the fluctuations of transient things the saints lay all the senses of their body under contribution to the service of their creator[17] with their eyes ever on the Lord,[18] desiring to hear the sound of his praise and to recount all his wonderful works,[19] considering his words sweeter to their throats than honey and the honeycomb to their mouths,[20] running after the odour of his ointments,[21] and while there is breath left in them and the spirit of God in their nostrils, they do not speak evil with their lips nor utter folly with their tongue,[22] and thus going on their way *with the armour of righteousness on the right hand and on the left*[23] they succeed in receiving the heavenly denarius which the supreme master of the household has promised to the workers in his vineyard.[24]

13.8 And the two cherubim formed one work because the writers of both documents served God with one and the same purity of work and devotedness of love and proclaim God with one harmonious voice and belief, and what the New Testament relates as accomplished facts regarding the Lord's incarnation, passion, resurrection and ascension, the calling of the gentiles, the expulsion of the Jews and the manifold affliction of the Church, these same facts the Old Testament, rightly

---

[16] cf. Rm 5:5

[17] *infra* 15 **

[18] cf. Ps 24:15

[19] cf. Ps 25:7

[20] cf. Ps 118:103

[21] cf. Sg 1:3

[22] cf. Jb 27:34 and Jb 6:30

[23] 2 Co 6:7

[24] cf. Mt 20:1–2

understood, truthfully foretold as events that were to happen. But
the coming of antichrist, the end of the world, the critical moment of
the last judgement, and the eternal glory of the good and punishment
of the wicked, both testaments demonstrate with harmonious truth.
The reason why the inner wings of the cherubim touched each other
above the ark was that the testaments are in full agreement in their
testimony about the Lord. Moreover, with their outer wings, one of
them touched one wall, the other touched the second because the
Old Testament was written specifically for the ancient people of God,
whereas the New was written for us who arrived at the faith after   *[183]*
the Lord's incarnation and we are rightly compared to the second
wall, i.e. the north wall, for to us it was granted to know the light
of truth after the figure and the darkness of idolatry. For even
though the primitive Church bloomed mainly from Jewish soil and
one may believe that all Israel is to be saved near the end of the
world, nevertheless the majority of believers of this age are drawn
from the gentiles to receive the mysteries of the Gospel, and to them
God has also given this gift, namely, that the eyes of their heart have
been unveiled so that they can recognize clearly that the letter of the
Old Testament is full of the mysteries of the grace of the Gospel. The
cherubim have their faces turned towards the outer house because
for our sake who are still standing outside and *are saved* not in fact
but *in hope,*[25] the divine books were written because their writers,
who are already reigning with the Lord and praising him together
in heaven, have our salvation at heart and appeal to his compassion
for our aberrations. The cherubim are overlaid with gold because
the authority of the testaments is enhanced by the illustrious works
of the writers. After the knowledge of the divine scriptures or the
inner glory of the heavenly hosts (for the two cherubim, as we have
said, denote both the angels and the testaments) had been spread
throughout the world, many at once began to convert to the faith
and abound in good works.

14. THE CARVING OF THE WALLS AND OVERLAYING OF THE FLOOR WITH GOLD

14.1   Whence it is aptly added:
⟨6:29⟩ **And the Temple walls all round he carved with various**

---

[25] Rm 8:24

figures and etchings. All the walls of the temple all the way round are all the peoples of the holy Church laid upon the foundation of Christ; with these he has filled the earth's entire circle, and the building of the faith which was begun, does not cease to this day to increase by the new progeny of its members, by the addition, as it were, of precious stones. For these walls are carved with various figures since *to one is given through the Spirit the utterance of wisdom, and to another the utterance of knowledge according to the same Spirit, to another faith by the same Spirit, to another gifts of healing by the one Spirit, to another the working of miracles, to another prophecy, to another the ability to distinguish between spirits, to another various kinds of tongues, to another the interpretation of tongues.*[1] And to come to those virtues which we can all have, *love, joy, peace, forbearance, patience, kindness, goodness, gentleness, self-control*[2] and the other fruits of the Spirit, what ⟨are these⟩ but the carved figures of the temple walls which are the adornment of the minds of the people of God? These walls are also chased with carvings when the faithful are endowed with a spirit ready to do all that the Lord has commanded,
[184]   to suffer all that he permits, saying from the heart, whatever befalls them, *I shall bless the Lord at all times,*[3] and, *My heart is ready, O God, my heart is ready, I shall sing and say a psalm to the Lord.*[4] They are chased with carvings when they concentrate their efforts on virtues alone so that they cannot be turned away from the pursuit of them by any obstacles posed by circumstances or by any enticements. For since the sculptor both excels the other arts in speed, and himself observes the rule by which he completes the work without going wrong, by this ⟨rule⟩ is designated the devout life of the saints which is ever ready to obey the will of God and has learnt by long practice of the virtues to fulfil this obligation of obedience without deviation. Hence the holy Church too in the Canticle of Canticles in admiration of the virtues of her spouse and redeemer said, *His hands are turned and as of gold, full of hyacinths.*[5] His hands are turned in the sense that the power and wisdom of God[6] appearing in the flesh wrought

---

[1] 1 Co 12:8–10
[2] Ga 5:22
[3] Ps 33:2
[4] Ps 56:8
[5] Sg 5:14
[6] cf. 1 Co 1:24

whatever cures and miracles he wished without any hesitation or
delay and without any tardiness due to error. ⟨His hands⟩ are of gold
because, being full of divine power, he effected internally what he
had ordered externally by his word. His hands are full of hyacinths
because he referred to the Father's glory all that he did, since by
the works he performed he raises up our senses to seek the things
of heaven. Therefore, all the walls of the temple round about are
chased with figures and carvings when the whole Church throughout
the world devotes itself with eager zeal and absolutely unswervingly
to the practice of spiritual virtues. Here are fittingly added the words:

**14.2   ⟨6:29⟩ And he made cherubim and palm-trees in them, and
various representations, as it were, in relief and protruding from the
wall.**[7] Solomon makes cherubim in the temple walls when the Lord
grants to his elect to guide their lives according to the rule of the
holy scriptures which contain a great store of knowledge. He makes
cherubim when he teaches them to imitate in this world, according
to their limited capacity, the chastity of the life of angels, and this is
done particularly by vigils and the divine praises, by sincere love of
the creator and the neighbour. He makes palm-trees when he fixes
in their minds the thought of their eternal reward so that the more
they have the reward of righteousness ever before the eyes of their
hearts, the less likely are they to fall from the pinnacle of uprightness.
He makes several representations, as it were, standing out in relief
from the wall when he assigns to the faithful the manifold functions
of the virtues, for instance, *compassion, kindness, lowliness, patience
and self-restraint to show forbearance towards one another and forgive
one another and above all these things* to have *love which is the bond*
[185]   *of perfection.*[8] That is to say, these virtues when they become such
a habit with the elect that they seem, as it were, to be naturally
ingrained in them, what else are they than the pictures of the Lord's
house done in relief as if they were coming out of the wall, because
they no longer learn the words and works of truth extrinsically from
others but have them deeply rooted within themselves, and, holding
them in constant readiness, can bring forth from their inmost hearts
what ought to be done and taught.

---

[7] *infra* 16.1 **
[8] Col 3:12–14

14.3 ⟨6:30⟩ **And he also overlaid the floor of the house with gold
both inside and outside.** Inside and outside mean in the oracle and
in the temple itself. Now we have said above[9] that the evenness
of the floor denoted the humble harmony of the holy brotherhood
where, though there are Jews and gentiles, barbarians and Scythians,
freeborn and slaves, high-born and low-born,[10] they all boast of being
brothers in Christ, all boast of having the same Father who is in
heaven, for no one may doubt the perfectly harmonious humility of
the heavenly citizens. The reason why Solomon overlaid the floor of
the house with gold inside and outside is that our king of peace[11] has
filled the angels and the souls of the righteous in heaven perfectly
and fully with the gift of love and has set apart the citizens of the
same heavenly homeland who are in pilgrimage in this world from
the baseness of the rest of mortals by the hallmark of love, saying,
*By this shall all know that you are my disciples, if you have love one for
another.*[12]

15. THE ENTRANCE OF THE ORACLE OR TEMPLE

15 ⟨6:31–32⟩ **And in the entrance to the oracle he made little doors
of olive-wood and five-cornered posts and two doors of olive-wood.**
As regards the first part of his statement, namely, *he made little doors
of olive-wood,* he seems to have wanted to explain this more clearly
when he added: *and two doors of olive-wood.* For there was one
entrance to the oracle but this entrance was closed by two doors
and was opened again when they were unlocked, just as the temple
and the portico before the temple no longer had an entrance, which
gives rise to a certain mystery because ⟨since there is⟩ *one Lord, one
faith, one baptism, one God,*[1] we must hope for one entrance into
the present Church after baptism and one entrance into the heavenly
kingdom through works of faith. For that the oracle had one entrance
is attested by the fact that further on it is written of the ark: *And as
the shafts protruded, the ends of them were seen outside the sanctuary*

---

[9] *supra* 9.1 **
[10] cf. Col 3:11
[11] cf. 1 Paralip 22:9
[12] Jn 13:35
[1] Ep 4:5–6

in front of the oracle, but were not to be seen further out.[2] Here, unless
I am mistaken, it is clearly shown that there was one entrance to the
oracle and this was made opposite the ark which was in the middle of
this oracle. And the little doors of this entrance can be interpreted in
many different ways. For as well as designating very aptly the angelic
spirits by whose assistance we are introduced into the dwelling of our   *[186]*
heavenly homeland, they equally prefigure the apostles and apostolic
men to whom were given the keys of the kingdom of heaven and who,
by the power of binding and loosing received from the Lord,[3] both
admit the worthy ones inside the gates of the kingdom, and debar
by excommunication or anathema the stubborn, the unclean and the
arrogant from entering eternal life. The works of righteousness also,
whereby one merits to attain the heavenly kingdom can rightly be
typified by the gates through which one entered the Holy of Holies
according to what is written in the Book of Wisdom: *And giving heed
to her laws is assurance of immortality, and immortality brings one near
to God; so the desire for wisdom leads to an everlasting kingdom.*[4]
In harmony with all this is the fact that these doors were made of
olive-wood, because, of course, both angels and perfect human beings
prove themselves glorious in the house of God by the fruit of mercy
and the works of light. Indeed all the elect open for themselves a
way to the heavenly homeland by the armour of light and godliness.
Now the reason why there are two little doors is either that angels
and holy people alike love the Lord and their neighbours, and no
one can enter the gate of life except through this twofold love, or
that this gate of life is unlocked to the faithful of both peoples, i.e.
Jews and gentiles. They have five-cornered posts because the court
of heaven not only admitted the souls of the elect but also opened its
doors to bodies endowed in the judgement with immortal glory. For
there are five senses of our body which we mentioned above,[5] sight,
hearing, taste, smell and touch, or if you like, each of the two posts
of the oracle was five cubits, because the entrance to the heavenly
homeland lay open only to those who strove to serve the Lord with
all the senses of their body and heart: that is, of their body, when
they do something for him through these senses, and of their heart

---

[2] 3 K 8:8
[3] cf. Mt 16:19
[4] Ws 6:19–21
[5] *supra* 8.4 **; 13.7 **

when they think soberly and justly and with piety on those things which they decide to do through these bodily senses.

16. THE MAKING OF THE CHERUBIM

16.1 ⟨6:32⟩ **And he carved upon them figures of cherubim, and figures of palm-trees, and carvings in high relief, and he overlaid them with gold.**[1] *Anaglyfa* in Greek are what are called *celaturae* in Latin. Now all these items, i.e. cherubim and palm-trees and carvings in the adornment of the temple walls, have been set forth and explained above[2] according to our ability, and there is no need to go to the trouble of adding anything further because the works of virtue which the Church performs throughout the world in her holy and perfect members should be pursued with all diligence by those especially to whom the care of the faithful has been committed and the keys of the kingdom of heaven granted, so that to the extent that *[187]* they rank higher than the rest, they should also excel them in merit of good actions. For they have the image of the cherubim engraved on them when they imitate, both in thought and action, the life of angels on earth insofar as mortals can. They resemble palm-trees when they keep their minds ever steadfastly intent on the gifts of their heavenly reward. For it is with the palm that the hand of a victor is adorned. They have carvings in bold relief when they show to all who observe them the clearest proofs of good works, proofs which no one can misconstrue. And all these works are covered with sheets of gold[3] when, as has often been said and must always be said, the brightness of love outshines the rest of the flowers of virtue especially in the eminent members of the Church.

16.2 That a veil also was added to these little doors the Chronicles tell us: *He also made a veil of violet, purple, scarlet and silk, and embroidered cherubim on it.*[4] This, of course, was done for decorative effect so that the all-silk hanging also might shimmer between the gilded walls, but with the same significance as the little doors. It was hung between the ark and the entrance of the oracle so that, as

---

[1] *supra* 14.2 **; *infra* 16.8 **
[2] *supra* 14.2 **
[3] cf. 3 K 6:35
[4] 2 Paralip 3:14

the little doors were opened at suitable hours, the veil too might be drawn back as often as those who had to enter the Holy of Holies arrived. Therefore, the constant drawing back of this veil according to the law signifies the opening of the heavenly kingdom which has been granted us through the incarnation of our Lord and saviour. Hence on the one hand, the heavens were opened at his baptism[5] to show that it was through the baptism which he himself hallowed for us that we must enter the door of our heavenly homeland, and on the other hand, at his death on the cross this same *veil was rent in two from top to bottom*[6] that it might be clearly taught that the figures of the law thereupon came to an end and the truth of the Gospel and the heavenly mysteries and the very entrance to heaven were no longer a matter of prophecy or figurative meaning but were on the very point of being opened to all who from the beginning of the world to that moment of time had passed from the world in the true faith. For on the fortieth day after the Lord's resurrection they all repaired to heaven with him and with every veil removed they were each according to their merits allotted one of the manifold mansions in their Father's house. But for us too who were still to come, the entrance to that heavenly city and house of our Father was unlocked already at that same moment. Of course, one does not go up to this city except through internal desires of eternal goods, through faith and the mysteries of the Lord's passion, through the fervour of pure love, through the mortification of carnal passion and through the daily assistance of the angels.

[188]   **16.3**   Hence it is appropriately recorded that this veil under which one entered the oracle was made of violet, purple, scarlet and silk, and that cherubim too were wrought in it. For violet which imitates the colour of the sky is aptly compared to the desires of heavenly things.[7] Purple which is made from the blood of shellfish and has even the appearance of blood is justifiably taken as a figure of the mystery of the Lord's passion in which we ought to be initiated and which we ought to imitate by carrying our cross. By scarlet which is of a glowing red shade is expressed the virtue of love, of which the disciples who had walked with the Lord said in wonder, *Was not our*

---

5 Mt 3:16
6 Mt 27:51; Lk 23:45
7 cf. Isid., *Etymol.* 19.22.11; 28.1–4

heart burning within us while he spoke on the way and opened to us the scriptures?[8] Silk which is produced from a seed which springs green from the earth and which, as a result of a lengthy process applied by silk-workers, sheds its natural greenness and is given a bleached appearance, fittingly suggests the chastening of our flesh. For the inborn moisture, as it were, of the flesh we are bidden to dry out by the Apostle when he says, *Mortify, therefore, your members that are upon the earth: fornication, uncleanness, lust, evil concupiscence and covetousness which is the service of idols;*[9] to what a degree of brightness he wants this grace to be brought he shows elsewhere when he says, *I beseech you, therefore, brethren, by the mercy of God, that you present your bodies a living sacrifice, holy, pleasing to God; the worship you owe as sensible people.*[10] They embroider cherubim on the veil and they are composed of these same four choice colours when in everything which we do devoutly, we are, by God's gift, shielded from the poisoned darts of the demons by the protection of the angels; they embroider cherubim on the veil when in the good things we do we unceasingly make use of the great store of knowledge, constantly turning to the words of God, and when we guide our steps by unbroken contemplation of these words lest we happen to stray from the path of virtue.

16.4 ⟨6:33–34⟩ **And in the entrance to the temple he made quadrangular posts of olive-wood and two doors of cypress, one on either side. And each door was double, and so opened with folding leaves.** Just as the entrance to the oracle by which one reached the ark of the Lord and the cherubim signifies the entrance to the kingdom of heaven whereby we hope and desire to be introduced to the vision of our creator and the heavenly citizens, so the entrance into the temple shows in type the beginnings of our life oriented on God when we enter the Church of this present time. The latter entrance denotes our entry into the faith, the former our entry into vision. Hence the posts of this entrance were foursquare because of the four books of the holy Gospel by whose teaching we are instructed in the true faith, or because of the four cardinal virtues of prudence, fortitude,   *[189]* temperance and justice, on whose most firm foundation, as it were,

---

[8] Lk 24:32
[9] Col 3:5
[10] Rm 12:1

every edifice of good actions rests; prudence by which we learn what
we ought to do and how we ought to live; fortitude through which we
carry out what we have learnt must be done; and the prophet briefly
sums up these virtues in one verse saying, *the Lord is my light and
my salvation*[11], light, that is, to teach us the things we ought to do,
salvation to strengthen us to do them; temperance by which we have
discretion so as not to find ourselves giving more or less than the right
amount of attention to prudence or fortitude; and since anyone who
exercises prudence, fortitude and temperance will be proved beyond
dispute to be just, the fourth virtue which follows after prudence,
fortitude and temperance is justice.

16.5   The two doors which were made in this entrance are love of
God and the neighbour. And they are appropriately said to have
been made on either side because they face each other so that there
is no question of having one without the other. *Every one who believes
that Jesus is the Christ is a child of God, and every one who loves the
parent loves the child;*[12] and as he says another time, *he who does
not love his brother whom he has seen, how can he love God whom
he has not seen?*[13] Hence the outer door is rightly to be understood
as fraternal love, the inner one as love of God because the former
is first in time, the latter is loftier in dignity and through the former
one enters the latter because in love of the neighbour one learns how
the creator ought to be loved. Each of the doors was double and was
attached to the other when opened because in each of the two loves
there are two things we must chiefly observe. For in the love of God
we need to have true faith and the purity of good action, *for without
faith it is impossible to please God;*[14] and *faith without works is dead.*[15]
But in love of the brethren patience and kindness must be observed
as the Apostle says, *love is patient, is kind,*[16] i.e. patient in order to
put up with annoyances and wrongs from neighbours, kind in order
to forgive from the heart and do good to those from whom it suffers
wrongs. This is the kind of love the Lord wanted us to have when

---

[11] Ps 26:1
[12] 1 Jn 5:1
[13] 1 Jn 4:20
[14] Heb 11:6
[15] Jm 2:26
[16] 1 Co 13:4

he said, *Forgive and you shall be forgiven, give and it shall be given to you;*[17] forgive their wrongs to those who harm you, give the support of compassion to those whose wrongs you pardon; this is the kind of love he himself desires us to practise who has taught us to say in the [190] prayer, *Give us this day our daily bread, and forgive us our trespasses as we forgive those who trespass against us.*[18] Each of the two doors was double because each of the two loves is perfected in a twofold order; each door was attached to the other as it was opened because the virtues are joined and cannot be separated from each other. For neither faith without works nor good works without faith can please God, nor similarly does it suffice for one to endure wrongs, if he has thought it beneath him, even though able to do so, to give the one whom he puts up with the things he needs, nor is it enough for one with material wealth to give of this wealth to a needy neighbour unless he also condones with a sincere heart those annoyances which the person may have caused him.[19]

16.6 As for what is said about each of those doors being attached to each other while being opened, this opening does not denote a separation of spiritual virtues from each other but rather indicates that through the combination of these virtues our way into the holy Church becomes wider and wider so that the richer we are in them the more truly we are associated with the company of the saints, just as the parting of the Red Sea, after the people of God had escaped the pursuing Egyptian, did not signify a division of the one and only baptism but rather signified the opening by which, after all our sins have been blotted out, we cross over to the shore and desert of the virtues. Or at all events the doors which were attached to each other are opened when through the ministry of a preacher one discerns what properly pertains to the knowledge of the faith and what pertains to purity of life. Yet, because of their connection, these two things cannot be separated to the same extent as the difference between putting up with the wrongs of neighbours and giving them the benefit of our goods, since these things are most certainly wont to remain inseparable in one and the same heart of the perfect. It is to be noted, of course, that in the entrance of the oracle there

---

[17] Lk 6:37–38
[18] Mt 6:12; Lk 11:3
[19] cf. Greg., *Hom. in Ezech. PL* 76:1013B

are indeed said to have been two doors, but these double doors are
not said to have been in the real entrance of the temple, i.e. of the
first house; the two doors were such that each of the two was double,
that is, because in the present Church we must enter and live a life
of such a kind that we practise the love of God and our neighbour
through faith and works, through patience and kindness. But in the
life to come where we shall see the Lord and our neighbours in the
light of eternal blessedness, we shall exercise the very same twofold
love without the slightest hardship, and what is more we shall enjoy
it in the great abundance of divine sweetness. Hence the entrance
of the inner house had indeed two doors but this had single ones.
For faith is not necessary where we shall see in a clear light all that
we now believe and hope for; the effort of performing works is not
necessary where we shall be granted an everlasting reward for the
things we toil at here; patience is not necessary where no one inflicts   *[191]*
any harm, the generosity of kindness is not necessary where no one
is in need.

16.7   We have thus discussed the figure of the gates according to
our limited capacity, following in the footsteps of the Fathers. But,
according to the form of the work for the purpose of adornment,
provision was made that in one and the same entrance of the temple
there should be two doors. For it was necessary that the walls of the
house which were a hundred and twenty cubits high should also have
some cubits of thickness and in the thickest part of this the doors
were placed so that both doors should be flush with the wall, and
whether one looked at the door from a position inside or outside the
temple, the entire wall would appear to be one continuum throughout. Likewise the cedarwood wall also, since it was twenty cubits in
length and height, had to be considerably thick. Wherefore in its
entrance also two doors were made, in order, that is, that the door
might appear flush with the wall on either side, i.e. inside or outside.
And since the door had the same representations on it as the wall,
the wall would give the impression of being really one wall all the
way along without a break, presenting one appearance for aesthetic
reasons while prefiguring something different for the purposes of the
mystery.

16.8   But the verse that follows the description of the doors of the
temple, namely,

⟨6:35⟩ **And he carved cherubim and palm-trees, and did carving in high relief; and he overlaid the whole evenly with gold leaf in square work,** has already been expounded above,[20] because the same representations or carvings were wrought on the walls of the house and on the inner doors, and the meaning of the figure is obviously that the first door of the temple actually received the same representations and carvings and the same cherubim as the inner parts. The reason for this is that the same mysteries of faith, hope and charity which the sublime and the perfect each grasp in a sublime manner and which all the elect in heaven fully understand in the divine vision, are handed on also in the instruction of the unlettered for each one to learn and confess, in as much as those who have been initiated into the mysteries sometimes also succeed in understanding what they have devoutly believed.

---

[20] *supra* 13.1 **; 16.1 **

BOOK TWO

17. THE COURTS OF THE LORD'S HOUSE

17.1 ⟨6:36⟩ **And he built the inner court with three rows of polished stones and one row of cedar beams.** Of the inner court he speaks briefly; of the outer one he seems to say nothing at all. But mention is made of both in the Chronicles where it is written as follows: *He also made the court of the priests, and a great hall, and doors in the hall, which he covered with bronze.*[1] But the inner court, which is called the court of the priests because the priests and Levites ministered in it, was completely surrounded by the temple but on the east, from where one entered the temple, it was much further removed from the temple than on the other three sides, because, of course, it was on that side, i.e. at the front of the temple, that the sacred functions were performed. There it was that the bronze altar for offering victims to the Lord was situated, there the ten wash-basins for washing these victims, and there the Bronze Sea for washing the hands and feet of the priests when they went to perform their duties. Moreover, this court was three cubits high, as Josephus relates,[2] to exclude the others from admittance into the temple and show that this was permissible to the priests alone; and there was a door on the east side which was the point to which the people used to bring in their victims and sacrifices to be taken from there by the priests and brought forward to the altar. But of the outer court which the Chronicles call the great hall, Josephus writes as follows: *Outside of this temple he built another court in quadrangular form, erecting very large wide porticoes*[3] *in it and setting up high spacious gates at the four quarters of the globe, each facing one of the quarters from the four corners where he put the golden doors;* and a little further on ⟨he writes⟩, *Into this sacred precinct would enter all the people who had fulfilled the requirements of ritual purity and observance of the prescriptions of the law.*[4]

---

[1] 2 Paralip 4:9

[2] cf. Josephus *Ant.* 8.3.9.

[3] Here 'porticoes' is the word used in the Loeb translation to render the Greek word *stoás*.

[4] The Latin of this sentence is: *In hoc sacrarium omnes populi quibus purgatio et observatio legitimorum inerat introibant.* As it stands the clause *quibus . . . inerat*

17.2   Now, in point of fact, as he mentions himself in his commentary on the Psalms, Cassiodorus Senator,[5] in the picture of the temple which he put in the pandect[6] distinguished three ranks in these colonnades, i.e. placing the first outside the court of the priests in a square, the second similarly outside the innermost colonnade and surrounding it, ⟨and⟩ likewise the last one on each side of the previous colonnades all the way round. And in this way the temple was walled all round by the protection of structures of three kinds: a paving of marble in the open between the individual structures; and the walls of the houses on the inside i.e. those facing the temple, built in the form of a colonnade, but the outer ones solid; and so it was that the entire   *[193]* architectural configuration of the temple was judiciously organized to correspond to the differences in rank. For the high priest used to go into the Holy of Holies, the purified priests together with the Levites into the temple itself, the purified and non-purified together with the Levites and cantors into the court, the purified men of Juda into the innermost court of the greater hall, standing and praying in the open

---

cannot be translated literally into tolerable English.   I have felt it necessary to paraphrase but have done so in the light of the Greek text of Josephus which turns neatly into English without recasting: 'all of the people who were distinguished by reason of their purity of life and observance of the prescriptions of the law.'

5   The name 'Senator' is usually written like this as an integral part of Cassiodorus's name which is rendered in English as Cassiodorus Senator rather than as 'the Senator Cassiodorus'; Romans had two basic names, a *praenomen* or personal name and a *nomen* the name of their *gens*, i.e. their clan or family group. In addition they were given extra personal names, some denoting physical peculiarities (Naso), others occupations (Pictor), others public offices (Censorinus or Senator). cf. OCD s.v. *NOMEN.*

6   cf. Cassiodorus *Exp. in Ps.* 86.I *CCSL* 98:789, 40–43. The words 'in the pandect' translate Bede's phrase *in pandecte.* The nominative form *pandectes,* is a transliteration of the Greek παυδέκτης (lit. 'an all-receiver', from πᾶυ = 'all' + δέχομαι = 'I receive'). It was 'a book containing everything', a sort of encyclopaedia, and in Christian parlance it was used to denote the Bible, just as the word *bibliotheca,* 'a library' or 'collection of books', was used by St Jerome. Here it means Cassiodorus's complete and therefore large (hence *Codex Grandior*) copy of the entire Latin bible, now lost, which apparently Ceolfrith brought back from Rome to Wearmouth/Jarrow and Bede saw with his own eyes. So there were close links between it and the well-known *Codex Amiatinus,* now at the Laurentian Library in Florence, a copy of Jerome's Latin Vulgate (i.e. popular) version which was made at Wearmouth/Jarrow and was being carried to the Pope in Rome by Abbot Ceolfrith when he died in northern Italy. For more on the *Codex Amiatinus* and its relationship to the *Codex Grandior* cf. Bruce-Mitford, (1969).

air, if it was fine, if not, going into the colonnades nearest them, the purified women of Juda into the outer court, the gentiles, and the Jews who had recently come from the gentiles, into the outermost court until the sixth day of purification. These distinctions which we have found in Cassiodorus's picture we have taken care to note here briefly, reckoning that he learnt them from the Jews of old and that such a learned man had no intention of proposing as a model for our reading what he himself had not first found to be true.

17.3   These are the places recorded in the last gradual psalm which begins thus: *Come, bless the Lord, all you servants of the Lord who stand in the house of the Lord, in the courts of the house of our God.*[7] In these colonnades Jeremiah[8] and other prophets, in them too the Lord and the apostles, used to preach the word to the people. In one of these the Lord sat teaching when the adulterous woman was brought before him for judgement by the captious Pharisees;[9] in them he found the ones who were selling and buying sheep and cattle and doves and drove them with their wares out of the temple.[10] In them Peter and John found the lame man and healed him and brought him with them as they went in to pray.[11] In them the whole multitude of the people were praying when, as Zachary was offering incense, the angel appeared to him at the altar of incense and informed him on the birth of the precursor of the Lord.[12] However, these courts with their colonnades could not hide the view of the temple from those who looked at it from a distance because the place where the temple was situated was much higher than the place where the colonnades had been erected. For as Josephus writes,[13] *the outermost buildings of the courts, although they had been erected to a height of four hundred cubits, reached only to the top of the mountain on which the temple was built.*[14]

---

[7] Ps. 133:1
[8] cf. Jr 19:14
[9] cf. Jn 8:2
[10] cf. Mt 21:12; Jn 2:14
[11] cf. Ac 3:18
[12] cf. Lk 1:5ff
[13] Josephus *Ant* 8.3.9
[14] This quotation from Josephus's *Antiquities*, while it reflects substantially the original Greek of the passage cited, does not render that original exactly as we have it today.

17.4   These items of information on the structure of the temple, in our opinion, should indeed be passed on to the keen reader. But among them let us seek out figures of whatever mysteries sacred scripture has thought fit to relate and the rest let us use purely for

[194] historical knowledge. The temple building inside the court of the priests, then, represents the life of the perfect and those of sublime sanctity in the holy Church, that is to say, of those who by the excellence of their virtues are wont to approach the Lord and also provide guidance to others in the way of salvation by word and work. For the priest has got his name in Latin from the fact that he ought to offer sacred guidance to those lower than him. In the scriptures this name comprises not only the ministers of the altar, i.e. bishops and priests, but indeed all who are outstanding by reason of the loftiness of their good life and salutary teaching, and are of benefit not only to themselves but to a great many others as well. For while they offer their *bodies as a living sacrifice, holy and pleasing to God,*[15] they truly exercise the priestly ministry spiritually. After all, it was not just to bishops and priests alone but to all God's Church that the apostle Peter was speaking when he said, *But you are a chosen generation, a kingly priesthood, a holy nation, a people for his possession.*[16] And the ancient people of God were also singled out by the honour of this dignity as he himself said to Moses, *Thus shall you say to the house of Jacob, and tell the children of Israel;*[17] and a little further on, *And you shall be to me a kingdom of priests and a holy nation.*[18]

17.5   But the large hall which was outside the court of the priests and in which the whole multitude of the people was wont to worship or gather to hear the word, suggests figuratively the life and behaviour of the carnal in the holy Church to whom the Apostle says, *But I, brethren, could not address you as spiritual people, but as people of the flesh, as babes in Christ, I fed you with milk, not solid food.*[19] These are aptly denoted by the great hall because without any doubt the

---

One must conclude either that it is a paraphrastic rendering which omits what is not relevant to the author's point, or that it is based on a different text from that now available to us.

[15]   Rm 12:1
[16]   1 P 2:9
[17]   Ex 19:3
[18]   Ex 19:6
[19]   1 Co 3:1–2

number of such people in the holy Church is far greater than that of the perfect, but the more they outnumber them, the lower they are in merit. Hence it is fitting that this great hall, even though it holds the majority, does not, for all that, admit them to the inner parts of the gilded temple, or to the service of the altar or even to the priests' court itself, because even though all the carnal and weak who are still in the Church have a share in the lot of the elect through the merit of pure faith and of piety which is dedicated to God, nevertheless, they are far from being fit to put on a par with those who have convincingly proved their fidelity. *For I will not venture to speak of anything except what Christ wrought through me, to win the obedience of the gentiles, by word and deed;*[20] and again, *I have fought a good fight; I have finished my course; I have kept the faith. Henceforth there is laid up for me a crown of righteousness.*[21]

17.6 The common people, it is true, came as far as the court of the priests, brought their sacrifices as far as this door and, when these had been accepted by the priest and offered on the altar, followed them with their eyes. Moreover, they directed their gaze from a distance into the temple itself when it was opened but they had no permission to enter the court of the priests. However, they cried to the Lord from the lower areas of ⟨the temple⟩ because the simplicity even of the carnal in the Church is not spurned by the Lord when they offer up with faith such prayers as they can. They direct their eyes from a distance into the temple of God when they earnestly rejoice in learning about and admiring the life of the sublime, and embrace with the affection of pious veneration those whom they cannot follow in the imitation of their virtue. They see the priests' sacrificial victims being consumed by sacred fire on the altar because they recognize that the great performance of august works is graciously accepted by the Lord through the Holy Spirit. They also bring their sacrificial offerings to the court of the priests to be offered to the Lord by them, while, in doing the good things which are of greater worth, they are encouraged by the exhortation of greater and more learned people and are commended ⟨to God⟩ by their intercession. They also offer their sacrifices to the priests to be commended by them to God whenever, with a view to the supreme reward, they give the

[195]

---

[20] Rm 15:18
[21] 2 Tm 4:7–8

necessities of this world, which they themselves have in abundance, to any of the saints in need, as the Lord urges when he says, *Make friends for yourselves of the mammon of iniquity, that when you fail they may receive you into everlasting dwellings.*[22] *And whosoever,* he says, *shall give one of these little ones a cup of cold water to drink only in the name of a disciple, amen, I say to you, he shall not lose his reward;*[23] and so one and the same person takes up the sacrifices of both on the altar of God when the Lord judges the alms of the rich by which they minister to the saints together with the great virtues of the same saints worthy of his regard and reward. Therefore, the multitude of the believers, who left their possessions and served the Lord with one heart and mind, are the temple of God and the place inside the court of the priests specially consecrated to him.

17.7   Again the great hall and those praying in it in a circle round the court of the priests are a figure of those of the gentiles who were believers in Syria and Antioch and the other provinces and cities[24] on whom the apostles and elders who were in Jerusalem imposed no further burden than that they refrain *from that which has been offered to idols and from blood and from things strangled and from fornication.*[25] However, they wished that the poor among the saints who were in Jerusalem be supported by their offerings so that those who put their worldly possessions at the disposal of these poor people could become sharers in their spiritual wealth.[26] But Barnabas and Paul with their companions who received these people's offerings and [196] brought them to Jerusalem, are the priests who accepted the sacrifices and brought them to the altar of the Lord for consecration, because they brought the gifts of their charity to the saints who were obliged to pray for them. Therefore, the court, which was situated midway between the place for the common people and that for the priests, signifies the division which separates the carnal ones in the holy Church, who indeed are only beginners in the way of righteousness, from the pinnacle of the perfect, which was determined not by lot but by the greatness of their merits. For the carnal ones feel it is

---

[22] Lk 16:9
[23] Mt 10:42
[24] cf. Ac 15:22–29
[25] Ac 21–25
[26] cf. Rm 15:26–27

enough for them to have faith, hope and charity, as well as purity of conduct. The perfect on the other hand, as well as having these, also labour in preaching the word, distribute all their goods to the poor, give themselves to vigils, fasting, hymns and spiritual canticles, as well as to sacred reading, endure persecutions and dangers for righteousness' sake, and with prompt zeal perform the other things which Paul with his companions boasts of having done.[27]

17.8 Hence it is aptly noted that the priests' court was constructed of three courses of polished stones and one course of cedar beams. For the three courses of polished stones are faith, hope and charity, and the expression 'of polished stones' is appropriate because each one needs a certain amount of intelligence to discern how he ought to believe, and what he ought to hope for as well as love. But the one course of cedar beams is good works performed without being vitiated by outward show, since, if this condition is lacking, faith, hope and charity cannot be genuine. For it has often been said that, on account of their pleasant fragrance and naturally incorruptible quality, cedar beams symbolize the enduring character and good repute of works of piety.[28] All the elect who aim at pleasing God by faith, hope, love and action get as far as this court. Beyond it climb the perfect by the exalted grace of their merits since they reach such a peak of virtue that they can say to their hearers, *Be imitators of us as we also are of Christ,*[29] and boast and say, *Do you not know that we shall judge the angels? How much more the things of this world?*[30]

18. HOW MANY YEARS THE TEMPLE TOOK TO BUILD

18.1 ⟨6:37–38⟩ **In the fourth year the foundation of the house of the Lord was laid in the month of Zio. And in the eleventh year in the month of Bul (which is the eighth month) the house was finished in all its parts and according to all its specifications. He was seven years in building it.** The allegorical meaning of the fact that the house of the Lord was built in seven years is plain because, of course, the holy Church is being built of the souls of the elect for the entire

[27] cf. 2 Co 11:18–28
[28] *supra* 8.3 **; 11.1 **; Isid., *Etymol.* 17.7.33
[29] 1 Co 11:1
[30] 1 Co 6:3

duration of this world which is also completed in a period of six days
and it too brings its growth to an end with the end of the world.   *[197]*
Or, at all events, it is built in seven years on account of the import
of the grace of the Spirit through which the Church alone gets the
authority to be the Church. For Isaiah enumerates the seven gifts of
the Holy Spirit without which no one can either become a believer
or keep the faith or by the merit of faith attain the crown.[1] On the
other hand, the fact that it was in the eighth year and in the eighth
month of that year that the house was completed in all its parts and
all its specifications, has to do with the world to come and the day
of judgement when the holy Church will already have reached such a
degree of perfection that it will not be possible to find anything to add
to it. For it will then have what that dutiful devotee suppliantly asked
of the Lord saying, *Lord, show us the Father, and it is enough for us.*[2]
For it is well known that the day of judgement is often represented
typologically in the scriptures by the number eight from the fact that
it follows this world which lasts for seven days. Which is also why the
prophet gave the title 'For the eighth' to the psalm he used to sing
through fear of this severe judge, beginning with the words, *Lord,
rebuke me not in your indignation, nor chastise me in your wrath* and
so forth.[3]

18.2   But there arises the rather important question as to how the
house of the Lord is said to have been completed in all its parts in
the eighth month and in all its specifications, whereas in what follows
one reads that its dedication was completed in the seventh month.[4]
On the other hand, it is not credible that Solomon, though he built
the temple in seven years and completed it in the eighth month of the
eighth year, nevertheless, deferred the dedication of the completed
building until the seventh month of the ninth year. Hence it seems
more likely that the house was built in seven years and seven months
so that the solemn ceremony of dedication might be celebrated in the
same seventh month, and, as the Chronicles relate:[5] on the twenty-
third day of that month Solomon sent the people away to their tents,

---

[1] Is 11:2–3
[2] Jn 14:8
[3] Ps 6:1–2
[4] cf. 3 K 8:2
[5] cf. 2 Paralip 7:10

and thus after one week when the eighth month had come round, the house of the Lord was found to be complete and already finished, that is to say, both in all its parts and in its actual dedication. Unless perhaps one should think that after the dedication of the temple some extra features were added for its services up to the beginning of the eighth month, the king speeding up the work so that the temple would be dedicated in the seventh month, at all events, which was entirely solemn, and that in this way the two things might turn out to be true, namely, both that the temple had been completed in the eighth month in all its parts and specifications, and that it had been dedicated in the seventh month.

18.3 ⟨7:13–14⟩ **And king Solomon sent and fetched from Tyre, Hiram, the son of a widow of the tribe of Nephtali, whose father was a Tyrian, a craftsman in bronze, and full of wisdom, understanding, and skill in making any work in bronze. And when he came to king** *[198]* **Solomon, he did all his work.** And this was done on account of the mystery. For the Tyrian craftsman whom Solomon employed to help in his work stands for the ministers of the word chosen from the gentiles. The allusion to this man as a craftsman is a beautiful touch because he was the son of a widow of Israel, a person who is sometimes wont to be taken as prefiguring the Church of the present day for whom her husband, namely, Christ, after having tasted death, rose and ascended into heaven, leaving her meanwhile to sojourn on the earth. However, there is no need to labour the explanation of how the sons of this widow are preachers since all the elect individually profess themselves children of the Church, and also since in regard to these preachers of the New Testament a special promise is made in the words of the prophet: *Instead of your fathers, sons are born to you; you shall make them princes over all the earth.*[6] Now Hiram did all Solomon's work, that is to say, because the holy teachers, while they devote themselves faithfully to the ministry of the word, do indeed do the work of God, since by speaking outwardly they open the way of truth to those whom he himself has predestined to eternal life by enlightening them inwardly. *I,* he says, *planted, Apollo watered; but God gave the increase.*[7] Moreover, he made the work of bronze because the energetic teacher seeks to entrust the word to those who,

---

[6] Ps 44:7

[7] 1 Co 3:6

on the one hand, desire to receive it with reverence and keep it to the end, and who also by preaching to others do their utmost to spread more widely whatever right doctrine they have learnt themselves; for it is common knowledge that bronze is a metal which is very durable and produces all kinds of sounds.

18.4 ⟨7:15⟩ **And he cast two pillars in bronze. Each pillar was eighteen cubits high, and a line of twelve cubits compassed both pillars.** These are the pillars of which Paul says, *James and Cephas and John, who were regarded as pillars, gave to me and Barnabas the right hand of fellowship, that we should go to the gentiles, and they to the circumcised.*[8] In these words he seems to expound, as it were, the mystery of the material pillars and what they stand for and why two of them were made. For they signify the apostles and all spiritual teachers, those, that is, who are strong in faith and work and elevated to heavenly things by contemplation. Moreover, there are two of them so that they may bring both gentiles and circumcised into the Church by preaching. They stood in the portico in front of the doors of the temple and strikingly adorned its entrance on both sides by their elegance and beauty. The temple door, on the other hand, is the Lord because no one comes to the Father except through him,[9] and as he says elsewhere, *I am the door. If anyone enter by me, he shall be saved.*[10] That is to say, the pillars placed there stand around this door on either side when the ministers of the word show both groups of people the way into the heavenly kingdom so that each of them, whether they come to the faith of the Gospel from the light of the knowledge of the Law or from the ignorance of heathendom may have people at hand to show them the way of salvation both by word and example.

[199]

18.5 Or at all events, because in the Book of Paralipomenon it is written of these pillars as follows: *These pillars he put at the entrance of the temple, one on the right hand, and the other on the left,*[11] the reason why the two pillars were made and were so positioned was to teach us that both in prosperity and adversity we must keep the

---

[8] Ga 2:9
[9] cf. Jn 14:6
[10] Jn 10:9
[11] 2 Paralip 3:17

entrance to our heavenly homeland before the eyes of our mind. This indeed is why Paul, who was, of course, a most eminent pillar of the house of the Lord, earnestly admonishes us by his own example and that of his followers that we must fortify ourselves *by the armour of righteousness on the right hand and on the left,*[12] so that whether basking in prosperity or broken in spirit by adversity we may not deviate in any direction from the royal road of life by which we must make our way to the inheritance of the heavenly homeland promised to us. It is to be noted, of course, in this sentence from Paralipomenon which I have quoted, that this portico of the temple is also called the vestibule of the temple, and what we read in the prophets: *Between the vestibule and the altar the priests prayed,*[13] is to be understood as between the portico and the altar.

18.6   Moreover, it is properly recorded that both pillars are eighteen cubits high. For three sixes make eighteen. But the three refers to faith on account of the holy Trinity, and the six to works, because the fact that the world was made in that number of days is clearer than daylight. And three is multiplied by six when *the righteous person ⟨who⟩ lives by faith*[14] acquires knowledge of pious belief by the performance of good works. For the pillar before the temple doors is eighteen cubits high when each eminent preacher openly intimates to all, that it is only through faith and the works of righteousness we can attain the joys of heavenly life. Although this can also be understood in the more profound sense that the name of Jesus begins from this number among the Greeks. With them the first letter of this name means ten and the second eight. And fittingly are the pillars of the house of God eighteen cubits high because holy teachers, indeed all the elect, pursue this objective by living well that they may merit to see their creator face to face, for they will have nothing further to seek when they reach him who is above all things.

18.7   ⟨6:15⟩ **And a line of twelve cubits compassed both pillars.** The   *[200]* line of twelve cubits is the norm of apostolic teaching. This line compasses both pillars when each teacher, whether sent to preach to the Jews or to the gentiles is careful to do and teach only what

---

[12] 2 Co 6:7
[13] Ezk 8:16; Jl 2:17
[14] Rm 1:17

the holy Church has received and learnt through the apostles. For anyone who wants to live or preach otherwise and prefers either to despise the apostolic decrees or propose something novel according to his own whim, is not a pillar fit for the temple of God, for since he thinks it beneath him to follow the apostolic decrees, by the thinness, as it were, of his laziness or the grossness of his pompous arrogance, he is out of accord with the line of twelve cubits. The Lord, doubtless, put these lines around the pillars of his temple when, as he sent his disciples to teach and baptize all nations, he said to them, *teaching them to observe all that I have commanded you.*[15] Whoever, therefore, observes and teaches everything the Lord commanded the apostles, without either adding anything further or omitting any of them, such a one is indeed a pillar in God's house which is the Church and a bulwark of truth such as the apostle Paul admonished Timothy to be.[16] But because without a knowledge of the scriptures neither the teachers' manner of life nor their word can be sound, it is fittingly added:

18.8 ⟨7:16⟩ **He also made two capitals of molten bronze, to be set upon the tops of the pillars (the height of one capital was five cubits, and the height of the other capital was five cubits).** The tops of the pillars, that is, their highest part, are the hearts of faithful teachers whose God-centred thoughts guide all their actions and words as the head guides the members of the body. On the other hand, the two capitals which were placed on these pillar-tops are the two testaments, which holy teachers are totally bound both in mind and body to meditate and observe. It is appropriate, then, that both capitals were five cubits high because the scripture of the Mosaic Law comprises five books and furthermore the entire collection of Old Testament writings embraces the five ages of the world. But the New Testament does not proclaim to us something different from what Moses and the prophets had said should be proclaimed: *If you believed Moses you would believe me, for he wrote of me.*[17] For Moses

[201] wrote much about the Lord not only in figure but also quite plainly as when he relates what had been promised to Abraham in the Lord's

---

[15] Mt 28:20
[16] cf. 1 Tm 3:15
[17] Jn 5:46

words: *in your seed shall the families of the earth bless themselves,*[18] and when in his own words he says to the Israelites, *the Lord will raise up for you from among your brethren a prophet like me; him you shall hear according to all things whatsoever he shall speak to you.*[19] Of this prophecy the voice of the Father from heaven reminded the disciples when, as the Lord appeared to them in glory between Moses himself and Elijah on the holy mountain, it rang out saying, *This is my beloved Son in whom I am well pleased; listen to him.*[20] Therefore, with the admirable harmony of divine activity, the grace of the New Testament was hidden under the veil of the Old at first, but now the mysteries of the Old Testament are revealed by the light of the New, as if the reason why the capital of each of the two pillars was five cubits high was that it is manifest that the grace of the perfection of the Gospel too is innate in the Old Testament whose mysteries are noted beforehand in the five books of the Law or are all comprised more fully in the five ages ⟨of the world⟩; and so it happens that each eminent preacher, whether destined to be sent to the Jews or to the gentiles, fortified with the harmonious testimony of the word of God, keeps the sure and correct rule of faith and conduct free from error, and in the course of his teaching knows how to draw forth *out of his treasure-house, new things and old.*[21] Not only do the testaments harmonize with each other in their account of the divine mysteries, but also all the elect who are written about in the books of these testaments are endowed with the one faith and are bound to each other by the same charity. Hence with reference to the making of these capitals it is fittingly added:

18.9 ⟨7:17⟩ **And a kind of network and chain-work wreathed together with wonderful artistry. Both of the capitals of the pillars were cast.** And the same thing is written in the Book of Paralipomenon as follows: *He also made, as it were, little chains in the oracle and he put them on the tops of the pillars.*[22] The shape of the chains and the likeness of the network on the capitals is the variety of spiritual virtues in the saints which is sung of to the Lord in the psalms:

18 Ac 3:25
19 Ac 3:22
20 Mt 17:5
21 Mt 13:52
22 2 Paralip 3:16

The queen stood on your right hand, in gilded clothing, surrounded with variety,[23] i.e. in the clothing of shining love, arrayed in the variety of the different charismata. At all events, the multiple intertwining of chains and the expansion of the network suggests the many different characters among the elect, who, when they faithfully adhere to the words of the holy preachers by listening and obeying, show forth to all who behold them, like the network and the little chains placed upon the tops of the pillars, the miracle of their interconnection. For these *[202]* chains are woven together with wonderful craftsmanship because it is thanks to the absolutely marvellous grace of the Holy Spirit that the lifestyles of believers, quite removed from each other though they may be in space, time, rank, status, sex and age, are nevertheless linked together by one and the same faith and love. That this common fraternal bond of the righteous, separated in space and time, is effected by the union of the gift of the Spirit, is also shown by the following words, when, with reference to the making of the capitals, it is further remarked:

18.10 ⟨7:17⟩ **Seven rows of nets were on one capital, and seven nets on the other capital.** For the number seven is conventionally used to denote the grace of the Holy Spirit, as attested in the Apocalypse by John, who, after saying that he had seen *the lamb with seven horns and seven eyes,* went on to add, by way of explanation, *which are the seven spirits of God sent into the whole world.*[24] This the prophet Isaiah more clearly explains when, speaking of the Lord who was to be born in the flesh, he says, *and the spirit of the Lord shall rest upon him, the spirit of wisdom and of understanding, the spirit of counsel and of fortitude, the spirit of knowledge and of godliness. And he shall be filled with the spirit of the fear of the Lord.*[25] The reason why there were seven rows of nets in both capitals is that it was through the grace of one and the same septiform Spirit that the Fathers of both testaments received the privilege of election.

18.11 ⟨7:18⟩ **And he made the pillars, and two rows right round each network to cover the capitals, and he did the same to the other capital.** True, there were two rows of networks right round the capital

---

[23] Ps 44:10

[24] Rv 5:6

[25] Is 11:2–3

but both rows were repeated seven times over until the capital was encircled and the row rejoined itself after going full circle. Nor is the figure of the mystery obscured by the fact that there are two rows of network since it is well known that the virtue of love consists of two distinct aspects, namely, when we are bidden to love God with our whole heart, our whole mind and our whole strength, and our neighbour as ourselves.[26] But both of those rows have seven rows of nets because without the grace of the Holy Spirit neither God nor the neighbour can be loved. For the statement, *because the love of God has been poured into our hearts through the Holy Spirit who has been given to us,*[27] remains true. But where the love of God is, there, assuredly, the love of the neighbour also is poured into the hearts of the faithful because, of course, the one cannot be had without the other. Furthermore these networks were made to cover the capitals, i.e. to encircle them completely, because, rightly understood, every page of holy writ echoes throughout with the sound of the grace of love and peace. For the capitals are indeed the volumes of the divine word, the networks are the bonds of mutual love and the capitals are covered with networks when the sacred words, if I may say so, are shown on all sides to be clothed with the gift of love. For even in the things which we do not understand in the scriptures, love is abundantly in evidence.

[203]

18.12   But regarding these networks or capitals the following words have properly been added:

⟨7:18⟩ **that were upon the top, with pomegranates.**   For pomegranates, whose nature it is to encase many seeds inside them with a single rind outside, are aptly offered as a figure of the holy Church which is wont to include the countless ranks of the elect within the universal pale of the one faith. But it can also apply to each individual righteous person's life and conduct, which contains many ornaments of spiritual thoughts and virtues like a great many seeds inside one rind, and is careful to erect around them a secure rampart of faith and humility in case they should trickle away.[28] And by a quite apt mystical figure the tops of the pillars were encircled all round with pomegranates because holy teachers must recall the memory of for-

---

[26]   cf. Mk 12:30–31

[27]   Rm 5:5

[28]   *infra* 18.15 **

mer believers and ever following their example reinforce their actions and words in every respect, lest, by living or teaching in a manner at variance with their norm, they should go astray. Therefore, as the admirable interconnection of the networks symbolizes the unity of the faithful which is in the bond of peace,[29] so also do the pomegranates suggest typologically this same unity which holds countless peoples throughout the world together in the one rule of catholic faith. Or at all events, the marvellous interlinking of networks demonstrates the manifest harmony of all the faithful; the position of the pomegranates expresses the Spirit's interior virtues which others cannot see at all, namely, humility, kindness, self-restraint and other such things.[30] And, as it were, the surface of the fruits is outwardly visible but the store of seeds encased within is not, when the devout behaviour of the saints is on public display for all, but the inward grace of faith, hope and love and of the other good things of the Spirit, is not visible. Therefore, since the words, *to cover the capitals that were upon the top with pomegranates,* referred to the networks, it seems that, according to the order of the work itself, the pomegranates were put round the capitals from underneath and out of these pomegranates rose the networks with which they were partly covered; and it is clear from the representation of the mystery why the networks with which the capitals were bound were covered with pomegranates. These have almost the same meaning whether applied to spiritual persons or spiritual virtues. For we know that virtues beget virtues and saints   *[204]* progress from virtue to virtue until the God of gods is seen in Sion.[31] And no greater virtue than this is attainable. That is why the Apostle also says, *Knowing that tribulation produces patience, and patience trial, and trial hope.*[32] But in the universal assembly of the elect various righteous persons succeed each other and the lesser ones are glad to follow faithfully in the footsteps of the greater and of their predecessors, and to rely on their sayings or writings, lest perchance they should lapse into error. Therefore, the networks are placed above the pomegranates when the harmony of love is added to perfect works and when from both gifts of virtue, i.e. both actions and love, the life of the saints begins to shine forth, the additional interlinking of

---

[29] cf. Ep 4:3
[30] cf. Col 3:12
[31] cf. Ps 83:8
[32] Rm 5:3–4

the networks accompanies, as it were, the circle of pomegranates on the capitals. And since all the gifts of virtues in this life have as their object the glory of the eternal reward which is promised and ministered to us through the Gospel, it is aptly added:

18.13 ⟨7:19⟩ **And the capitals that were upon the top of the pillars were of lily-work in the portico, of four cubits.** What else can the lilies mean but the glory of the heavenly homeland and the beauty of immortality fragrant with the flowers of paradise? What else can the four cubits mean but the word of the Gospel which promises us entry into eternal happiness and shows us the road by which we may reach it. Therefore, when holy teachers show us the promised threshold of the heavenly kingdom in the four books of the holy Gospel, it is as if the tops of the pillars display the lily-work of four cubits that is upon them. Taking this text literally, it should be noted that when the lily-work on the capitals is recorded as having been of four cubits and the words 'in height' or 'in width' are not added, it is, of course, left to the reader's judgement whether this ought to be understood as referring to height or to width. It is agreed beyond the slightest doubt that a pillar which a rope of twelve cubits spanned would be four cubits thick. For the circumference of every circle is three times the length of its diameter. Finally because the Bronze Sea was ten cubits in diameter, as we read in what follows, it was thirty cubits in circumference.[33] But because the lily-work is said to have been four cubits, whether this means in width or in height, at all events, the meaning of the figure is clear, because it is only through the Gospel that the voice most ardently longed for has sounded: *Do penance, for the kingdom of heaven is at hand.*[34]

18.14 But the statement that follows, namely,   [205]
⟨7:20⟩ **And again other capitals in the top of the pillars above, according to the measure of the pillar over against the network,** is made according to the measure of a pillar of the same height as it; but the height of this pillar is not stated. Now these capitals, whatever kind or size they were, for the scripture text does not indicate their dimensions clearly, seem to have been placed in front of the lilies. Regarding the structure of these, if one enjoys delving into mystical

---

[33] cf. 3 K 7:23
[34] Mt 4:17

matters, one may, not inappropriately, describe it as that sublimity of
the everlasting kingdom which *neither eye has seen nor ear heard nor
has it entered into the heart of man what things God has prepared for
those who love him.*[35] For behind the four-cubit lilies were ranged
other capitals, whose height is not stated, because, while it is true
that in the Gospel we read a lot about heavenly beatitude, namely,
how the clean of heart will see God there,[36] how they will be equal
to the angels of God,[37] how they will neither marry nor be given
in marriage,[38] how they cannot die any more, how, wherever Christ
is, his ministers will also be,[39] how he will show himself to them,
how he will tell them plainly about his Father,[40] how no one will
take away from us the joy of his vision,[41] nevertheless, the actual
form of the things we have mentioned, what the actual conditions
and mode of life are like in that heavenly homeland, is clear only to
those of its citizens who have gained entrance to it. Therefore, the
structure or height of these capitals which were above the lily-work
⟨is⟩ appropriately ⟨mentioned⟩ so that some inkling may be given
as to how awesome to earthly beings is the nature of the heavenly
abode. And yet concerning this abode this much is no secret, namely,
that in it all share in the enjoyment of the vision of God, each one
to a more sublime degree according as the eyes of one's heart are
more purified in order to see him. For he who said, *He has blessed all
that fear the Lord, both little and great,*[42] also said, *For you will repay
everyone according to his works.*[43] Therefore, all the elect will share
a common blessing,[44] but in accordance with the different quality of
their works there are many mansions for the blessed in one and the
same eternal house of the Father in heaven.[45] Which is also, in my
opinion, indicated mystically in the formation of these pillars where it

---

[35] 1 Co 2:9
[36] cf. Mt 5:8
[37] cf. Lk 20:36
[38] cf. Mt 22:30
[39] cf. Jn 12:26
[40] cf. Jn 14:21; 16:25
[41] cf. Jn 16:22
[42] Ps 113:21(13)
[43] Ps 61:13
[44] cf. Greg., *Hom. in Ezech. PL* 76:977A
[45] cf. Jn 14:2; see note on this text at the end of Prol.2 above.

is said: *And again other capitals in the top of the pillars above, according to the measure of the pillar over against the network.* For the capitals are made on top according to the dimensions of the pillar when holy teachers, indeed all the righteous who follow the footsteps of these [206] teachers, receive the rewards of heavenly recompense according to the merits of their good work. Moreover, these capitals are made over against the network because it is according to the measure of the love by which the holy brotherhood is bound together in this life that the presence of their creator too will be linked with the fellowship of the heavenly citizens in heaven. But because this fellowship of heavenly citizens is granted to the faithful of both peoples, it is rightly added:

18.15 ⟨7:20⟩ **And of the pomegranates there were two hundred in rows right round the other capital.** We have said that the pomegranates were a type of either the whole Church or of each individual believer,[46] but the number a hundred which was originally applied to the right hand was sometimes wont to be used as a figure of eternal beatitude.[47] There were twice this number of pomegranates around the second capital to suggest mystically that the people of both testaments who were to be unified in Christ were to be brought in to receive the crown of eternal life. In keeping with this figure are the words written about the apostles fishing after the Lord's resurrection when they saw him standing on the shore: *for they were not far from the land, but, as it were, two hundred cubits, dragging the net with the fish.*[48] For the disciples indeed drag the net full of large fish for two hundred cubits to the Lord who is already on the shore showing the effects of his resurrection when holy preachers entrust the word of faith to both Jews and gentiles and drag the elect of both peoples from the waves of this present world and lead them to the glory of the peace and immortality to come. The circumference, therefore, of the second capital has two rows of pomegranates when the sublimity of the heavenly kingdom assembles the elect of both peoples in one citadel of peace.

18.16 ⟨7:21⟩ **And he set up two pillars in the portico of the tem-**

---

[46] cf. *supra* 18.12 **
[47] Bede, *De temp. rat.* ed. Jones 179:18ff
[48] Jn 21:8

ple. **And when he had set up the pillar on the right hand, he called its name Jachin, firmness; likewise he set up the second pillar, and called its name Booz, in strength.** As we have said above, the right-hand pillar represents figuratively the teachers who formed the primitive Church in Jerusalem; the second is a figure of those who were destined to preach to the gentiles; or, at all events, the right-hand pillar signifies those who in prophecy had predicted the Lord who was to come in the flesh; the second one those who bear witness that he has already come and has redeemed the world by his blood. And both pillars were appositely given the same name, since one was called 'firmness' and the other 'in strength' to show that in all teachers there was the one staunchness of faith and practice, and to *[207]* note tacitly the sluggishness of our time when some want to have the appearance and name of being teachers, priests and pillars of the house of God though they have absolutely none of the firm faith needed to despise worldly ostentation and make invisible goods their ambition, none of the strength needed to administer correction, none of the diligence even to understand the errors of those to whom they have been preferred.

19. THE BRONZE SEA

19.1 ⟨7:23⟩ **He also made a molten sea of ten cubits from brim to brim, completely round.** This molten Sea was made as a figure of the laver of salvation in which we are cleansed for the remission of our sins. For priests were washed in it, as the Chronicles assure us;[1] but it is agreed that all the elect are called priests in a typological sense in the scriptures since they are members of the high priest Jesus Christ. And rightly has scripture given the name of Sea to this vessel, in memory, that is, of the Red Sea in which once, through the destruction of the Egyptians and the deliverance of the people of God, the form of baptism was anticipated, as the Apostle explains when he says, *that our fathers were all under the cloud, and all passed through the sea, and all in Moses were baptized in the cloud and in the sea.*[2] Now the sacrament of baptism both requires of us purity of life in this world and promises us the glory of eternal life in the world to come. Both of which things are denoted in this Bronze Sea in one

---

[1] cf. 2 Paralip 4:6

[2] 1 Co 10:1–2

sentence where it is said to be ten cubits from brim to brim. For by the ten commandments in the Law the Lord expressed all that we must do. Likewise by the denarius he indicated the reward of good deeds when he foretold that it was to be given to those working in the vineyard.[3] The reason why the Sea was ten cubits from brim to brim was that the whole choir of the faithful from the first one baptized in the name of Jesus Christ to the last to believe and be baptized at the end of the world must enter upon one and the same way of truth, and hope for a common crown of righteousness from the Lord. It was completely circular in order to signify that the whole universe all the way round was to be cleansed in the laver of life from the filth of its sins.

19.2   In this regard the remark is well made that
⟨7:23⟩ **its height was five cubits,** because, of course, whatever fault we have committed by the sense of sight or hearing or smell or taste or touch, all this the grace of God washes away for us through the ablution of the life-giving font.[4] But the remission of past sins is not enough if one does not thereafter devote oneself to good works; *[208]* otherwise, if the devil, after leaving a person, sees such a one to be lacking in good actions, he comes back in greater numbers and makes *the last state of that person worse than the first.*[5] Hence it is fittingly added:

19.3   ⟨7:23⟩ **And a line of thirty cubits compassed it all the way round.** For by the line can fittingly be meant the discipline of the heavenly precepts with which we are restrained from the indulgence of our passions since scripture says that *a threefold cord is not easily broken*[6] because, of course, the observance of the commandments of God, which is established in the hearts of the elect by faith, hope and the love of an eternal reward, cannot be frustrated by any obstacle of temporal things. And the line encircles the Sea when by works of piety we strive to enhance the sacrament of baptism which we have received. Now this line is aptly said to be three cubits long. For five times six make thirty. By the number six in which the Lord both made

---

[3] cf. Mt 20:2
[4] *infra* 20.2 **
[5] Lk 11:24–26
[6] Qo 4:12

mankind when it did not exist and remade it when it had perished, our good actions are also rightly represented, and six is multiplied by five to make thirty, when we humbly subject all our bodily senses to divine things. However, there is also another sense in which we can quite appropriately take this number thirty as applying mystically to the Sea. For three tens make thirty. And after the flood, from the issue of Noah's three sons, the human race filled the whole expanse of the universe;[7] for the tribe of Shem occupied Asia, Ham's descendants occupied Africa and the progeny of Japheth occupied Europe and the islands of the sea. And because, together with the performance of good works and the hope of heavenly rewards, the sacrament of baptism was to be administered to all the nations, it was fitting that a line of thirty cubits should encircle the Sea, in which the water of baptism was prefigured. But it must also be said that the Lord at the age of thirty years came to the Jordan to be baptized by John.[8] For since by his baptism which he received at the age of thirty he consecrated for us the water of the laver of salvation, it is right that a line should encircle the Sea which is a figure of our baptism, so that, by the gift of him who underwent baptism without sin, it might be signified that baptism was specifically given to all of us who believe in him for the remission of our sins.

19.4 ⟨7:24⟩ **And a carved work under its brim surrounded it, encircling the Sea for ten cubits. There were two rows cast of chamfered sculptures.** Since it has been said above that a line of thirty cubits encircled the Sea and it is now added that this carved work under the brim went round it for ten cubits, it is obvious from both accounts that the vessel was bent backwards and spread out like a bowl, because from a circumference of thirty cubits which it measured at the brim, it narrowed to ten cubits. The chamfered sculpture is one which represents some historical events. Hence also the chamfered sculptures surrounding the Sea rightly denote examples of former times which we must judiciously ponder to see by what works the saints have pleased God from the beginning, and with what obstinacy the reprobate persisted in crimes and with what wickedness they perished because of their crimes; how in the beginning of the nascent world Cain was condemned for the malice of envy, and Abel crowned for

[209]

---

[7] cf. Gn 9:18–19

[8] cf. Lk 3:23

the merit of his uprightness;[9] how Lamech was cursed for his adultery and murder, and Enoch[10] brought back to paradise for the grace of his piety;[11] how after the flood Ham was detested by his father for his lack of filial piety, and the peoples of Shem and Japheth were granted a perpetual blessing for their reverential obedience;[12] how Abraham was made the heir of the divine promise in recognition of his faith[13] while the numerous other nations were left in their ancestral unbelief; how when the Lord came in the flesh, Judaea was rejected for the offence of unbelief and the gentiles brought back to salvation by the grace of faith, and other things of the kind in both testaments, which, when judiciously and devoutly contemplated, are of great profit to all earnest-minded people. And that perhaps is the reason why two orders of chamfered sculptures were made in the Bronze Sea, namely, that those who were immersed in the font of baptism may listen carefully to the stories of both testaments; and the reason why they were ten cubits in circumference was that they might strive to imitate whomsoever they perceived in these stories to have been committed to carrying out the heavenly commands and totally rapt up in the pursuit of heavenly rewards. Moreover, the text which follows is apt:

19.5 ⟨7:25⟩ **And it stood upon twelve oxen, of which three looked towards the north and three towards the west and three towards the south and three towards the east.** For that by the oxen we must understand the apostles and evangelists and indeed all the ministers of the word, we know from the teaching of the Apostle. Expounding the commandment of the law in which it is said: *You shall not muzzle the mouth of the ox that treads out the grain,* he says, *Is it for oxen that God is concerned? Does he not speak entirely for our sake? This is written for our sakes; because the one who ploughs should plough in hope, and the one who threshes in hope of receiving fruit.*[14] The   *[210]* twelve oxen, then, are the twelve apostles and all who take their place in ruling the holy Church in Christ. These oxen indeed carry

---

[9] cf. Gn 4:3–16
[10] cf. Gn 5:24
[11] cf. Gn 4:19–24
[12] cf. Gn 9:20–27
[13] cf. Gn 15:4–6
[14] 1 Co 9:9–10

the Sea which was laid upon them when the apostles and the apostles' successors do their utmost to carry out with prompt devotedness the task imposed on them of preaching the Gospel, and three of them face towards the north, and three towards the west, three towards the south, and three towards the east when they preach belief in the holy Trinity to all quarters of the four-cornered universe. For the apostles too, who by this mystery were twelve, i.e. four times three, were chosen to proclaim belief in and acknowledgment of the holy Trinity throughout the four corners of the world and baptize all nations in the name of the Father and of the Son and of the Holy Spirit.[15] May we, then, in this present life, be quite easily able to see, or learn of by reading, the words, deeds and sufferings of these apostles and their successors, even though we cannot yet see what a glorious reward awaits them in the world to come. Hence it is aptly added:

19.6 ⟨7:25⟩ **And their hindquarters were all hidden inside.** For all the hindquarters of the oxen are hidden inside because the reward which is bestowed upon holy teachers for eternity is already determined in the decision of the interior arbiter, but to us who are still outside, it remains entirely hidden. But then it cannot in any way be hidden because everyone who receives the bath of baptism for salvation must also have faith, hope and love, and without these three virtues no one can any longer do anything to enter into life. Hence it is rightly added:

19.7 ⟨7:26⟩ **And the laver was a handbreadth thick.** The thickness of the laver in the Sea is the solidity of virtue in baptism; and this thickness is a handbreadth when the reception of baptism is enhanced by the strength of faith, hope and love. Nor is there any way of showing that it profits the recipients unless the solid assurance of these virtues together with good works strengthens the recipients' spirit. The bath of baptism is received and celebrated after the example of the Lord's passion and resurrection from the dead according to what the Apostle says in his exposition, *that all of us who have been baptized in Christ Jesus were baptized in his death. For we were buried together with him by baptism into death, so that, as Christ was raised from the dead by the glory of the Father, we too might walk in newness of life. For if we have been planted together in the likeness of his death, we shall be so too in*

---

[15] cf. Mt 28:19

the likeness of his resurrection.[16] And this too is indicated typologi-
[211] cally in the making of the Bronze Sea when immediately afterwards
it is added:

19.8 ⟨7:26⟩ **And its brim was like the brim of a cup, or the leaf
of a crisped lily.** For by the brim of a cup is expressed the taste
of the Lord's passion, and by the leaf of a crisped lily the glory
of his resurrection is openly revealed.[17] For that the chalice of his
passion is indicated in the cup is attested by the Lord himself who, on
approaching his passion, prayed to his Father saying, *Father, if you are
willing, remove this chalice from me;*[18] but the lily, which, in addition
to the grace of a most pleasant fragrance, displayed a white colour
on the outside and a golden colour on the inside, appositely suggests
the glory of the resurrection of him who both showed the disciples
the immortality of his body externally and at the same time taught
that there was within him a soul shining with divine light. One can
also fittingly take the crisped lily as the *mediator of God and men*[19]
himself crowned with glory and honour[20] on account of the suffering
of his death, who prior to his passion was still, as it were, a closed
lily and shone forth as an illustrious human being by reason of his
signs and wonders, but after his resurrection and ascension showed
himself to the citizens of the heavenly homeland as a crisped lily
because he showed forth in his assumed humanity the power of the
divine glory which he had with the Father before the world was.[21]
Hence too in the Canticle of Love he wanted to be designated by
the word 'lily' saying, *I am the flower of the fields and the lily of the
valleys.*[22] So the reason why the brim of the Sea in which the priests
were washed was, so to speak, the brim of the cup and the leaf of
the crisped lily, was that the laver of salvation whereby we are made
members of the High Priest purifies us in the faith of his most august
passion from the stain of all our sins and admits us thus purified to
the vision of his eternal glory. It is doubtless in this laver that both

---

[16] Rm 6:3–5
[17] *infra* 24.4 **
[18] Lk 22:42
[19] 1 Tm 2:5
[20] cf. Ps 8:6
[21] cf. Jn 17:5
[22] Sg 2:1

groups of people, i.e. circumcised and uncircumcised, are made one in the Lord through faith, hope and love, as he himself attests while preaching specifically to the circumcised, when, among other things, he says, *And other sheep I have that are not of this fold; them also I must bring. And they shall hear my voice, and there shall be one fold and one shepherd.* [23] And this was also prefigured typologically in this Sea for it is added:

19.9 ⟨7:26⟩ **It contained two thousand bates.** For the number one thousand is customarily used in the scriptures to signify perfection, because, of course, it is the cube of the number ten. For ten times ten make a hundred. That is, this figure, though already a square, is still one-dimensional; but to have it rise up and become solid, you have to multiply a hundred by ten and it becomes a thousand, and by this number, of course, is indicated the steadfast and invincible and, so to speak, fully squared conscience of the righteous. Whichever way you turn it, a square will stand up. [24] Likewise the mind of the elect is incapable of being overturned from its stance of uprightness by any onset of temptation. A bate is a measure of the Hebrews, which they themselves call a bath, which holds three bushels; [25] the same is true of an oephi which they also call an epha, but the oephi has to do with the measurement of various grains: wheat, barley and pulse; but a bate is used for liquids: wine, oil and water. And so a bate which is a standard measure denotes the works of equity and justice in which those who are baptized for the remission of sins must be apprenticed; and the Sea held a thousand bates when the water of baptism washed the Jewish people and transported them into the heavenly kingdom; it held a thousand more when it made the multitudes of the gentiles, who had been reborn in the same font and established in the works of righteousness, sharers in the same everlasting kingdom.

19.10 True it must be noted here that there are people who think we are prohibited by God's law from carving or painting, in a church or any other place, representations of either humans or animals or objects of whatever kind, on the grounds that he has said in the Ten Commandments of the Law, *You shall not make for yourself a carved*

[212]

---

[23] Jn 10:16

[24] cf. Greg., *Hom. in Ezech.* PL 76: 1044C-D

[25] cf. Isid., *Etymol.* 16.26.12

thing, or the likeness of anything that is in heaven above, or in the earth beneath, or of those things that are in the waters under the earth.[26] But they would not think any such thing if they called to mind either the work of Solomon by which he made palm-trees and cherubim with various carvings inside the temple[27] and pomegranates and network on its pillars and also twelve oxen and chamfered sculptures on this Bronze Sea;[28] as well as that, on the supports of the lavers, as we read in what follows, he made lions and oxen, palm-trees, axles and wheels with cherubim and various kinds of paintings;[29] or, at any rate, ⟨they would not think so⟩ if they considered the works of Moses himself who at the Lord's command first of all made cherubim on the propitiatory[30] and later a brazen serpent in the desert so that by gazing at it the people might be healed of the poison of wild serpents.[31] For if it was permissible to raise up the brazen serpent on a tree that the Israelites might live by looking at it, why is it not permissible that the exaltation of the Lord our saviour on the cross whereby he conquered death be recalled to the minds of the faithful pictorially, or even his other miracles and cures whereby he wonderfully triumphed over the same author of death, since the
[213]   sight of these things often tends to elicit great compunction in the beholders and also to make available to those who are illiterate a living narrative of the story of the Lord. For in Greek too a painting is called ζωγραφία, i.e. 'living writing'. If it was permissible to make twelve bronze oxen carrying the Sea that had been laid upon them to face in threes towards the four quarters of the universe, what objection is there to depicting how the twelve apostles went and taught all nations, baptizing them in the name of the Father and of the Son and of the Holy Spirit,[32] or representing this in a living scripture, as it were, for all to see. If it was not against this law for chamfered sculptures of ten cubits to be made in this Sea all the way round, how could it be considered contrary to the law if we carve or paint in pictures the stories of the saints and martyrs of Christ,

---

[26] Ex 20:4

[27] cf. 3 K 6:29

[28] cf. 3 K 7:15–25

[29] cf. 3 K 7:29

[30] cf. Ex 25:17–20

[31] cf. Nb 21:8–9

[32] cf. Mt 28:19

seeing that we have merited through the protection of the divine law
to attain the glory of everlasting reward?

19.11   Yet if we examine the words of the law more carefully, perhaps it will become apparent that it is not making images of objects
or animals that is forbidden. Rather what is entirely prohibited is
making them for the purpose of idolatry. Finally, as the Lord on
the holy mountain was about to say, *You shall not make for yourself a
carved thing,* he first said, *You shall not have strange gods before me,*
and then added, *You shall not make for yourself a carved thing, or the
likeness of anything that is in heaven above, or in the earth beneath, or
of those things that are in the waters under the earth;* and he concluded
as follows: *You shall not adore them or serve them.*[33] These words are
a clear statement that what people are forbidden to make are those
images which the impious are in the habit of making for the worship
of alien gods and which the gentiles have misguidedly devised for
service and worship. Moreover, in my opinion, no prescription of the
divine law forbids making these; otherwise even the Lord in response
to the Pharisees who put him to the test on rendering to Caesar the
coin of tribute on which, they said, Caesar's name and image was
depicted, would certainly not have said the words, *Render to Caesar
what are Caesar's and to God what are God's.*[34]   Rather he would
have corrected their error and said, 'It is not lawful for you in the
minting of your gold to make the image of Caesar because the divine
law forbids such sculpture.' For when the coin of tribute was shown
him, it would have been an opportunity for him to say so, if Caesar's
image had been misrepresented upon it for purposes of idolatry and
not rather in token of his royal authority.

20. THE TEN BASES AND LAVERS

20.1   ⟨7:27⟩ **And he made ten bases of bronze; every base was four
cubits in length, and four cubits in breadth, and three cubits high.**
Variously and in many ways the selfsame mysteries of our salvation
are prefigured. For the same apostles and apostolic men who were
denoted by the oxen supporting the Sea are also denoted by the bases
which had been fitted for the purpose of supporting the wash-basins,

[214]

---

[33] Ex 20:3–5
[34] Mt 22:21

just as the wash-basins themselves were a type of the same spiritual laver as was also typified by the Sea.[1] For as the Chronicles relate, they washed in them all the things they were going to offer as a holocaust. Now the holocaust of the Lord can be taken in general to mean the whole multitude of the elect that, according to the voice of the precursor, was baptized by him with the Holy Spirit and fire.[2] Therefore, just as the priests who were washed in the Sea represent those who through baptism are made sharers in the high priesthood which is in the Lord Jesus Christ, so also do the holocausts most aptly present an image of these same people when through the washing of baptism they are filled with the grace of the Holy Spirit. For the victim is washed in the laver when the water of baptism is poured over one of the faithful; but it is offered as a holocaust when through the imposition of the hands of the bishop one receives the gift of the Holy Spirit. Although the evangelist Philip was preaching and baptizing in Samaria,[3] what was he washing but the victims of the Lord in the laver of the temple? However, because the Holy Spirit had not yet begun to come down upon any of them, but they had been baptized only in the name of the Lord Jesus,[4] like washed victims they had not yet got as far as the fire of the most sacred altar. But when Peter and John were sent there and began to lay hands on the baptized, and these began to receive the Holy Spirit and speak in tongues,[5] then the victims reached the fire of the altar to become a holocaust which means in Latin 'whole-burnt', because, that is, the grace of the Holy Spirit filling their conscience made them begin to glow with divine love.[6] But the fact that ten bases were made to support the lavers could thus be interpreted mystically to mean that the ministers of the laver of life call those whom they immerse to the joys of eternal beatitude, which is usually represented figuratively by the number ten.[7]

20.2   But because these lavers are written about individually in what

---

[1] cf. 2 Paralip 4:6
[2] cf. Mt 3:11
[3] cf. Ac 8:4–5
[4] cf. Ac 8:14–17
[5] cf. Ac 19:6
[6] cf. Greg., *Hom. in Ezech. PL* 76:1037C
[7] *infra* 20.11 **

follows,[8] i.e. because five of them were placed on the right-hand side of the temple and five on the left, we must rather consider in them the mysteries of the number five. For the laver bases were placed on both sides of the temple to show that the grace of the sacred font was to be made accessible to both peoples of God, and there are five on *[215]* either side to show, just as we have already said in the explanation of the Sea which is five cubits deep,[9] that in a typological sense all their transgressions committed through the five bodily senses are to be remitted to the faithful through the laver of baptism. Therefore, as in one Sea laid upon twelve oxen is expressed the unity of baptism which was to be preached by the apostles all over the world, so also by means of two sets of lavers is mystically shown that the gentiles were to be assembled with Judaea into the one fellowship of the faith through the water of baptism. For although the victims were washed in twin lavers, some on the right of the court, some on the left, they were nevertheless consumed by the one altar fire so as to become a holocaust; because whether one receives the bath on the side of the circumcised or of the uncircumcised, all are sanctified by the one Spirit so that they can become children of God. This indeed is why the Apostle says, *But you have received the spirit of adoption, enabling us to cry out, 'Abba, Father!'*[10] 'You have received,' he says, 'one Spirit by which you may all become children of adoption, the Spirit, namely, whereby we cry, "Abba, Father"; "Abba", that is, we who come from the Hebrews to the faith, "Father", we who come from the gentiles, with different languages, it is true, according to the diversity of nations, but invoking one and the same God the Father because of the gift of the one Spirit.

20.3 However, that each of the bases was four cubits long and four cubits wide and three cubits high is easy to understand. For the length refers to the patience of long endurance, the width to the expansiveness of love, the height to the hope of heavenly reward.[11] Moreover, there are four principal virtues on which the rest of the structure of the virtues depends, namely, prudence, fortitude, temperance and justice, and the reason why the length and width of the

---

[8] cf. 3 K 7:39

[9] *supra* 19.2 **

[10] Rm 8:15

[11] cf. Greg., *Hom. in Ezech.* PL 76:957C, 963A–B, 1034C, 1047D–1048B, 1067D–1069B

bases was four cubits was that holy preachers, whether they endure outwardly the adversities of the world, the lengthy exile and present labours, or expand their heart in the love of their creator and of their neighbours with inward joy, always pay attention to the virtues, i.e. by prudently distinguishing between good things and evil, courageously bearing adversity, restraining their heart from its desire of pleasures, and maintaining uprightness in their manner of acting. But the height of the bases is three cubits when, through the exercise of the virtues which they practise by the endurance of evils and the love of what is good, they strive with sustained resolve to attain the vision of the holy Trinity.

20.4 ⟨7:28⟩ **And the work of the bases was itself embossed, and** *[216]* **there were carvings between the joinings.** This seems to mean the joinings which linked the boards of the lavers, that is to say, in order to form one base of four or five boards. What kind of carvings they had between these joinings, i.e. on their sides fore and aft, on the right and on the left and also on top, is made clear by the addition of the next verse:

20.5 ⟨7:29⟩ **And between the little crowns and the ledges were lions and oxen and cherubim, and in the joinings likewise above.** Hence the surface of the bases was not level at any point, but whichever side one turned, it was carved with mystical figures because the minds of the saints, indeed their whole way of life, displays the charm of the virtues in everything, and not an empty or idle hour passes them by that they fail to have time for good works or words or, at all events, thoughts. They have little crowns carved upon them when they yearn with untiring longing for entry into eternal life; they have ledges when, amid their longing for the life of heaven which is above, they never undo the bonds of fraternal intercourse which is at hand; they have lions between the little crowns and ledges when they so raise their minds to hope for heavenly things and so open them out to the love of their neighbour that they do not shirk the zealous exercise of stern denunciation upon any sinners entrusted to their charge.[12] In addition to lions they have oxen when they employ even the invective of correction in a spirit of meekness, when, in the heat of rebuking, they never cease to have the cloven hoof of prudent

---

[12] cf. Greg., *Hom. in Ezech. PL* 76:1054B–D

action and word, or to roll the words of divine reading around in the mouth as if ruminating upon them. Finally, blessed Stephen, the one who was the pillar par excellence of the Lord's temple, seemed to show the fierce teeth and claws of a lion when he said to his persecutors, *You stiff-necked people, uncircumcised in heart and ears, you always resist the Holy Spirit; which of the prophets did your fathers not persecute?* and so forth;[13] but in saying this he showed how much of the compassion of bovine meekness he nurtured in his heart within, when, for these same persecutors raging to kill him, he knelt and said, *Lord lay not this sin to their charge.*[14] But because we can have neither hope of things eternal in heaven, nor love of neighbour on earth, nor the fervour of trenchant zeal, nor the gentleness of compassionate restraint, without knowledge of the holy scriptures, it is aptly remarked that, after crowns and ledges, after lions and oxen, cherubim too were carved. For it is generally accepted that cherubim *[217]* are a type of sacred scripture, whether because the two cherubim on the propitiatory of the ark[15] were fashioned as a figure of the two testaments which sing in harmony of Christ, or because the name itself means 'much knowledge'.[16] However, the more assiduously one gives oneself to reading the pages of God's word, the more necessary it is that in all one's acts or judgements one should fear the scrutiny of the inner witness or judge, lest, either by overstepping the bounds of justice in reproving sinners or by pardoning without the restraint of proper discretion, one should incur the wrath of the just judge. *For he who adds knowledge adds labour also.*[17] Hence here too after the carvings of the cherubim it is suitably added:

20.6 ⟨7:29⟩ **And above the lions and oxen, as it were, bands of bronze hanging down.** For bands hang down above the lions and oxen when holy teachers, both in the severity and rigour with which they judge sinners and in the gentleness and leniency with which they pardon penitents, fear the judgement of their creator, lest perhaps by unjustly binding or loosing anyone they deserve to be bound themselves by him whose judgement cannot err.

---

[13] Ac 7:51–52
[14] Ac 7:60
[15] Ex 25:17–20
[16] cf. Jer., *Nom. Hebr. CCSL* 72:74, 20
[17] Qo 1:18

20.7 ⟨7:30⟩ **And every base had four wheels and axle-trees of bronze; and at the four sides were shoulderings under the laver which were cast and facing one another.** The four wheels are the four books of the Gospels which are very aptly compared to wheels because, just as the wheel's whirling motion can travel with the greatest rapidity wherever it is steered, so with the Lord's help through the instrumentality of the apostles the word of the Gospel filled all the regions of the world in a short space; as the wheel raises from the earth the chariot laid upon it, and when raised carries it where the driver steers it, so the preaching of the Gospel lifts up the minds of the elect from earthly cravings to heavenly desires and, having lifted them up, guides them to progress in good works or to the ministry of preaching, in whichever direction the helping grace of the Spirit wills. For since, in the text that follows, it says that *they were the kind of wheels usually designed for a chariot,*[18] and moreover, we read of the saints, *The chariot of God is attended by ten thousands; thousands of them that rejoice,*[19] why, then, is it that the wheels of the bases are compared to the wheels of chariots, unless it is that one and the same word of the Gospel makes some of those whom it teaches chariots of God, and others pillars of God's temple? For all who were sent far and wide as teachers to spread the word of the Gospel in the world were *[218]* chariots of God, and very fast ones too, because, as they sped about from one place to the next, they brought God into the hearts of believers; but the ones who remain in one place announce the word of salvation to their neighbours and light their way to the laver of life, which is received either in baptism or in the compunction of tears, these are, as it were, the bases of the temple which support the lavers for washing the sacrificial victims. For they exercise the ministry of salvation on the faithful in their charge in such a way that they do not undergo the hardships of travelling rather long distances to get new communities of people. So the reason why the wheels of the bases are like chariot wheels is that the same books of the Gospels, which send these teachers to preach the true faith to the ignorant, order them to stay among those who have already been taught and imbued with the heavenly mysteries in order to strengthen them further.[20] The four wheels supported the base of the laver when the Gospels ordered

---

[18] 3 K 7:33
[19] Ps 67:18
[20] cf. Rufinus, *Hist. Eccl.* 2:23 *GCS* 9.165.1314

James the brother of the Lord to reside in Jerusalem to strengthen the Church; wheels like these were placed under God's chariots and prepared them to run when these Gospels wished Paul and Barnabas to travel around everywhere to preach to the gentiles.[21] The wheels placed underneath to support the laver of the temple raised the base from the ground when the blessed Pope Gregory recently in our own day ruled the Roman Church on the strength of the words of the Gospel; the same wheels fitted beneath God's chariot transported people long distances when the most venerable Fathers, Augustine, Paulinus and the rest of their companions backed by the oracular sayings of the Gospel came to Britain at his command and a short while ago entrusted the word of God to unbelievers.

20.8   If then the bases of the lavers are the holy teachers who administer to us the bath of life, and the four wheels of the bases are the four books of the Gospels, what else are the axle-trees of the wheels that support the bases but the very hearts of these teachers which, while earnestly intent on the precepts of the Gospel, raise them above their craving for what is lowest, just as the axles inserted into the wheels raise the base up further from the ground. Furthermore the shoulderings which were put outside the wheels to prevent them from slipping off the axles, are the proclamations of the prophets which lend weight to the evangelical and apostolic writing lest it should be doubted by any of its readers. And the apostle Peter speaking of the Lord says, *And we have the prophetic word made more sure, to which you will do well to pay attention,*[22] and moreover, all the evangelists and apostles were in the habit of mentioning the law and [219]   the prophets in what they wrote. Finally, Mark begins as follows: *The beginning of the Gospel of Jesus Christ, the Son of God, as it is written in the prophet Isaiah;*[23] and Matthew: *Now all this was done that the scriptures of the prophets might be fulfilled.*[24] It is well said that the shoulderings which had been placed under the laver on four sides were facing each other because, of course, all prophetical scripture is consistent inasmuch as it is the product of the one Spirit of God. Now for each of the four bases there were four shoulderings, that is,

---

[21] cf. Ac 13:2ff

[22] 2 P 1:19

[23] Mk 1:1–2

[24] Mt 26:56

corresponding to the number of wheels, not because there are only four prophetical books but because in everything that the prophets and Moses said they bore testimony to the sayings of the four evangelists so that as a result of the harmony of both, our common faith and love of Christ might strengthen the hearts of all.

20.9 ⟨7:31⟩ **Also the mouth of the laver inside was on the top of the capital. And what appeared outside measured one cubit all round; and it was one cubit and a half in all.** The mouth of the laver was one cubit on account of the unity of confession and faith because we are all baptized in the confession of the Father and of the Son and of the Holy Spirit, as the Apostle says, *One Lord, one faith, one baptism, one God and Father of all.*[25] And the mouth itself was at the top of the capital to teach that the way to the heavenly kingdom had been opened to us through baptism. But the actual laver was a cubit and a half in size, in view, no doubt, of the perfection of good works and the beginning of contemplation.[26] For the whole cubit in the laver denotes the perfection of good works. And this, without any doubt, that man had of whom the Lord said to the ancient tempter, *Have you considered my servant Job, that there is none like him on the earth, a blameless and upright man, who fears God and turns away from evil?*[27] But there is the other cubit of the vision of God which to a certain degree used to be granted to believers even while they were still detained in this life; as this man Job, speaking with the Lord after defeating the adversary, says, *With the hearing of the ear I have heard you, but now my eye sees you,*[28] as the Lord appeared to Moses face to face,[29] as he appeared to Isaiah[30] seated on his royal throne with the heavenly citizens surrounding him with due praise, as he often appeared to the other prophets, as the gates of heaven opened and the glory of God was shown to blessed Stephen in the moment of his passion,[31] as the mysteries of the entrance to Paradise and the

---

[25] Ep 4:5–6

[26] cf. Greg., *Hom. in Ezech. PL* 76:1048A–B

[27] Jb 1:8

[28] Jb 42:5

[29] cf. Ex 33:11

[30] cf. Is 6:1–3

[31] cf. Ac 7:55

third heaven were disclosed to Paul;[32] but all these were on a very
modest scale in comparison with the glory which is to be revealed in   *[220]*
the world to come.[33] Therefore, after the cubit of good works, which
can be achieved in this life in the saints, begins the cubit of heavenly
contemplation which, as we well know, is finally to be achieved in the
life to come in all the elect.

20.10   This measurement of one and a half cubits applied not only
to the lavers but also to their wheels and bases. For it is written in
what follows:
⟨7:32⟩ **The height of a wheel was a cubit and a half;** and a little
further on, ⟨7:35⟩ **And on the top of the base there was a round band
of half a cubit, fashioned in such a way that the laver might be set
upon it.** For the lavers measured a cubit and a half because we are
washed by such faith in the font of life that we may merit through
works of righteousness to enter into eternal life, and that, although
we cannot be without sin while we live here, we may be able partly
to taste and love the sweetness of the life of heaven in this interim
life, but not, of course, enjoy perfect vision. The wheels too measure
a cubit and a half because the text of the Gospel reading shows how
those who wish to be perfect ought to live, and holds out to us the
hope of eternal reward in the present time, but promises us that the
actual quality of that reward is to be revealed to us and bestowed upon
us in the time to come. And the bases themselves were a cubit and a
half in size at the top where they held the lavers because the teachers
themselves and chief ministers were eminent for their perfection in
this life by reason of the work of administering the bath of salvation,
but they partially enjoyed the light of contemplation and so they say,
For *our knowledge is imperfect and our prophesying is imperfect; but
once perfection comes, all imperfect things will disappear.*[34]

20.11   ⟨7:37–38⟩ **After this manner he made the ten bases of the one
casting and measure, and of similar carving; he also made ten lavers
of bronze.** Why ten bases were made and the same number of lavers
laid upon them has already been told.[35] But the reason why there

---

[32] cf. 2 Co 12:4
[33] cf. 1 P 5:1
[34] 1 Co 13:9–10
[35] *supra* 20.1 **

was one casting and measure and a similar carving for all the bases
or lavers was not to signify that the merits of all teachers could be
equal, but rather that there is one Gospel faith in which they are
instructed, one sacrament of baptism by which they are washed, one
same Spirit by which all the elect are consecrated, even though they
have different gifts in this Spirit who distributes them to each one as
he wishes.[36]

20.12 ⟨7:38⟩ **One laver contained forty bates.** The number forty   *[221]*
conventionally typifies great perfection because, of course, four tens
make forty; now there are ten precepts whereby our whole code of
conduct is laid down in the divine law, but four books of the Gospels
in which entry into our heavenly homeland was opened to us through
the plan of the Lord's incarnation. And because all who are involved
in the ministry of sacred baptism must, together with the faith and
mysteries of the Gospel, show the fruits of upright conduct, it is fitting
that each of the lavers in which the holocausts were washed should
hold forty bates.

20.13   But as regards what follows, i.e.
⟨7:38⟩ **and was of four cubits,** whether it means in height or in
width, the meaning of the mystery is obvious. For one laver was
four cubits either because of the four books of the holy Gospel in
which the form of baptism is laid down for us, or else on account
of the four cardinal virtues in which each believer, if he is not to
be a believer in vain, must be formed, or, at all events, on account
of the four quarters of the world in which the bath of salvation is
administered, as the psalmist says, *Whom he has redeemed from the
hand of the enemy, and gathered out of the countries, from the rising
and from the setting of the sun, from the north, and from the sea.*[37] But
as regards what he said above: *and together it was one cubit and a
half,*[38] (and not even there did he add whether he meant height or
width), it seems that he wished it to be understood that the bottom
of the laver itself was this width. Unless I am mistaken, this can very
easily be inferred from the measurement of the base on which each
laver was placed which is described thus: *And on the top of the base*

---

[36]   cf. Rm 12:6; 1 Co 12:11
[37]   Ps 106:2–3
[38]   3 K 7:31

there was a round band of half a cubit, fashioned in such a way that the laver might be set upon it.[39] So the width of the lavers at the bottom was a cubit and a half, but the actual capacity of the lavers was four cubits. But whether he means in height or width or both is for the one who knows to say.

20.14 ⟨7:39⟩ **And he set the ten bases, five on the right side of the temple, and five on the left.** He is speaking of the right and left side of the temple not on the inside of the temple itself but in front of the temple, i.e. towards the east in the inner court which was properly called that of the priests. Now he set five on the right side of the temple because of the Jews who in ancient times used to make use of the sun of justice on account of the teaching of the law, and five at the left because of us who for a long time clung blind-heartedly to the slavery of him[40] who says, *I will set my throne in the north,*[41] which, to put it in plain language, means 'I desire to abide in those hearts which I consider to be strangers to the light of truth and the flame of divine love.'

[222] **20.15** ⟨7:39⟩ **And the sea he set on the right side of the temple facing the east southwards.** And this was placed in the same court to the east. His words, *on the right side of the temple,* he repeats when he says, *southwards.* For those who entered the court from the east had first to turn southwards where the Sea stood in the very corner ready for the priests to wash, then as they proceeded inside they were met by lavers placed on either side for washing the victims; inside these was a bronze dais five cubits long and five cubits wide and three cubits high, on which Solomon stood when dedicating the temple;[42] then as they proceeded further they came to the altar of holocaust facing the south side of the court, then the temple porticoes or vestibule in which were bronze pillars around the door of the temple. Therefore, the fact that he placed the Sea at the right side of the temple signifies that it is through the bath of baptism we must reach the kingdom of heaven which is properly represented by the term 'right hand'. For

---

[39] 3 K 7:35
[40] cf. Greg., *Hom. in Ezech. PL* 76:1008D–1009A
[41] Is 14:13
[42] cf. 3 K 8:63–64

He who believes and is baptized shall be saved.[43] For where right as well as left hand are taken in the positive sense, they indicate either Judaea and the gentiles, as we have said above in the explanation of the bases, or the present and future life of the Church, or the happy and sad things of the world, or something of the sort, but where the right hand by itself is used in the positive sense, it more frequently stands for eternal joys. But the fact that he made the Sea face eastwards has virtually the same significance, namely, that the splendour of internal glory is revealed to us through the bath of the holy font; the fact that it was at the south side of the court signifies that the faithful are wont to be kindled into a blazing fire of genuine love through the reception of the Holy Spirit; for in the scriptures the heat of the noonday sun customarily meant the ardour of love and the light of the Holy Spirit, through whom this love is poured forth[44] in the hearts of the elect.

21. THAT THE VESSELS OF THE LORD WERE MADE IN THE JORDAN REGION

21.1 ⟨7:45–46⟩ **All the vessels that Hiram made for king Solomon for the house of the Lord were of fine bronze. In the plains of the Jordan the king cast them, in the clay ground.** It is appropriate that the vessels of the Lord's house were cast in the region of the Jordan, namely, in the river in which our Lord deigned to be baptized[1] and by his immersion in the waves of its waters changed the element for us into a bath for sins, because every baptism of the faithful in which they are consecrated to the Lord is celebrated on the model of his baptism whereby he himself sanctified the waters. It is proper that the vessels of the Lord's house should have been made in the country of the Jordan, for there is no other way for us to become vessels of election and mercy than by looking to his baptism which *[223]* he underwent in that river and making sure that we too are washed in that life-giving river. However, it must be noted that he says these vessels were made not only in the country around the Jordan but also in its plains to signify the multiplication of the faithful which was to take place not only in Judaea but also in the wide world of

---

[43] Mk 16:16
[44] cf. Rm 5:5
[1] cf. Mk 1:9

all the nations in fulfilment of the prophecy which says, *The plains and everything in them will rejoice.*[2] A similar idea is expressed by the same psalmist regarding the mysteries of the Lord's incarnation, when, speaking in the person of those who came to the faith after the mysteries of this incarnation had been fulfilled, he says, *Behold we have heard of it in Ephrata; we have found it in the fields of the wood.*[3] For we have heard in Ephrata, i.e. in Bethlehem, the mysteries of the Lord inasmuch as we have read the promise of the patriarch David,[4] who was from the same city, that Christ would come in the flesh from the fruit of its womb; we have found it in the fields of the wood inasmuch as we ourselves have come to know, we ourselves have seen, we ourselves have been made partakers in what was revealed throughout the universe in the wide world of the gentiles. Therefore, the king cast the vessels of the Lord's house in the plains of the Jordan, inasmuch as the Lord filled it with the baptism of salvation that he might make from it vessels of mercy throughout the whole wide world.

21.2   As for the clay ground of which the moulds for casting the vessels of the Lord's house were made, how better can we understand it than as the sacred scripture from which we receive the norm of good living? For, as it were, the clay hardened in the fire shows what shape, size and kind the vessels of the Lord ought to be when scripture shows us the norm of righteousness which we are to follow, and sets before us for our imitation in all things the examples of the saints who persevered unflinchingly in the fire of tribulation. If we desire to be chosen and precious vessels in the Lord's house ⟨let us remember that⟩ bronze too when melted by fire goes into moulds of clay so that the vessel may be made suitable for the heavenly services, when, after being humbled for our good and softened by the flame, whether of divine love or of human adversity as well, we ourselves enter on the path of our predecessors by performing good works that we may attain our predecessors' rewards by running well. For it is not always necessary for us to be issued with rules of good behaviour, but when our work has been performed, the goodly palm of a blessed reward is to be hoped for, because, for that matter, vessels were not always

---

[2] Ps 95:12
[3] Ps 131:6
[4] cf. Ps 131:11

kept enclosed in clay moulds either; instead, when they had reached the point of completion, the casings of the moulds were broken and *[224]* they were brought out into the light and each of them arranged in its proper place in the temple of the Lord. Now we say this, not because the works of the saints are ever to perish, but because by the time they receive the crown of righteousness which they have earned by their good works, there should be an end to every obligation of performing toilsome works. After all who is to suffer martyrdom for belief in Christ in that life, where, having repulsed their adversaries, all the elect rejoice in the presence of Christ? Who is to bury the dead there where it is the land of the living only? Who is to console the mourner where *God will wipe away every tear from the eyes of the saints* ?[5] Who is to open his house to the stranger and the guest where all the elect together have their dwelling from God, *a house not made with hands, eternal in the heavens* ?[6] Who is to bring me bread when I am hungry or drink when I am thirsty[7] where the *Lord feeds me and I shall want for nothing?*[8] So when the vessels' moulds which were once necessary, are broken, the vessels themselves shine resplendent in the house of the Lord inasmuch as, when, at the end of the world, there is an end not only to the persecutions which of their own accord they suffer for righteousness' sake but also to the laborious works of righteousness at which the elect toil and sweat for eternal blessedness, they will rejoice in the vision of the creator in the glory of the immortality they have obtained.

22. THE TWO ALTARS

22.1 ⟨7:48⟩ **And Solomon made all the vessels for the house of the Lord: the altar of gold, and the table of gold upon which the loaves of proposition**[1] **should be set.** The altar of gold signifies the hearts of the perfect righteous ones, shining with the light of inner love and

---

[5] Rv 7:17

[6] 2 Co 5:1

[7] cf. Bede, *In Luc.* 3 *CCSL* 120:226, 2370–2372; Greg., *Hom. in Ezech. PL* 76:954A

[8] Ps 22:1

[1] The 'loaves of proposition', more commonly known to readers of the English Bible as the 'showbread', are variously termed in Hebrew: (1) הפנים לחם (*leḥem happānîm*) 'the bread of the face (of God)' or 'the bread of the Presence' because it was placed before the presence of Yahweh; and (2) המערכת לחם (*leḥem hamma'areket*) 'the showbread' or lit. 'bread of disposition or arrangement or setting forth in order'. It

chastity, whose sublimity even the position of this altar is well fitted to express. For it stood in front of the door of the Holy of Holies, as we can plainly read in the construction of the tabernacle.[2] That is to say, on this altar it was not the blood of the victims nor the libations that were burned but only the incense, the smoke of which went up and covered the ark and oracle and filled it with a sweet fragrance.[3] In this was portrayed a figure of the saints, who, disregarding their cravings for temporal things and concentrating all their efforts on the quest for heavenly things, stand, as it were, inside close by the oracle; nor are they far removed from the veil by which the temple and the Holy of Holies are separated from each other, inasmuch as they dwell on earth in body only, but in their inner selves spend their whole life in heaven, and the smoke of the incense rises from this altar inside the Holy of Holies where the ark is hidden, when the saints' prayers, prompted by the flame of love, reach all the way to heaven *where Christ is seated on the right hand of God.*[4] For on this altar it is not [225] the blood of victims that is burned but only the incense, inasmuch as such men have not the works of flesh and blood to immolate on the altar of their heart and sacrifice to the Lord, but offer him only the votive offerings of tears and prayer in token of their desire for the heavenly kingdom.

---

is this second expression that is reflected in Septuagint Greek 'ἄρτοι τῆς προσφορᾶς (*ártoi tês prosphorâs*) 'loaves of presenting or offering or setting forth' which in turn is reflected in the Vulgate version *panes propositionis*, the word *propositio* meaning, *inter alia*, 'a setting forth for public view.' The Douay's 'loaves of proposition' was a close imitation of the Vulgate. I have retained it both because Bede was using the Vulgate and because the specific plural 'loaves' sits better with Bede's text than the generic singular 'bread'. These loaves (cf. de Vaux (1973), 422) consisted of 12 cakes of pure wheaten flour laid out in two rows on a table in front of the Holy of Holies each week on the eve of the sabbath; after a week they were replaced by fresh ones and eaten by the priests but were not placed on the altar. (cf. Lv 24:5–9). They were a pledge of the Covenant between the 12 tribes of Israel and Yahweh; however, incense was placed beside each row as a 'memorial-offering' and was burnt (on the altar of perfumes) when the loaves were changed. The presence of incense on the table with them shows they were something like a sacrificial offering. We know from some magical texts and ritual tablets that in the Ancient East it was a very common custom to set bread before the deity.

[2] cf. Ex 30:1–6; 40:5, 24

[3] cf. Greg., *Hom. in Ezech. PL* 76:1070A–D

[4] Col 3:1

22.2 However, because no one suddenly reaches the top, but climbs to the point of heavenly desire by conscientiously sacrificing carnal pleasures, scripture in its mystical construction of the Lord's house has not neglected to include the figure of those who struggle to cauterize with the flame of heavenly fear the carnal passions still in them *which war against the soul,*[5] in order to be able to rise to higher things as a result of eradicating these from heart or body and offer to God the incense of spiritual prayers and compunction. For another altar was made to offer victims on, a much bigger one it is true, but as inferior in situation and quality of metal as it was superior in size. For one thing it was made of bronze, and for another it was sited before the temple doors. On it were depicted figuratively those, doubtless, who serve the Lord with a devotedness of such a kind that their flesh still lusts against the spirit and their spirit against the flesh,[6] and that they are wont to say, 'we serve the law of God in our minds but the law of sin in our flesh'.[7] And when by frequent fasting they strive to curb the promptings of the flesh, restrain the dissoluteness of wanton behaviour, and rise upwards in a manner worthy of God by prayer, vigils and alms and the other fruits of the Spirit to the peace which comes from abstinence, what else are they doing but immolating to him the victim of their devotedness, in fulfilment of the saying of the Apostle which beseeches us through God's mercy to offer up our bodies as a living sacrifice, consecrated to God and worthy of his acceptance?[8] And since they are aflame with the fervour of spiritual love but have not yet emerged triumphant from the conquest of their carnal passions, the altar of holocaust, though it has the sacred fire from heaven, has the appearance of bronze and not of gold. But because the carnal in the holy Church outnumber the spiritual, and those who hold the allurements of vice in check by practising restraint outnumber those who have won the battle with their vices and laid them to rest and have the joy of being secure in the attainment of virtue, the altar of holocaust was quite rightly said to be much bigger than the a altar of incense.[9] For it is written of it in the Book of Paralipomenon: *He also made an altar of bronze twenty cubits long,*

---

[5] 1 P 2:11
[6] cf. Ga 5:17
[7] cf. Rm 7:25
[8] cf. Rm 12:1
[9] cf. Greg., *Hom. in Ezech. PL* 76:983A–B

of bronze twenty cubits long, and twenty cubits broad, and ten cubits
[226]   *high.*[10] And indeed Moses made the altar of incense in the desert
a cubit in length and another in breadth and two in height.[11] How big
Solomon made this, the scripture does not say. All it says is that
he made an altar of gold. It is evident, however, that he could not
make it as big as that of the holocaust, for if it had been made twenty
cubits in length and breadth, it would have stretched the entire width
of the temple. Therefore, to the extent that the altar of holocaust
was sited in a more public place than that of the incense, and was
less imposing by reason of the kind of offering made upon it and the
baseness of the metal it was made of, to that extent it excelled in the
amount and number of victims offered on it, doubtless because the
number of those to whom it is said: *If you wish to enter into life, keep
the commandments,*[12] is far greater than the number of those who
are attracted by the call, *If you wish to be perfect, go, sell what you
have,* and so forth.[13]

22.3   Nevertheless the dimensions of this altar are not without a
mystical explanation. For it is twenty cubits long and as many cubits
broad and ten cubits high, a number which, in fact, we have spoken
of above in our commentary on the temple and its vestibule.[14] But it
must also be briefly added here that if the altar of holocaust is a type
of those in the Church who seek to consecrate their body and soul to
God through the fire of his love, the perseverance of these others in
good works is represented by the length of the altar, the generosity
of their love of God and their neighbour by its width, their hope in
expecting the vision of God by its height. The fact that the length
and breadth of the altar was twenty cubits denotes how truly great
was the perfection of this untiring patience and genuine love which
is given us through the observance of both testaments. For four fives
make twenty; now the books of the Mosaic law are five and those
of the liberty of the Gospel are four; when we attain to the spiritual
understanding and observance of the law by the light of the grace of
the Gospel, we truly complete the number twenty; and this number

---

[10] 2 Paralip 4:1
[11] Ex 30:1–2
[12] Mt 19:17
[13] Mt 19:21
[14] *supra* 6.1 **

the hearts of the elect, with the guidance of both testaments and the help of the selfsame author of both testaments, remain steadfast in the performance of good works even in persecution, and display the cheerfulness of love even towards those who persecute them. The number ten conventionally designates the hope of heavenly rewards, as the Lord affirms when he declares that those who worked in the vineyard of the great householder are to be remunerated;[15] and this

[227]   number is rightly used as a figure of the eternal reward in which our nature is eternally united to God in vision, because in this number the divine and human nature together are mystically expressed. For God is a trinity, but man is made up of the number seven, i.e. of four on account of his body which comprises four elements, and of three on account of the threefold interior difference which holy scripture shows us when it bids us love God with our whole heart, our whole soul and our whole strength.[16] This is why in the decalogue of the Law there are three commandments which spur us on to the service of divine love, and seven which enjoin love of the neighbour.[17] Hence those who observe the decalogue by loving God and the neighbour, deservedly receive the reward of this observance in the simultaneous vision of God and the neighbour; and those who in this life love both the neighbour whom they see and God whom they do not see,[18] will in the next life *see* both God, *the king in his beauty,*[19] and the neighbour glorified and beautified in God. And that is why the altar, which was made as a figure of the elect with a view to signifying their everlasting life, was ten cubits high. But after it was said that Solomon had made the altar of gold, it was immediately added:

22.4 ⟨7:48⟩ **And the table of gold upon which the loaves of proposition should be set.** The table of gold is the sacred scripture, rich in the light of spiritual understanding of which the psalmist says to the Lord, *You have prepared a table before me in the presence of those who afflict me.*[20] For lest our enemies who afflict us should divert us into the path of error, our creator has prepared us a table of knowledge

---

[15]   cf. Mt 20:1–2
[16]   cf. Mk 12:30
[17]   cf. Ex 20:2–17
[18]   cf. 1 Jn 4:20
[19]   Is 33:17
[20]   Ps 22:5

to strengthen us in the true faith.[21] For the loaves of proposition are the holy teachers whose salutary words or works, anyone who searches in the divine pages will find proposed to us as a model for living. Hence it was prescribed in Exodus that twelve of these loaves be made,[22] i.e. on account of the twelve apostles through whose ministry both the New Testament scripture was written and the mysteries of the Old Testament revealed by the condescension of the Lord. That is to say, this number designates not only these apostles but also all who, by proclaiming the word, administer the nourishment of life to the faithful, because, of course, all follow the same norm of teaching as the apostles received from the Lord. Moreover, we read of these loaves in Exodus[23] that they had to be changed every sabbath, and new ones set out in place of the old on the Lord's table, and it was laid down that they must be produced in the one size and *[228]* from the same kind of flour. From all this the mystical meaning of the internal refreshment shines forth clearer than the light of day. For new loaves are substituted after the old ones are removed when, after some of the faithful teachers are taken from this life, the holy Church ordains others in their place, and this only on the sabbath day, because everyone who fights the good fight, finishes the course, and keeps the faith, will at the time of his death enter into the rest of a blessed eternity.[24] The reason why the loaves were always made the one size and not of different flour was that it was one and the same form of truth and faith which the apostles first put before their audience and which thereafter their successors and all faithful teachers to the end of the world never failed to preach to the churches of Christ throughout the world.

23. THE TEN GOLD TABLES OF THE LORD'S HOUSE

23.1 Regarding what we read in the Chronicles that Solomon made *ten tables and set them in the temple, five on the right side, and five on the left; also a hundred bowls of gold,*[1] one cannot believe that these tables were made both to carry the loaves of proposition and

---

[21] cf. Greg., *Hom. in Ezech. PL* 76:1045A–1046C

[22] cf. Ex 25:30; Lv 24:5–6; cf. also Bede *De tab.* 1,7 *CCSL* 119A: 1, 851–878

[23] cf. Lv 24:8

[24] cf. 2 Tm 4:6–7

[1] 2 Paralip 4:8

the vessels of the Lord, i.e. the bowls which the scripture also reports were made, and the censers, the thuribles, the little mortars and other things which we read about in what follows.[2] For as regards what is introduced a little further on in the same Book of Chronicles, *and Solomon made all the vessels for the house of God, and the altar of bronze, and the tables upon which the loaves of proposition lay,*[3] either he used the plural number for the singular according to the very common practice in the scriptures, as in Joshua son of Nun: *But the children of Israel transgressed the commandments, and took for their own use some of the devoted things,*[4] when it was Achan alone and not several of the sons of Israel who did so; or at least because the loaves of proposition used to be baked before the sabbath so that they could be placed on the table of proposition first thing on the sabbath, it could be that the newly baked loaves were put out on the tables directly and were kept covered there that night until the old loaves were removed at dawn; then these were put out while still warm. But these ten tables do not differ in figurative meaning from this table of proposition. For just as one table laden with twelve loaves symbolizes the unity of the whole scripture, a harmony guaranteed by the authority of the apostles, so, not implausibly, do the ten golden tables figuratively proclaim the words of the divine law and the prophets, which either offer us the refreshment of God's word like the loaves of proposition, or else put before us the examples, glory and miracles of the faithful vessels of the Lord which, so to speak, are placed upon them.

23.2   And rightly are there two sets of five tables, not only because   *[229]* the lawgiver wrote five volumes, but also because the whole set of Old Testament books comprises the five ages of the world. The number of five tables is doubled and five are placed on the right and five on the left when, after the incarnation of the Lord, either the same scripture is entrusted to both peoples of God, i.e. Jews and gentiles, or is shown as full of Gospel figures which it was once felt must only be taken literally by the ancient people of God.[5] For when, as we read in the

---

[2] cf. 2 Paralip 4:22

[3] 2 Paralip 4:19

[4] Jos 7:1

[5] cf. Greg., *Hom. in Ezech. PL* 76:969C–970A

holy scripture, for instance, of Abel[6] being crowned with martyrdom, or of Enoch taken up out of the world, or how Noah was miraculously saved when the world was perishing,[7] or how, with the wiping out of the wicked men, Lot's hospitality had been rewarded from on high,[8] how in return for his obedience Abraham was appointed father of all nations,[9] how after being sold as a slave, Joseph was immediately exalted in return for his chastity and innocence;[10] when we take these and countless things of the kind as models of virtue, what is it that holds them up before us but the five golden tables or vessels of the Lord or the loaves of proposition still on the left side of the temple? For, taken in the historical sense, the divine scriptures open to us both the door to proper living and the eternal rewards to be hoped for from the Lord. But when on a deeper understanding of these things, we catch echoes of either the plan of the Lord's incarnation or some other mysteries of the holy Church, we find, as it were, the five other tables for carrying the vessels of election and the food of the life of the spirit on the right side of the temple, because we recognize that these very same words of sacred history, which are to us an entirely new lightning-flash of heavenly wisdom, open the door to a new understanding of the old. In which figure also, of course, are included the five lampstands made in the temple.

24. THE TEN LAMPSTANDS

24.1   For when scripture said that king Solomon had made the table on which the loaves of proposition were placed, it later added: 'of gold' and said,

⟨7:49⟩ **And the golden lampstands, five on the right hand, and five on the left, over against the oracle, of pure gold, and the flowers like lilies, and the lamps over them of gold.**   For just as the tables are rightly used as a type of holy scripture because they both minister righteousness to those hungering for the bread of the word and bear the vessels of the heavenly ministry, i.e. they propose for our imitation the actions of the righteous, so also by these lampstands the words of

---

[6] cf. Gn 4:8; 5:24; Sir 44:16ff

[7] cf. Gn 6:18

[8] cf. Gn 19:1ff

[9] cf. Gn 17:4–6; 22:16–18

[10] cf. Gn 37:28ff

God are symbolized, i.e. because they give the light of wisdom to the erring. That is why the psalmist says, *A lamp to my feet,* and so forth;[1] *[230]* that too is why Solomon says, *Because the commandment is a lamp, and the law a light.*[2] Moreover, the reason why five lampstands were placed on the right and five on the left is quite easy to see from our discussion of the tables. But when he said five on the right and five on the left, he added fittingly: *over against the oracle.* For the oracle where the ark was, as has often been said, stands for the way to the heavenly homeland *where Christ is seated at the right hand of God,*[3] privy, that is, to his Father's secrets. And the temple lampstands of gold were placed opposite the oracle because the words of God always have in view the abode of the heavenly city that they may instil into our hearts the knowledge and desire of it, and fire those who take their fleshly origin from the earth to long for and to merit a place of everlasting abode in heaven.

24.2 On the other hand, regarding what is said about the lampstands,

⟨7:49⟩ **five on the right hand and five on the left,** there are people who think this is to be taken in the sense that five were on the right of the lampstand which Moses made in the desert[4] and five on the left of it, but that both were to the south where the one lampstand which Moses made was supposed to stand. But they should apply the same interpretation to the ten tables, all of which, it is true, were positioned on the north side but five on the right of the Mosaic table and five on the left. Yet if you consider the words of sacred scripture where it says, *And the golden lampstands five on the right hand, and five on the left over against the oracle,*[5] it is obvious, unless I am mistaken, that both sets of five alike faced the oracle inasmuch as they were placed opposite it, close to either side of the temple. For if all the lampstands had been placed right along the south side of the temple they would not be said to have been placed opposite the oracle but rather, facing north or facing the tables, if the tables too stood there, as was said in Exodus of the one lampstand, which without any doubt

---

[1] Ps 118:105
[2] Pr 6:23
[3] Col 3:1
[4] cf. Ex 26:35
[5] 3 K 7:49

stood on the south side: *He set the lampstand also in the tabernacle of the testimony, facing the table on the south side;*[6] and also in the Book of Numbers: *When you set up the seven lamps facing in that direction they shall give light in front of the lampstand.*[7] The reason why there were both lampstands and tables on either side of the temple was that divine scripture was composed for the enlightenment and refreshment of both peoples of God, and in prosperity and adversity, on sad occasions and joyous, it has been wont to refresh us lest we   *[231]* weaken, and to enlighten us lest we remain blind; furthermore, it sets forth for the benefit of both peoples the vessels of mercy laid upon it, i.e. the deeds of the righteous recounted in it, that we too may be encouraged in the performance of righteous actions.

24.3   But if you ask what the difference in type is between the lampstands and their lamps, we can rightly take the lamps to mean saintly people into whom the oil of the Holy Spirit has been poured so that they not only are themselves aflame with the fire of love in their hearts, but show the light of knowledge to their neighbour in their words; the lampstands, on the other hand, which hold these lamps aloft so as to be seen in the Church, we can take to mean the sacred scripture which, when read, shows us the virtues and teaching of the saints. And this interpretation is supported by the Lord's word in which he says of John, *He was a burning and a shining light.*[8] Thus we can also very fittingly say that the lamps are the words of God according to the saying of the psalmist which we have already quoted earlier, *Your word, O Lord, is a lamp to my feet.*[9] On the other hand, the lampstand for these lamps are all the saints who with ever humble intent subject their hearts and bodies to the burden of the Lord's commandments. For whoever takes care not to follow his own will in anything but is attentive in everything to what holy scripture may say, and strives to be submissive to its commandments and listen to its promises, is like the golden lampstand of God's house which holds its lamps, because he strives to make the chaste members of his body and the chaste thoughts of his mind submissive to God's commands, and in order to do this with the same fixed resolve as the lampstand,

---

[6] Ex 40:22
[7] Nb 8:2
[8] Jn 5:35
[9] Ps 118:105

it is necessary to keep this firmly raised up to heavenly things to preserve the lamps placed upon it not only from falling but also from
any change in condition. But after saying, *And the golden lampstands,
five on the right hand, and five on the left, over against the oracle, of
pure gold,* he added:

24.4 ⟨7:49⟩ **And the flowers like lilies, and the lamps over them of
gold.** Taken literally it seems that the top portion of the lampstands
was bent backwards like a lily which, as we read, is what happened
in the tabernacle lampstand, for both its centre stem and the reeds
which protruded from it are described as having had a great many
lilies with cups and little globes.[10] Now the flowers of the lily, as has
often been said, represent the beauty of the evergreen land of the
living[11] of which blessed Peter says that we have been regenerated
by the Lord *unto a lively hope, unto an inheritance, incorruptible,
undefiled and unfading, reserved in heaven.*[12] And well have golden
lily flowers been wrought in the lampstand of God's house because   *[232]*
divine scripture is habitually urging us to spurn temporal joys and seek
the good things of our heavenly homeland, and just as the lampstand
holds the lily flowers aloft and has golden lamps on top, so all the
elect who are contained in this sacred scripture are shown to have
had their thoughts elevated to the things above and to have sought
and received the good things of heaven from the Lord. We have
treated rather fully of the table and lampstand and the two altars and
the vessels of the Lord's house in the books which we have written
on the construction of the tabernacle and of the priestly vestments.[13]
So if anyone desires information on these matters according to our
capacity to interpret them which draws upon the tradition of the
Fathers, let him consult that work.

25. THE DOOR HINGES AND THE COMPLETION OF THE
    HOUSE OF THE LORD

25.1 There follows the verse:
⟨7:50⟩ **And the hinges for the doors of the inner house of the Holy**

---

[10] cf. Ex 25:31–36
[11] *supra* 19.8 **
[12] I P 1:3–4
[13] cf. Bede, *De tab.* 1, 633.977; 2, 1361; 3, 1240

of Holies and for the doors of the house of the temple were of gold. If
the doors of the inner house of the Holy of Holies are the ministries
of angels which unlock the entrance to celestial life for us when we
have left the body, and the doors of the house of the temple are the
holy teachers and priests who throw open to us the first thresholds of
the present Church by teaching, baptizing and communicating to us
the mysteries of the Lord's body and blood, what are the hinges of
both doors but the minds and hearts of these angels or saints by which
they cleave fixedly to the contemplation and love of their creator so
that those who never turn their gaze from the will of him whom they
serve may thereby properly fulfil the ministry entrusted to them? For
the gates are opened and closed at the appropriate time, but at no
time do they leave their hinges, because both angels and holy people,
whether they receive the faithful and the elect in this life of faith, or
in the other life of vision, keep their minds ever firmly rooted in love.
These hinges are well said to have been made of gold for this reason,
namely, either because of the merit of their own glory or because of
the love they have for God.

**25.2　⟨7:51⟩ And Solomon finished all the work that he did in the
house of the Lord.** Solomon finishes the work he did in the house
of the Lord when on the last day our peaceable king glorifies all the
elect with the immortality of the resurrection. Otherwise as long as
the condition of this world continues, Solomon does indeed do the
work of the Lord's house but does not yet finish it, because the Lord
inspires and helps the hearts of the elect to perform good works, but
does not grant immunity from sin to anyone who is only a sojourner
in this life, for he reserves this gift for the blessedness of the life to
[233]　come. But he finishes all the work of his temple and renders it fit
for dedication when he takes to his eternal kingdom his elect who
have been transferred from this life. And this is well illustrated both
in the fact that the temple was built in seven years but finished and
dedicated in the eighth. For the whole of this time runs through
a cycle of seven days; the eighth is the day of judgement and the
resurrection to come from which the sixth and eleventh psalms get
their title.[1] And indeed what follows aptly applies to this time:

25.3　⟨7:51⟩ And he brought in the things that David his father had

---

[1] cf. Ps 6:1; Ps 11:1

dedicated, the silver and the gold, and the vessels, and stored them in the treasuries of the house of the Lord. For silver applies to the clarity of eloquence, gold to the brilliance of wisdom, and vessels generally to rational creatures; and David, Solomon's father, sanctifies the silver when God the Father strengthens speakers with the grace of the Holy Spirit to speak the word of the Gospel; he sanctifies the gold when he enlightens those endowed with natural ability by filling them with his Spirit in order to contemplate the wonders in his law; he sanctifies the vessels too when, having bestowed the grace of this Spirit on all the Church's children in general that they may love the gifts of eternal salvation, he fires them with a desire for them. This silver, this gold, these consecrated vessels Solomon brings into the temple, when, after the universal judgement is over, our Lord brings into the joy of his heavenly kingdom all the elect, i.e. the company both of teachers and the rest of the faithful, and he lays up the various kinds of vessels, silver or gold, in the treasuries of the Lord's house when he hides in the covert of his countenance away from the bustle of human beings those who have merited to enjoy the abundance of his sweetness.[2] It is fitting that the treasuries in which the vessels of election should be hidden are many, whereas the house of the Lord in which these treasuries were is one; for on the one hand, the Church in which all the elect are contained is one, however much they may differ in merits, and on the other hand, the heavenly homeland promised to all the elect is one and not of different kinds, even though, just as *star differs from star in glory, so also is the resurrection of the dead.*[3] Both of these things the Lord, the very judge and distributor of rewards, has shown in one sentence when he says, *In my Father's house there are many mansions.*[4] The reason why Solomon made one house of the Lord but furnished it with many treasuries to accommodate the vessels of various kinds, though it was sanctified with only one blessing, was that there is one

[234] house of the Father not made with hands that will last eternally in heaven,[5] but many mansions in it to receive all who fear him, and the Lord blesses those that love him, both little ones and great.[6] Amen.

---

2 cf. Ps 30:20–21
3 1 Co 15:41–42
4 Jn 14:2
5 cf. 2 Co 5:1
6 cf. Ps 113:21(13)

SELECT BIBLIOGRAPHY

PRIMARY SOURCES

Aldhelm, *De virginitate, (prosa)*, ed. R. Ehwald, *MGH AA* 15 (Berlin, 1919); tr. M. Lapidge and M. Herren, in *Aldhelm: The prose Works*, (Cambridge and Totowa, N.J., 1979).

Augustine, *De civitate Dei*, ed. B. Dombart and A. Kalb, *CCSL* 47–8 (Turnhout, 1955); same ed. with tr. by G. E. McCracken, W. M. Green, D. S. Wiesen, P. Levine, E. M. Sanford, and W. C. Greene, *LCL*, 7 vols. (London and Cambridge, Mass., 1957–72); also ed. E. Hoffmann, *CSEL* 40, 2 vols. (Vienna, 1899–1900); tr. H. Bettenson (*Penguin Classics*, Harmondsworth, 1972); also tr. M. Dods, *NPNF*, 1st ser., 2 (Buffalo, 1887; reprinted Grand Rapids, 1956); D. B. Zema , G. G. Walsh, G. Monahan, and D. J. Honan, *FOTC* 8, 14, and 24 (New York, 1950–4).

————, *Enarrationes in psalmos*, ed. D. E. Dekkers and J. Fraipont, *CCSL*, 38–40 (Turnhout, 1956); tr. A. C. Coxe (New York, 1888, repr. Grand Rapids, 1950).

Bede, *De schematibus et tropis*, ed. C. B. Kendall, *CCSL*, 123A (Turnhout, 1975); tr. G. H. Tannenhaus in *Readings in Medieval Rhetoric*, ed. J. M. Miller, M. H. Frosser, T. W. Benson (Bloomington and London, 1973) 96–122.

————, *De tabernaculo*, ed. D. Hurst, *CCSL*, 119A (Turnhout, 1969). tr. A. G. Holder, *Translated Texts for Historians Series*, (Liverpool University Press, 1994).

————, *De templo*, ed. D. Hurst, *CCSL,* 119A (Turnhout, 1969).

————, *De temporum ratione*, ed. C. W. Jones and T. Mommsen, *CCSL*, 123B (Turnhout, 1977).

————, *Historia ecclesiastica gentis Anglorum*, ed. and tr. B. Colgrave and R. A. B. Mynors (Oxford, 1969).

————, *The Ecclesiastical History of the English People. The Greater Chronicle. Bede's Letter to Egbert*, ed. J. McClure and R. Collins (Oxford, 1994).

————, *Historia abbatum,* ed. C. Plummer, *Ven. Baedae opera historica,* 1; tr. D. H. Farmer in *The Age of Bede* (Harmondsworth, 1983).

————, *Homiliae euangelii,* ed. D. Hurst,, *CCSL,* 122 (Turnhout, 1965); tr. L. T. Martin, and D. Hurst, 2 vols. *Cistercian Studies Series,* 110–11 (Kalamazoo, 1991).

————, *In Esram et Neemiam,* ed. D. Hurst *CCSL,* 119A (Turnhout, 1969).

————, *In Lucam,* ed. D. Hurst *CCSL,* 120 (Turnhout, 1960).

Biblia Sacra iuxta uulgatam uersionem, ed. R. Weber, 2 vols. (Stuttgart, 1969; 2nd ed., 1975)

Cassiodorus, *Expositio in Psalmos,* ed. M. Adriaen, *CCSL,* 97–98.

————, *Institutiones,* ed. R. A. B. Mynors (Oxford, 1937); tr. L. W. Jones, *An Introduction to Divine and Human Readings* (New York, 1946).

Eddius Stephanus, *The Life of Bishop Wilfrid,* ed. B. Colgrave (Cambridge, 1927).

Eusebius/Rufinus, *Historia Ecclesiastica,* ed. in *GCS* 9.

Gildas, *The Ruin of Britain and Other Works,* ed. M. Winterbottom (London and Chichester, 1978).

Gregory the Great, *Homiliae in Euangelia,* ed. in *PL* 76; tr. D. Hurst *Cistercian Studies Series* 123; (Kalamazoo, 1990).

————, *Homiliae in Ezechielem,* ed. in *PL* 76; ed. M. Adriaen, *CCSL,* 142 (Turnhout, 1971); ed. with French tr.) C. Morel, *SC* 327, 352, 360 (Paris, 1986–90); tr. T. Gray, *The Homilies of Gregory the Great on the Book of the Prophet Ezekiel* (Etna, Calif., 1990).

————, *Regulae pastoralis liber,* ed. C. Morel, *SC* 381–2 (Paris 1992); tr. H. Davis, *Gregory the Great. Pastoral Care* (Westminster, Md., 1950).

Isidore, *Etymologiae,* ed. W. M. Lindsay *Scriptorum classicorum bibliotheca Oxoniensis,* (Oxford, 1911).

Jerome, *de Situ Locorum,* ed. in *PL* 23.

————*de nominibus hebraicis,* ed. P. de Lagarde, *CCSL,* 72 (Turnhout, 1959).

Josephus, *Antiquitates Iudaicae,* Greek text edited and translated by H. St. J. Thackeray, in *LCL,* 6 vols. (London and New York, 1926); Latin translation of Bks 1–5 ed. F. Blatt in *The Latin Josephus (Acta Jutlandica)* 30, (Copenhagen, 1958).

Libri Carolini: ed. in *MGH, Concilia 2, Supplementum.*

Origen, *Homilies on Leviticus 1–16*, tr. G. W. Barkley (Washington 1990).
Vita Ceolfridi, ed. C. Plummer in *Ven. Baedae opera historica*, 1, 388–404 (Oxford 1896); tr. D. Whitelock in *English Historical Documents*, 1 (London and New York 1955, 2nd ed. 1979).
Virgil, *Aeneid*, ed. T. E. Page (London, 1894; St Martin's Press, New York, 1955).

SECONDARY WORKS

Alexander, J. J. G. (1978), *Insular Manuscripts: 6th to the 9th Century* (London, 1978).
Amos, T. L. (1987), 'Monks and Pastoral Care in the Early Middle Ages', in *Religion, Culture, and Society in the early Middle Ages: Studies in Honor of Richard E. Sullivan*, ed. T. F. X. Noble and J. J. Contreni (*Studies in Medieval Culture* 23; Kalamazoo, 1987), 165–80.
Bailey, R. N. (1983), 'Bede's Text of Cassiodorus' Commentary on the Psalms', in *Journal of Theological Studies* n.s. 34 (1983), 189–93.
————, (1991), 'St Wilfrid, Ripon and Hexham' in *Studies in Insular Art and Archaeology*, ed. C. Karkov and R. Farrell, *American Early Medieval Studies*, 1, (1991), 3–25.
Barrows, M. P. L. (1963), 'Bede's *Allegorical Exposition of the Canticle of Canticles:* A Study in Early Medieval Allegorical Exegesis', unpublished Ph.D. dissertation, University of California at Berkeley, 1963.
Berschin, W. (1989), '*Opus deliberatum ac perfectum:* why did the Venerable Bede write a second prose life of Cuthbert?', in *St Cuthbert, His Cult and His Community to AD1200*, ed. G. Bonner, D. Rollason, C. Stancliffe (Woodbridge, 1989) 95–102.
Beumer, J. (1953), 'Das Kirchenbild in den Schriftkommentaren Bedas', in *Scholastik*, XXVIII (1953), 50–51.
Blair, J. and Sharpe R., eds. (1992), *Pastoral Care Before the Parish, (Studies in the Early History of Britain,)* (Leicester, 1992).
Bolton, W. F. (1963), 'An Aspect of Bede's Later Knowledge of Greek', in *Classical Review*, 13 (1963), 17–18.
Bonner, G. (1966), *Saint Bede in the Tradition of Western Apocalyptic Commentary*, Jarrow Lecture, 1966).
————, ed. (1976), *Famulus Christi: Essays in Commemoration*

of the Thirteenth Centenary of the Birth of the Venerable Bede, (London, 1976).

————, *et. al.* ed. (1989) *St. Cuthbert, his Cult and Community to AD1200,* (London, 1989).

Brown, G. H. (1987), *Bede the Venerable (Twayne's English Authors Series* 443, (Boston, 1987).

Bruce-Mitford, R. L. S. (1967), *The Art of the Codex Amiatinus* (Jarrow Lecture, 1967). Reprinted in *Journal of the British Archaeological Association,* 3rd ser. 32 (1969), 1–25.

Burrows, J. A. (1988), *The Ages of Man: A Study in Medieval Writing and Thought,* (Oxford, 1988).

Cahn, W. (1994), 'Architecture and exegesis: Richard of St Victor's *Ezekiel* commentary and its illustrations', in *Art Bulletin,* 76, (1994), 53–68.

Campbell, J. (1966), 'Bede' in *Latin Historians,* ed. T. A. Dorey (London, 1966), 159–90. Reprinted in *Essays in Anglo-Saxon History,* (London, 1986), 1–27; cf. also 29–49.

————, (1971), 'The First Century of Christianity in England', in *Ampleforth Journal,* 76 (1971), 12–29. Reprinted in his *Essays in Anglo-Saxon History,* 47–67.

————, (1973) 'Observations on the Conversion of England: A Brief Commemorative Review Article', *Ampleforth Journal,* 78 (1973), 2, 12–26. Reprinted in his *Essays in Anglo-Saxon History,* 69–84.

————, (1979), *Bede's* Reges *and* Principes (Jarrow Lecture, 1979). Reprinted in his *Essays in Anglo-Saxon History,* (London, 1986), 85–98.

————, (1982), *The Anglo-Saxons,* (Oxford, 1982).

————, (1986), *Essays in Anglo-Saxon History,* (London, 1986).

Capelle, P. (1936), 'Le rôle théologique de Bède le Vénérable', in *Studia Anselmiana,* 6 (1936), 1–40.

Carroll, Sr. M. T. A. (1946), *The Venerable Bede: His Spiritual Teachings (Catholic University of America Studies in Mediaeval History* n.s. 9; Washington, D.C., 1946).

Charles-Edwards, T. M. (1983), 'Bede, the Irish and the Britons', in *Celtica,* 15 (1983), 41–52.

Colgrave, B. (1958), *The Venerable Bede and his Times* (Jarrow Lecture, 1958).

————, and Mynors, R. A. B., ed. (1969) & tr. *Historia Ecclesiastica Gentis Anglorum,* (Oxford, 1969).

Connolly, S. (1995), 'The power motif and the use of Scripture in Cogitosus' *Vita Brigitae*', in *Aquitaine and Ireland in the Middle Ages*, ed. J.-M. Picard (Dublin, 1995), 207–220.

Corsano, K. (1987), 'The first quire of the Codex Amiatinus and the *Institutiones* of Cassiodorus', in *Scriptorium* 41, (1987), 3–34.

Cowdrey, H. E. J. (1984), 'Bede and the "English People" ', in *Journal of Religious History*, 11 (1981), 501–23. Reprinted in his *Popes, Monks and Crusaders* (London, 1984), No.3.

Crépin, A. (1976), 'Bede and the Vernacular', in *Famulus Christi*, ed. G. Bonner, 170–193.

Daniélou, J. (1940), *From Shadows to Reality: Studies in the Biblical Typology of the Fathers* (tr. from *Sacramentum Futuri*, Paris, 1940; London 1960).

————, (1957), *The Angels and Their Mission*, tr. D. Heimann (Westminster, Md., 1957; reprinted 1987).

Davidse, J. (1976), *Beda Venerabilis' interpretatie van de historische werkelijkheid*, (Groningen, 1976). (cf. Schoebe, G., below).

————, (1983) 'The Sense of History in the works of the Venerable Bede', in *Studi Medievali*, 23 (1983) 647–95.

de Lubac, H. (1959–1964), *Exégèse médiévale: Les quatre sens de l'Écriture*, 2 vols. in 4 parts, (Paris, 1959–1964).

de Margerie, B. (1980–), Introduction à l'histoire de l'exégèse, 4 vols. to date, (Paris 1980–). Deshman, R. (1986), 'The imagery of the living *Ecclesia* of the English monastic reform', in P. Szarmach ed., *Sources of Anglo-Saxon culture*, (Kalamazoo, 1986), 261–82.

de Vaux, R. (1973), *Ancient Israel, Its Life and Institutions*, (London, 1973).

Douglas, I. M. ((1976), 'Bede's *De templo* and the Commentary on Samuel and Kings by Claudius of Turin', in *Famulus Christi* (London, 1976), 325–33.

Emmerson, R. and B. McGinn, ed., (1992), *The Apocalypse in the Middle Ages*, (Ithaca and London, 1992).

Farr, C. A. (1989), *Lection and Interpretation* = the Liturgical and Exegetical Background of the Illustrations in the Book of Kells. (Unpublished Ph.D. dissertation, University of Texas at Austin, 1989).

Farrell, R. T., ed. (1976), *Bede and Anglo-Saxon England: Papers in honour of the 1300th anniversary of the birth of Bede, given at*

Cornell University in 1973 and 1974, in British Archaeological Reports 46 (Oxford, 1976).

Ferber, S. (1976), 'The Temple of Solomon in Early Christian and Byzantine Art', in *The Temple of Solomon: Archaeological Fact and Medieval Tradition in Christian, Islamic and Jewish Art*, ed. Joseph Gutmann (Missoula, 1976).

Fischer, B. (1962), 'Codex Amiatinus und Cassiodor', in *Biblische Zeitschrift*, n.f. 6 (1962), 57–79.

Fisher, J. D. C. (1965), *Christian Initiation: Baptism in the Medieval West (Alcuin Club Collections* 47; London, 1965).

Foot, S. (1992), ' "By Water in the Spirit": The Administration of Baptism in Early Anglo-Saxon England', in Blair and Sharpe (1992), 171–92.

———, (1989), 'The Parochial Ministry in Early Anglo-Saxon England: The Role of Monastic Communities', in *The Ministry: Clerical and Lay*, ed. W. J. Sheils and D. Wood (*Studies in Church History* 26; Oxford and Cambridge, Mass., 1989), 43–54.

Fry, D. K. (1979), 'The Art of Bede: Edwin's Council', in *Saints, Scholars, and Heroes*, ed. M. H. King and W. M. Stevens (Collegeville MN, 1979), 191–207.

Gibson, M. (1993), 'The Place of the *Glossa ordinaria* in Medieval Exegesis', in *Ad Litteram: Authoritative Texts and Their Medieval Readers*, ed. K. E. Emery, Jr. and M. D. Jordan (Notre Dame, 1992), 5–27; reprinted in her *'Artes' and Bible in the Medieval West*, (Aldershot, Hants. and Brookfield, Vt., 1993).

Goffart, W. (1988), *The Narrators of Barbarian History, AD550–800*, (Princeton, 1988).

Gutmann, J. ed. (1976), *The Temple of Solomon. Archaeological fact and medieval tradition in Christian, Islamic and Jewish art*, (Missoula, Montana, 1976).

Halporn, J. W. (1980), 'Pandectes, Pandecta, and the Cassiodorian Commentary on the Psalms', in *Revue Bénédictine*, 90 (1980), 290–300.

Hamilton-Thompson, A., ed. (1935), *Bede, his Life, Times, and Writings: Essays in Commemoration of the Twelfth Centenary of his Death*, (Oxford, 1935).

Hanning, R. W. (1966), *The Vision of History in Early Britain*, (New York, 1966).

Henderson, G. (1980), *Bede and the Visual Arts* (Jarrow Lecture, 1980).

————, (1993), 'Cassiodorus and Eadfrith once again', in *The Age of Migrating Ideas* ed., R. M. Spearmann and J. Higgitt (Edinburgh, 1993), 82–91.

Holder, A. G. (1989a), 'Allegory and history in Bede's interpretation of sacred architecture', in *American Benedictine Review* 40, (1989a), 115–31.

————, (1989b), 'New Treasures and Old in Bede's *De tabernaculo* and *De templo*, in *Revue Bénédictine*, 99 (1989b), 237–249.

————, (1990), 'Bede and the tradition of patristic exegesis', in *Anglican Theological Review* 72, (1990), 399–411.

————, (1991) 'The Venerable Bede on the Mysteries of Our Salvation', in *American Benedictine Review* 42 (1991), 140–62.

Hunter Blair, P. (1959), *'Bede's Ecclesiastical History of the English Nation and its Importance Today'* (Jarrow Lecture, 1959). Reprinted in his *Anglo-Saxon Northumbria,* No. 7.

————, (1970a), *The World of Bede,* (Cambridge, 1970; reprinted London, 1970).

————, (1970b) 'The Historical Writings of Bede', in *Spoleto,* 17 (1970), 197–221. Reprinted in his *Anglo-Saxon Northumbria,* No. 10.

————, (1976a), 'From Bede to Alcuin', in *Famulus Christi,* ed. G. Bonner, (1976) 239–60. Reprinted in his *Anglo-Saxon Northumbria,* No. 12.

————, (1976b), *Northumbria in the Days of Bede,* (London, 1976).

Jenkins, C. (1935), 'Bede as Exegete and Theologian', in *Bede: His Life, Times and Writings,* ed. A. Hamilton Thompson (Oxford: Clarendon Press, 1935; reprinted 1969), 152–200.

Jeremias, J. (1969), *Jerusalem in the Time of Jesus,* (London, 1969).

Jones, C. W. (1969–70), 'Some Introductory Remarks on Bede's Commentary on Genesis', in *Sacris Erudiri* 19, (1969–70), 113–198.

Jones, P. F. (1929), *A Concordance to the Historia Ecclesiastica of Bede* (Medieval Academy of American Publication, 2; Cambridge, Mass., 1929).

Judic, B. (1985), 'La Bible miroir des pasteurs dans la *Règle pastorale* de Grégoire le Grand', in *Le monde latin antique et la Bible,* ed. J. Fontaine and C. Pietri (*Bible de tous les temps* 2; Paris, 1985), 455–73.

Kendall, C. B. (1978), 'Bede's *Historia Ecclesiastica:* the Rhetoric of faith', in *Medieval Eloquence: Studies in the Theory and Practice of Medieval Rhetoric,* ed. J. J. Murphy, (Berkeley, 1978), 145–72.

————, 'Imitation and the Venerable Bede's *Historia Ecclesiastica*', in *Saints, Scholars, and Heroes,* ed. M. H. King and W. M. Stevens (Collegeville, 1979), 161–190.

King, M. H. and W. M. Stevens (1979), *Saints, Scholars and Heroes: Studies in Medieval Culture in Honour of Charles W. Jones,* (Collegeville, 1979).

Kitson, P. (1983), 'Lapidary Traditions in Anglo-Saxon England: part II, Bede's *Explanatio Apocalypsis* and related works', in *Anglo-Saxon England,* 12 (1983), 73–123.

Krautheimer, R. (1942), *Introduction to an 'Iconography of medieval architecture',* (New York, 1969) 115–50.

Krinsky, C. (1970), 'Representations of the Temple of Jerusalem before 1500', in *Journal of the Warburg and Courtauld Institutes,* 33, 1–19.

Kühnel, B. (1986–87), 'Jewish symbolism of the Temple and the Tabernacle and Christian symbolism of the Holy Sepulchre and the heavenly Tabernacle', in *Jewish Art,* 12/13, (1986–87) 147–68.

Ladner, G. B. C. (1942), 'The symbolism of the biblical cornerstone in the medieval west', in *Medieval Studies,* 4, (1942) 43–60. Repr. G. Ladner, *Images and Ideas in the Middle Ages. Selected Studies in History and Art,* (Rome 1983) I, 171–96.

Laistner, M. L. W. (1935), 'The Library of the Venerable Bede', in *Bede, His Life, Times, and Writings,* ed. A. H. Thompson (Oxford, 1935; reprinted New York, 1966), 237–266; reprinted in *Intellectual Heritage of the Early Middle Ages,* ed. C. G. Starr (Ithaca, N.Y., 1957), 93–116.

————, (1957) 'Bede as a Classical and a Patristic Scholar', in *The Intellectual Heritage of the Early Middle Ages* (Ithaca, N.Y., 1957), 93–116.

Lapidge, M. ed. (1995), *The Jarrow Lectures,* 1 (London, 1995).

Leclercq, J. (1961), *The Love of Learning and the Desire for God,* (New York, 1961).

Leonard, W. (1952), 'The Epistle to the Hebrews', in *A Catholic Commentary on Holy Scripture,* ed. Dom Bernard Orchard *et. al.* (London, 1952).

Levison, W. (1935), 'Bede as Historian', in *Bede: His Life, Times and Writings,* ed. A. H. Thompson (Oxford, 1935) 111–151.

McClure, J. (1983), 'Bede's Old Testament Kings', *Ideal and Reality,* ed. P. Wormald, D. Bullough and R. Collins, (1983) 76–98.

————, (1984), 'Bede and the life of Ceolfrid', *Peritia* 3, (1984) 71–84.

————, (1985), 'Bede's *Notes on Genesis* and the training of the Anglo-Saxon clergy' in Walsh, K. and D. Wood eds. (1995), 17–30.

Mackay, T. W. (1979), 'Bede's Biblical Criticism: the Venerable Bede's Summary of Tyconius' *Liber regularum'*, in *Saints, Scholars, and Heroes: Studies in Medieval Culture in Honour of Charles W. Jones*, ed. M. H. King and W. M. Stevens (Collegeville, 1979) 1:209–31.

Mann, J. (1994), 'Allegorical buildings in medieval literature', *Medium Aevum* 63, (1994) 191–209.

Markus, R. A. (1970), 'Gregory the Great and a Papal Missionary Strategy', in *The mission of the Church and the Propagation of the Faith*, ed. G. J. Cuming, *Studies in Church History*, 6 (1970), 29–38. Reprinted in his *From Augustine to Gregory the Great*, No.2.

————, *Bede and the Tradition of Ecclesiastical Historiography*, (Jarrow Lecture). Reprinted in his *From Augustine to Gregory the Great*, No.2.

————, (1986), 'Pelagianism: Britain and the Continent', *Journal of Ecclesiastical History* 37 (1986), 191–204.

Martin, L. T. (1986), 'Bede's Structural use of Word-play as a Way to Teach' in *From Cloister to Classroom*, ed. E. R. Elder (Kalamazoo, 1986) 27–46.

Mayr-Harting, H. M. R. E. (1972, 3rd ed. 1991), *The Coming of Christianity to Anglo-Saxon England*, (London, 1972).

————,(1976), *The Venerable Bede, the Rule of St. Benedict, and Social Class*, (Jarrow Lecture, 1976).

Meyvaert, P. (1964), *Bede and Gregory the Great* (Jarrow Lecture, 1964). Reprinted in *Benedict, Gregory, Bede and Others*, (London, 1977), No. 8.

————, (1976) 'Bede the Scholar', in *Famulus Christi: Essays in Commemoration of the Thirteenth Centenary of the Birth of the Venerable Bede*, ed. Gerald Bonner (London, 1976), 40–69. Reprinted in *Benedict, Gregory, Bede and Others*, (London, 1977), No. 16.

————, (1979), 'Bede and the Church Paintings at Wearmouth-Jarrow', in *Anglo-Saxon England* 8 (1979), 63–77.

Nordhagen, P. J. (1977), 'The Codex Amiatinus and the Byzantine

Element', in *The Northumbrian Renaissance,* (Jarrow Lecture, 1977).

Olsen, G. W. (1982), 'Bede as Historian: The Evidence from his Observations on the Life of the First Christian Community at Jerusalem', in *Journal of Ecclesiastical History,* 33 (1982) 519–30.

Orchard, Dom B. ed. (1952), *A Catholic Commentary on Holy Scripture,* (London, 1952)

O'Reilly, J. (1992), 'St John as a figure of the contemplative life: text and image in the art of the Anglo-Saxon Benedictine reform' in N. Ramsay, M. Sparks, T. Tatton-Brown eds., *St Dunstan, His Life, Times and Cult,* (Woodbridge 1992) 165–185.

————, (1994), 'Exegesis and the Book of Kells: the Lucan genealogy', in F. O'Mahony ed., *The Book of Kells* (Aldershot 1994), 344–397. Repr. in T. Finn and V. Twomey eds., *Scriptural Interpretation in the Fathers,* (Dublin 1995), 315–355.

Ousterhout, R. (1990), 'The Temple, the Sepulchre and the Martyrion of the Saviour', in *Gesta,* 29, (1990) 44–53.

Parkes, M. (1982), *The Scriptorium of Wearmouth-Jarrow* (Jarrow Lecture, 1982).

Picard, J-M. (1984), 'Bede, Adomnaan and the writing of history', in *Peritia* 3, (1984) 50–70.

Plummer, C. ed. (1896, repr. 1946, 1956), *Epistola ad Ecgbertum,* in *Venerabilis Baedae Opera Historica (=VBOH)* (2 vols. Oxford, 1896; reprinted 1946, 1956) I. 405–23; (for tr. of 'Letter to Egbert' cf. *English Historical Documents,* Vol. 1, ed. D. Whitelock (1st ed. London,1955; 2nd ed. New York, 1979), 799–810.

————, ed. *Historia Abbatum,* in*(VBOH)* I. 364–87; for tr. cf. Webb, J. F. and Farmer, D. H. ed. & tr. *The Age of Bede,* (Penguin, 1983) 185–211.

————, ed. *Historia Ecclesiastica Gentis Anglorum* in vols. I and II. For translation cf. *supra* Colgrave, B. and Mynors, R. A. B.

Ray, R. D. (1976), 'Bede, the Exegete, as Historian', in *Famulus Christi,* (1976) 125–140.

————, (1980), 'Bede's *vera lex historiae*', in *Speculum,* 55 (1980) 1–21.

————, (1982), 'What do we know about Bede's Commentaries?', in *Recherches de Théologie ancienne et médiévale,* 49 (1982), 5–20.

————, (1985), 'Augustine's *De Consensu Evangelistarum* and the historical education of the Venerable Bede', in *Studia Patristica,*

16 (1985) 557–63.

————, (1986), 'The triumph of Greco-Roman rhetorical assumptions in pre-Carolingian historiography', in *The Inheritance of Historiography 350–900* ed. C. Holdsworth and T. P. Wiseman (Exeter, 1986) 67–84.

————, *The New Bede* (Boydell Press, in preparation).

Rosenau, H. (1979), *Vision of the Temple. The Temple of Jerusalem in Judaism and Christianity*, (London, 1979).

Roth, C. (1953), 'Jewish Antecedents of Christian Art', in *Journal of the Warburg and Courtauld Institutes*, 16 (1953).

Schoebe, G. (1965), 'Was gilt in frühen Mittelalter als geschichtliche Wirklichkeit? Ein Versuch zur "Kirchengeschichte" des Baeda Venerabilis', in *Festschrift Hermann Aubin*, ed. O. Brunner *et al.* (Wiesbaden, 1965), 625–51.

Smalley, B. (1952), *The Study of the Bible in the Middle Ages*, (Oxford, 1952).

————, Review of M. L. W. Laistner and H. H. King, *A Hand-List of Bede Manuscripts*, in *Journal of Theological Studies*, 45 (1944) 228–31.

Spicq, C. (1944), *Esquisse d'une histoire de l'exégèse latine au moyen âge* (Paris, 1944).

Stancliffe, C. (1983), 'Kings who opted out', in *Ideal and Reality*, ed. P. Wormald *et al.*, (Oxford, 1983) 59–94.

Sutcliffe, E. J. (1935), 'The Venerable Bede's Knowledge of Hebrew', in *Biblica*, 16 (1935) 301–306.

Taylor, H. M. and J. Taylor (1965), *Anglo-Saxon Architecture*, 3 vols (Cambridge, 1965).

Thacker, A. (1983), 'Bede's Ideal of Reform', *Ideal and Reality in Frankish and Anglo-Saxon Society: Studies Presented to J. M. Wallace-Hadrill*, ed. P. Wormald, D. Bullough and R. Collins (Oxford, 1983) 130–53.

————, (1992), 'Monks, preaching and pastoral care in early Anglo-Saxon England', in J. Blair and R. Sharpe (1992) 137–70.

Tugène, G. (1982), 'L'Histoire "ecclésiastique" du peuple anglais: réflexions sur le particularisme et l'universalisme chez Bède,' in *Recherches Augustiniennes*, 17 (1982) 129–72.

Verkerk, D. H. (1995), 'Exodus and Easter Vigil in the Ashburnham Pentateuch', in *Art Bulletin*, 77, 1995, 94–105.

Wallace-Hadrill, J. M. (1988), *Bede's Ecclesiastical History of the English People: A Historical Commentary*, (Oxford, 1988).

Walsh, K. and D. Wood eds. (1985), *The Bible in the Medieval World: Essays in Memory of Beryl Smalley* (Studies in Church History, Subsidia 4, Oxford, 1985).

Ward, B. (1990), *Venerable Bede, (Outstanding Christian Thinkers series)*, (London, 1990).

————, (1991), *Bede and the Psalter,* (Jarrow Lecture, 1991).

Webb, J. F. and D. H. Farmer, ed. & tr. (1983), *The Age of Bede,* (Penguin, 1983); cf. pp. 185–211 for tr. of *Historia Abbatum.*

Webster, L. and J. Backhouse eds. (1991), *The Making of England. Anglo-Saxon Art and Culture AD600–900,* (London, 1991).

Whitelock, D. (1976), 'Bede and His Teachers and Friends', in *Famulus Christi,* ed. G. Bonner (London, 1976), 19–39.

————, (1960), *After Bede,* (Jarrow Lecture, 1960).

————, ed. (1955), *English Historical Documents,* (1st ed. London, 1955; 2nd ed. New York, 1979); Vol. I contains tr. of 'Letter to Egbert' 799–810.

Willmes, A. (1962), 'Bedas Bibelauslegung', in *Archiv für Kulturgeschichte,* 44 (1962), 281–314.

Wormald, P. (1976), 'Bede and Benedict Biscop', in *Famulus Christi,* ed. G. Bonner (1976), 141–69.

————, (1983) 'Bede, the *Bretwaldas,* and the Origins of the *Gens Anglorum*', in *Ideal and Reality,* (Oxford, 1983), 99–129.

————, (1976) 'Bede, "Beowulf", and the Conversion of the Anglo-Saxon Aristocracy', in *Bede and Anglo-Saxon England,* ed. R. T. Farrell (Oxford, 1976).

————, D. Bullough and R. Collins eds. (1983), *Ideal and Reality in Frankish and Anglo-Saxon Society: studies presented to J. M. Wallace-Hadrill* (Oxford, 1983).

INDEX OF BIBLICAL QUOTATIONS AND ALLUSIONS

Genesis 1:31 .... 3.4; 6.1
2:1 .... 3.4
4:3–16 .... 19.4
4:8 .... 23.2
4:18–24 .... 19.4; 23.2
5:24 .... 19.4
6:9 .... 7.7
6:18 .... 23.2
9:18–19 .... 19.3
9:20–27 .... 19.4
15:4–6 .... 9.4
17:4–6 .... 23.2
19:1ff 23.2
22:2 .... 5.3
22:14 .... 5.3
22:16–18 .... 23.2
37:28ff 23.2
Exodus 12:2 .... 5.1
16:35 10
19:3 .... 17.4
19:6 .... 17.4
20:2–17 .... 22.3
20:3–5 .... 9.1
20:4 .... 9.10
25:8–9 .... 1.2
25:18–20 .... 13.5; 19.10
25:30 .... 22.4
25:31–36 .... 24.4
26:35 .... 24.2
30:1–2 .... 22.2
30:1–6 .... 22.1
31:18 .... 11.2
33:11 .... 20.9
37:7–9 .... 13.5

Exodus 40:5 .... 22.1
      40:22 .... 24.2
      40:24 .... 22.1
Leviticus 24:5–6 .... 22.4
      24:8 .... 22.4
Numbers 8:2 .... 24.2
      9:10–11 .... 5.2
      21:8–9 .... 19.10
Deuteronomy 2:7 10
      22:8 .... 8.4
      24:7 .... 5.1
Joshua 5:2–3 .... 11.2
      7:1 .... 23.1
3 Kings 5:1–12 .... 2.2
      5:6 .... 2.4
      5:13–14 .... 3.1
      5:14 .... 3.2
      5:15–16 .... 3.3
      5:17 .... 4.1
      5:18 .... 4.2,3
      6:1 .... 5.1
      6:2 .... 6.1
      6:3 .... 6.2
      6:4 .... 7.1
      6:5 .... 8.4
      6:5–6 .... 7.2
      6:6 .... 7.5
      6:7 .... 7.7
      6:8 .... 8.1
      6:9 .... 8.3
      6:10 .... 8.4; 5
      6:15 .... 5.1; 8.6; 9.1
      6:16 .... 9.2
      6:17 10
      6:18 .... 11.1; 2
      6:19 .... 12.1
      6:20 .... 9.2; 12.2; 3
      6:21 .... 12.4
      6:22 .... 9.1; 12.3; 5
      6:23 .... 13.1

3 Kings 6:24 . . . . 13.2
          6:25 . . . . 13.3
          6:27 . . . . 13.4
          6:28 . . . . 13.5
          6:29 . . . . 14.1,2; 19.10
          6:30 . . . . 14.3
          6:31–32 15
          6:32 . . . . 16.1
          6:33–34 . . . . 16.4
          6:35 . . . . 16.1; 8
          6:36 . . . . 17.1
          6:37–38 . . . . 18.1
          7:13–14 . . . . 18.3
          7:15 . . . . 18.4; 7
          7:15–25 . . . . 19.10
          7:16 . . . . 18.8
          7:17 . . . . 18.9,10
          7:18 . . . . 18.11,12
          7:19 . . . . 18.13
          7:20 . . . . 18.14
          7:21 . . . . 18.16
          7:23 . . . . 18.13; 19.1,2,3
          7:24 . . . . 9.4
          7:25 . . . . 9.5,6
          7:26 . . . . 9.7,8,9
          7:27 . . . . 20.1
          7:28 . . . . 20.4
          7:29 . . . . 20.5,6
          7:29–36 . . . . 19.10
          7:30 . . . . 20.7
          7:31 . . . . 20.9,13
          7:32 . . . . 20.10
          7:33 . . . . 20.7
          7:35 . . . . 20.10,12,13
          7:37–38 . . . . 20.11
          7:39 . . . . 20.2,14,15
          7:45–46 . . . . 21.1
          7:48 . . . . 22.1,4
          7:49 . . . . 24.1,2 (*bis*),4
          7:50 . . . . 25.1

3 Kings 7:51 .... 25.2,3
    8:2 .... 18.2
    8:8 15
    8:29–30 .... 9.3
    8:63–64 .... 20.15
4 Kings 1:2 .... 7.4
1 Paralipomenon 21:25–26 .... 5.5
    22:9 .... 14.3
    28:11–12 .... 8.2
    29:2 .... 4.5
2 Paralipomenon 2:2 .... 3.4
    2:17–18 .... 3.4
    2:18 .... 3.4
    3:1 .... 5.3
    3:4 .... 6.1,2; 12.5
    3:6 .... 9.1
    3:7 .... 7.6
    3:9 .... 12.4,5
    3:13 .... 13.6
    3:14 .... 16.2
    3:16 .... 18.9
    3:17 .... 18.5
    4:1 .... 22.2
    4:6 .... 19.1; 20.1
    4:8 .... 23.1
    4:9 .... 17.1
    4:19 .... 23.1
    4:22 .... 23.1
    7:10 .... 18.2
Job 1:8 .... 20.9
    6:30 .... 13.7
    27:3–4 .... 13.7
    42:5 .... 20.9
Psalms 6:1 .... 25.2
    6:1–2 .... 18.1
    8:6 .... 19.8
    11:1 .... 25.2
    16:15 10
    22:1 .... 21.2
    22:5 .... 22.4

Psalms 24:15 .... 13.7
25:7 .... 13.7
26:1 .... 16.4
26:13 .... Prol.3; 6.1
30:20–21 .... 25.3
30:21 .... 12.5
33:2 .... 14.1
33:8 .... 7.4
44:8 .... 13.1
44:10 .... 18.9
44:17 .... 18.3
56:8 .... 14.1
61:13 ....18.14
67:18 ....20.7
67:21 .... Prol.1
72:28 .... 12.4
75:3 .... 5.3
83:8 ....4.4; 18.12
90:15 .... 8.4
95:12 ....21.1
106:2–3 .... 10; 20.13
113:21(13) Prol.2; 18.14; 25.3
118:1 .... 7.7
118:103 ....13.7
118:105 ....24.1; 3
118:120 ....12.4
129:1 ....13.5
129:2 ....9.3
131:6 ....21.1
131:11 ....21.1
133:1 ....17.3
147:12–14 .... 8.4
Proverbs 6:23 ....24.1
10:7 ....Prol.1
Qoheleth 1:18 ....20.5
4:12 ....9.3
7:21 ....7.7
Song of Songs 1:3 ....13.7
2:1 ....9.8
5:14 ....14.1

Wisdom 6 : 19–21 15
Sirach 44 : 10 .... 13.7
    44 : 14 .... Prol.1
    44 : 16ff 23.2
Isaiah 2 : 2 .... 3.3; 5.3
    6 : 1–3 .... 20.9
    9 : 7 .... 2.2
    11 : 2–3 .... 18.1,10
    14 : 13 .... 20.14
    28 : 16 .... 1.1
    33 : 17 .... 12.2; 22.3
Jeremiah 19 : 14 .... 17.3
Ezekiel 8 : 16 .... 18.5
    10 : 5–8 .... 13.1
    27 : 8–9 .... 4.3
Joel 2 : 17 .... 18.5
Matthew 3 : 11 .... 20.1
    3 : 12 .... 5.5
    3 : 16 .... 16.2
    4 : 5 .... 7.2
    4 : 17 .... 18.13
    5 : 8 .... 18.14
    5 : 9 .... 5.5
    4 : 2 10
    4 : 5 .... 7.2
    5 : 6 10
    5 : 8 .... 18.14
    5 : 14 .... 5.3
    6 : 1 .... 3.1
    6 : 2–8 .... 3.1
    6 : 12 .... 16.5
    10 : 42 .... 17.6
    11 : 11 .... 8.5
    13 : 52 .... 18.8
    16 : 19 15
    16 : 24 .... 11.2
    17 : 5 .... 18.8
    19 : 17 .... 22.2
    19 : 17–18 .... 7.3
    19 : 18–19 .... 11.3

Matthew 19:21 .... 7.3; 11.3; 22.2
19:28 .... 11.3
20:1–2 .... 13.7; 22.3
20:2 .... 19.1
21:12 .... 17.3
22:21 .... 9.11
22:30 .... 7.3; 18.14
25:21 .... 9.2
26:56 .... 20.8
27:51 .... 16.2
28:19 .... 19.5; 10
28:20 .... 10; 18.7
Mark 1:1–2 .... 20.8
1:9 .... 21.1
12:30 .... 22.3
12:30–31 .... 8.4; 18.11
16:16 .... 20.15
Luke 1:5 .... 17.3
1:17 .... 8.5
3:23 .... 19.3
6:37–38 .... 16.5
10:1 .... 13.3
10:27 .... 13.2
11:3 .... 16.5
11:24–26 .... 9.2
16:9 .... 17.6
20:36 .... 18.14
20:35–36 .... 1.1
21:34 10
22:42 .... 9.8
23:45 .... 16.2
24:32 .... 16.3
John 2:14 .... 17.3
2:19 .... 1.1
2:21 .... 1.1
4:35–36 .... 5.4
5:35 .... 24.3
5:46 .... 18.8
8:2 .... 17.3
10:9 .... 6.2; 18.4

John 10:16 .... 9.8
    12:26 .... 18.14
    13:35 .... 14.3
    14:2 .... Prol.2; 18.14; 25.3
    14:6 .... 7.2; 18.4
    14:8 .... 18.1
    14:21 .... 12.4; 18.14
    16:22 .... 10; 18.14
    16:25 .... 18.14; 12.4
    17:5 .... 19.8
    19:34 .... 8.1
    21:8 .... 18.15
Acts of the Apostles 1:3–4 10
    1:15 .... 5.1; 8.2
    2:3–4 .... 8.2
    3:1–8 .... 17.3
    3:22 .... 18.8
    3:25 .... 18.8
    4:12 .... 4.1
    4:32 .... 7.3; 11.1
    6:1 .... 7.3
    7:51–52 .... 20.5
    7:55 .... 20.9
    7:60 .... 20.5
    8:4–5 .... 20.1
    8:14–17 .... 20.1
    13:2ff 20.7
    13:48 .... 3.3
    15:22–29 .... 17.7
    19:6 .... 20.1
    21:25 .... 17.7
Romans 1:17 .... 18.6
    1:28–32 .... 7.3
    5:3–4 .... 18.12
    5:5 .... 12.5; 13.7; 18.11; 20.15
    6:3–5 .... 9.7
    7:25 .... 22.2
    8:11 .... 1.1
    8:15 .... 20.2
    8:24 .... 13.8

Romans 8:39 .... 6.2
    12:1 .... 16.3; 17.4; 22.2
    12:6 ....20.12
    12:12 10
    13:10 .... 13.2
    15:4 .... Prol.1
    15:18 .... 17.5
    15:26–27 .... 17.7
1 Corinthians 1:24 ....14.1
    2:9 ....18.14
    3:1–2 ....17.5
    3:6 ....18.3
    3:11 ....4.1
    3:16 ....1.1
    6:3 ....17.8
    9:9–10 ....19.5
    10:1–2 ....9.1
    10:11 ....2.1
    11:1 ....11.1; 17.8
    12:2 ....5.5
    12:8–10 ....14.1
    12:11 ....20.12
    13:4 ....16.5
    13:9–10 .... 20.10
    15:28 ....8.2
    15:41–42 .... 25.3
2 Corinthians 2:15 ....8.7
    5:1 ....21.2; 25.3
    6:7 ....13.7; 18.5
    7:1 ....4.6
    11:1 ....11.1
    11:26ff 11.1
    11:18–28 .... 17.7
    12:2–7 ....11.1
    12:4 ....20.9
Galatians 2:9 ....18.4
    5:6 ....11.2
    5:17 ....22.2
    5:20–22 ....7.3
    5:22 ....14.1

Galatians 5:24 . . . . 12.4
         6:2 . . . . 3.4
         6:5 . . . . 3.4; 8.6
Ephesians 2:20 . . . . 1.1; 4.1
         3:19 . . . . 11.2
         4:3 . . . . 18.12
         4:5–6 . . . . 15; 20.9
         5:8 . . . . 5.5
Colossians 1:13 . . . . 3.3
         3:1 . . . . 22.1; 24.1
         3:1–2 . . . . 12.5
         3:5 . . . . 16.3
         3:11 . . . . 14.39
         3:12 . . . . 18.12
         3:12–14 . . . . 9.1; 14.2
I Thessalonians 5:14 . . . . 3.3
1 Timothy 1:5 . . . . 9.1
         2:5 . . . . 1.1; 12.5; 9.8
         3:15 . . . . 18.7
2 Timothy 4:6–7 . . . . 22.4
         4:7–8 . . . . 17.5
Hebrews 1:14 . . . . 13.6
         4:9 . . . . 3.4; 8.2
         9:1–9 . . . . 9.2
         9:6 . . . . 9.2
         11:36–38 . . . . 11.3
         11:6 . . . . 16.5
James 2:17 . . . . 11.2
         2:20 . . . . 11.2
         2:26 . . . . 16.5
         5:11 . . . . Prol.1*(bis)*
1 Peter 1:3–4 . . . . 24.4
         2:5–6 . . . . 1.1
         2:9 . . . . 17.4
         2:11 . . . . 22.2
         5:1 . . . . 20.9
2 Peter 1:19 . . . . 20.8
1 John 2:4 . . . . 8.1
         3:2 . . . . 13.1
         4:16 . . . . 12.5

1 John 4:20 .... 16.5: 22.3
     5:1 .... 16.5
Revelation 5:6 .... 18.10
     7:17 .... 21.2
    21:27 .... 7.7

INDEX OF PATRISTIC AND CLASSICAL SOURCES

Anonymus
Libri Carolini
(*MGH, Concilia 2, Supplementum*): 13.5
Bede
De tabernaculo (*CCSL* 119A):
    1, 513ff 13.1
    1, 633, 977ff 24.4
    2, 1361ff 24.4
    3, 1240ff 24.4
In Lucam (*CCSL* 120):
    3, 1897/1905 .... 13.3
    2370/2372 .... 21.2
De temporum ratione (ed. Jones):
    179:18ff 18.15
Cassiodorus
Expositio in Psalmos (*CCSL* 97–98):
    86.1 .... 17.2
Eusebius/Rufinus
Historia Ecclesiastica (*GCS* 9):
    165.13-14 .... 20.7
    169.17-21 .... 7.2
Gregory the Great
Homiliae in Ezechielem (*PL* 76):
    952D 3.4
    954A 21.2
    957C 6.1; 20.3
    963A–B 6.1; 20.3
    969C–970A 23.2
    977A 18.14
    983A–B 22.2
    992A 3.4
    1008D–1009A 20.14
    1013B 16.5
    1034C 20.3
    1034D–1048B 20.3

1037C 20.1
1044C 4.1
1044C–D 19.9
1045A–1046C 22.4
1047D–1048B 20.3
1048A–B 20.9
1054B–D 20.5
1067D–1069B 20.3
1070A–D 22.1

Homiliae in Euangelia (*PL* 76):
1139A 13.3

Isidore
Etymologiae:
16.26.12 .... 19.9
17.7.33 .... 8.3
19.22.11 .... 16.3
19.28.1–4 .... 16.3

Jerome
de Situ Locorum (*PL* 23):
884B 4.3
904C 5.5

de nominibus hebraicis (*CCSL* 72):
63.11 .... 13.1
67.13 .... 5.5
74.20 .... 20.59
83.29 .... 5.5
103.7 .... 13.1
107.25 .... 2.2
109.21 .... 3.2
119.20 .... 4.3
121.9–10 .... 5.5
138.5 .... 17.2

Josephus
Antiquitates Iudaicae in (*LCL*):
8.3.2 .... 4.6; 6.2; 8.2
8.3.9 .... 17.1

Rufinus see **Eusebius**
Virgil
Aeneid:
3.126–27 .... 4.5

TRANSLATED TEXTS FOR HISTORIANS
Published Titles

Gregory of Tours: Life of the Fathers
Translated with an introduction by EDWARD JAMES
Volume 1: 176pp., 2nd edition 1991, ISBN 0-85323-327-6

The Emperor Julian: Panegyric and Polemic
Claudius Mamertinus, John Chrysostom, Ephrem the Syrian
edited by SAMUEL N. C. LIEU
Volume 2: 153pp., 2nd edition 1989, ISBN 0-85323-376-4

Pacatus: Panegyric to the Emperor Theodosius
Translated with an introduction by C. E. V. NIXON
Volume 3: OUT OF PRINT

Gregory of Tours: Glory of the Martyrs
Translated with an introduction by RAYMOND VAN DAM
Volume 4: 150pp., 1988, ISBN 0-85323-236-9

Gregory of Tours: Glory of the Confessors
Translated with an introduction by RAYMOND VAN DAM
Volume 5: 127pp., 1988, ISBN 0-85323-226-1

The Book of Pontiffs (*Liber Pontificalis* to AD 715)
Translated with an introduction by RAYMOND DAVIS
Volume 6: 175pp., 1989, ISBN 0-85323-216-4

Chronicon Paschale 284-628 AD
Translated with notes and introduction by
MICHAEL WHITBY AND MARY WHITBY
Volume 7: 280pp., 1989, ISBN 0-85323-096-X

Iamblichus: On the Pythagorean Life
Translated with notes and introduction by GILLIAN CLARK
Volume 8: 144pp., 1989, ISBN 0-85323-326-8

Conquerors and Chroniclers of Early-Medieval Spain
Translated with notes and introduction by KENNETH BAXTER WOLF
Volume 9: 176pp., 1991, ISBN 0-85323-047-1

Victor of Vita: History of the Vandal Persecution
Translated with notes and introduction by JOHN MOORHEAD
Volume 10: 112pp., 1992, ISBN 0-85323-127-3

The Goths in the Fourth Century
by PETER HEATHER AND JOHN MATTHEWS
Volume 11: 224pp., 1992, ISBN 0-85323-426-4

Cassiodorus: *Variae*
Translated with notes and introduction by S. J. B. BARNISH
Volume 12: 260pp., 1992, ISBN 0-85323-436-1

The Lives of the Eighth-Century Popes (*Liber Pontificalis*)
Translated with an introduction and commentary by RAYMOND DAVIS
Volume 13: 288pp., 1992, ISBN 0-85323-018-8

Eutropius: Breviarium
Translated with an introduction and commentary by H. W. BIRD
Volume 14: 248pp., 1993, ISBN 0-85323-208-3

The Seventh Century in the West-Syrian Chronicles
introduced, translated and annotated by ANDREW PALMER
including two Seventh-century Syriac apocalyptic texts
introduced, translated and annotated by SEBASTIAN BROCK
with added annotation and an historical introduction by ROBERT HOYLAND
Volume 15: 368pp., 1993, ISBN 0-85323-238-5

Vegetius: Epitome of Military Science
Translated with notes and introduction by N. P. MILNER
Volume 16: 182pp., 2nd edition 1995, ISBN 0-85323-910-X

Aurelius Victor: De Caesaribus
Translated with an introduction and commentary by H. W. BIRD
Volume 17: 264pp., 1994, ISBN 0-85323-218-0

Bede: On the Tabernacle
Translated with notes and introduction by ARTHUR G. HOLDER
Volume 18: 224pp., 1994, ISBN 0-85323-378-0

Caesarius of Arles: Life, Testament, Letters
Translated with notes and introduction by WILLIAM E. KLINGSHIRN
Volume 19: 176pp., 1994, ISBN 0-85323-368-3

The Lives of the Ninth-Century Popes (*Liber Pontificalis*)
Translated with an introduction and commentary by RAYMOND DAVIS
Volume 20: 360pp., 1995, ISBN 0-85323-479-5

Bede: On the Temple
Translated with notes by SEÁN CONNOLLY,
introduction by JENNIFER O'REILLY
Volume 21: 192pp., 1995, ISBN 0-85323-049-8

Pseudo-Dionysius of Tel-Mahre: *Chronicle*, Part III
Translated with notes and introduction by WITOLD WITAKOWSKI
Volume 22: 192pp., 1995, ISBN 0-85323-760-3

Venantius Fortunatus: Personal and Political Poems
translated with notes and introduction by JUDITH GEORGE
Volume 23: 192pp., 1995, ISBN 0-85323-179-6

For full details of Translated Texts for Historians, including prices and ordering information, please write to the following:

All countries, **except the USA and Canada: Liverpool University Press, Senate House, Abercromby Square, Liverpool, L69 3BX, UK (*tel* 0151-794 2233, *fax* 0151-708 6502).**

USA and Canada: **University of Pennsylvania Press, Blockley Hall, 418 Service Drive, Philadelphia, PA 19104-6097, USA (*tel* [215] 898-6264, *fax* [215] 898-0404).**